THE EDUCATION
OF JOHN ADAMS

His Excellency JOHN ADAMS President
of the United States of America

Respectfully Dedicated to the   Lovers of their country
and firm Supporters   of its Constitution

The Education
of John Adams

R. B. Bernstein

OXFORD
UNIVERSITY PRESS

OXFORD
UNIVERSITY PRESS

Oxford University Press is a department of the University of Oxford. It furthers
the University's objective of excellence in research, scholarship, and education
by publishing worldwide. Oxford is a registered trade mark of Oxford University
Press in the UK and certain other countries.

Published in the United States of America by Oxford University Press
198 Madison Avenue, New York, NY 10016, United States of America.

© Oxford University Press 2020

Library of Congress Cataloging-in-Publication Data
Names: Bernstein, Richard B., 1956– author.
Title: The Education of John Adams / R.B. Bernstein.
Description: New York, NY : Oxford University Press, 2020. |
Includes index.
Identifiers: LCCN 2019042398 (print) | LCCN 2019042399 (ebook) |
ISBN 9780199740239 (hardback) | ISBN 9780197502723 (epub)
Subjects: LCSH: Adams, John, 1735–1826. | Presidents—United
States—Biography. | United States—Politics and government—1775–1783. |
United States—Politics and government—1783–1809.
Classification: LCC E322 .B47 2020 (print) | LCC E322 (ebook) |
DDC 973.4/4092 [B]—dc23
LC record available at https://lccn.loc.gov/2019042398
LC ebook record available at https://lccn.loc.gov/2019042399

1 3 5 7 9 8 6 4 2

Printed by LSC Communications, United States of America

Frontispiece: Engravings taught Americans what their presidents looked like. This melancholy
engraved portrait of President John Adams appeared at the height of his popularity. "His
Excellency John Adams President of the United States of America"; engraver: H. B. Houston;
publisher: D. Kennedy; Philadelphia, PA, 1798. *Mabel Brady Garvan Collection 1946.9.697; Yale
University Art Gallery, New Haven, CT (Public domain)*

This book is dedicated
To the sacred memory
Of my dear friend
Marilee b. Huntoon (1955–2011),
The best and wisest person
Whom I have ever known.

Her finely touched spirit had still its fine issues, though they were not widely visible. Her full nature, like that river of which Cyrus broke the strength, spent itself in channels which had no great name on the earth. But the effect of her being on those around her was incalculably diffusive: for the growing good of the world is partly dependent on unhistoric acts; and that things are not so ill with you and me as they might have been, is half owing to the number who lived faithfully a hidden life, and rest in unvisited tombs.

George Eliot
Middlemarch (last paragraph)

1871

CONTENTS

Preface

"Let us dare to read, think, speak and write"

In 1765, John Adams, a twenty-nine-year-old Massachusetts lawyer, pondered the crisis engulfing Great Britain and its North American colonies. In his view, the dispute's focus was how the British Empire was to be governed under the unwritten English constitution. To address that problem, Adams drafted a pamphlet, "A Dissertation on the Canon and Feudal Law." He likened Britain's abuse of its authority over the colonists to the enslavement of medieval Europe by kings and lords allied with the Roman Catholic Church. Juxtaposing dangers past and present, he warned that a new tyranny was on the horizon, but, he added, the colonists had means to resist it. Knowledge of American rights under the English constitution, he maintained, would bolster American resistance: "This spirit [of liberty], however, without knowledge, would be little better than a brutal rage. Let us tenderly and kindly cherish, therefore, the means of knowledge. Let us dare to read, think, speak and write."[1]

Adams's exhortation to his readers illuminated his life, his part in the American Revolution, and his role in the evolution of American constitutionalism. In the American Revolution, the Founding Fathers fought in different ways and using different means. Adams marshaled words and arguments in the American revolutionary cause. As a lawyer, politician, legislator, constitution-maker, diplomat, and executive, he mobilized legal and historical knowledge for the greater good, drawing on the best of the past to save the future:

> Let every order and degree among the people rouse their attention and animate their resolution. Let them all become attentive to the grounds and principles of government, ecclesiastical and civil. Let us study the law of nature; search into the spirit of the British constitution; read the histories of ancient ages; contemplate the great examples of Greece and Rome; set before us the conduct of our own British ancestors, who have defended for us the inherent rights of mankind against foreign and domestic tyrants and usurpers, against arbitrary kings and cruel priests, in short, against the gates of earth and hell.

Adams lived with books at his elbow and a pen in his hand. Insatiably curious about the world around him, he educated himself and sought to teach his contemporaries and posterity what he had learned. These lifelong processes of learning and teaching constitute the education of John Adams.[2]

Previous studies use one of two competing approaches to Adams, neither of them capturing his life's complexity or significance. Dazzled by his colorful personality, his self-awareness, and his revealing himself on paper, most biographers stress Adams's character, some reducing his constitutional and political advocacy and analysis to mere products of his internal conflicts.[3] The competing biographical school spotlights him as a constitutional and political thinker, rooted in an intellectual tradition extending from Greece and Rome to the Enlightenment—but pushing his nonpolitical life into the background.[4]

Deciding between character without ideas (reducing Adams to an idiosyncratic volcano but ignoring his intellectual depth) and ideas without character (seeing Adams as a learned intellectual but shortchanging his humanity) is a false choice. Juxtaposing his ideas

with his character, this book sets him within intersecting contexts—
personal, regional, lawyerly, political, and intellectual—that shaped
his vision of the world and of his place in it.[5]

Setting Adams in context deepens our understanding of his life's
personal dimension. Adams's resentments, explosions of temper, and
paroxysms of vanity become more comprehensible when we grasp
why he felt and expressed himself that way. His outbursts, voicing
his sense of his virtues and failings, had roots in and resonated with
his intellectual and cultural contexts. Given, for example, that he and
his contemporaries saw fame as this world's just reward for service to
the public good, and that his sense of fame resonated with the moral
heritage of his Calvinist roots, he had reasons to take personally
efforts to denigrate his labors. Those seeking to deny him fame, he
thought, were trying to take away what he had earned. By denigrating
him, they rejected the worth of his labors and his arguments.[6] His
battles with Benjamin Franklin, with Alexander Hamilton, and with
Thomas Jefferson were clashes of personality *and* of principled intellectual disputes about political theory and practice.

Attention to Adams's personal dimension illuminates interactions
between his private and family life and his intellectual and public
life. Heeding character and ideas gives us a clearer sense of his marriage to Abigail Smith Adams, for example, showing it as an intellectual and political partnership as well as a loving relationship.[7] It also
suggests why he so often sacrificed his and his family's happiness to
his sense of duty and his obligation to public service, and why he expected his family to understand the choices that he made.

Adams's regional origins also helped to shape him and to explain
his political behavior. Passionately loyal to his native land, Adams
saw himself as a son of Braintree, of Massachusetts, and of New
England. He represented and embodied his local, colonial, state,
and regional roots. In these commitments, he had much in common
with others of his state and region, and his conduct's regional context and sources help to explain what otherwise looks idiosyncratic, bringing to the biographical enterprise insights drawn from

scholarly analysis of local loyalties' effects on American politics.[8] For example, in the late 1770s and 1780s, during his diplomatic service in Europe, Adams shared with most New Englanders a strong suspicion of France—though France, the new nation's strongest ally, was the only European power able to counter British military and naval might. Influenced by their austere Calvinist Protestant/English heritage, they saw the French as corrupt, decadent, and mired in Catholic idolatry and superstition. Thus, letters written to Adams by fellow New Englanders (including Abigail), commiserating with his torments and echoing his suspicions that he was being undermined by the French and by fellow diplomats, resonated with and reinforced his resistance to the French Foreign Ministry and to Benjamin Franklin.

Adams's lawyerly identity is also central to understanding him. Not only was he one of his era's most learned and talented attorneys, but his self-definition as a lawyer was integral to his sense of what he should be as well.[9] The law suited him well as a career, meshing with his love of learning and study, his talent for public speaking and argument, and his capacity for hard work. Even after politics supplanted law as his calling in the 1770s, he remained a man of law, with a lawyer's perspective, learning, gift for oratory (and verbosity), ability to absorb and deploy vast amounts of research in a short time, contentiousness, and willingness to risk condemnation for the right cause. His legal cast of thought explains his penchant for conflict better than his supposed foibles or instability does.

As a diplomat, for example, Adams nearly always saw himself as a hick from Braintree who had moved from the Atlantic world's periphery to its center. Fears that he might be ill-equipped, even unqualified, to represent his country and defend its interests on the world stage plagued him; he drew on his lawyering skills to shape his work. Unfortunately, his hard-charging litigator's tactics backfired on Adams the envoy. This conflict between role and method even showed itself in his greatest diplomatic triumph. His negotiations led the Dutch to recognize the United States and to give the new nation vital loans, but the vexations he suffered led to his physical and emotional collapse.

Adams's diplomacy is notorious for collisions between himself and Franklin. One source of this conflict was Adams's concern for protecting Massachusetts in particular and America in general. Like other Americans, Adams feared that Franklin had spent too long in Europe, weakening his ties to home and his commitment to American interests.[10] Another source was Adams's formal, litigious, confrontational approach to diplomacy, which clashed with Franklin's conciliatory, informal methods.[11] Unlike the urbane Franklin, a master of the indirect approach, Adams plunged into disagreements with American colleagues, foreign counterparts, and Congress, sometimes all at once. Adams was a bull in a china shop who brought his own china shop with him.[12] Skeptical and envious of Franklin's skilled diplomacy, Adams measured himself against Franklin and brooded over the other man's faults—Franklin's laziness, love of popularity, administrative sloppiness, and even his amateurish spoken French. When supporters from New England warned him that Franklin was working with Adams's enemies in Congress to undermine him, he exploded in response, with near-catastrophic results.

Adams's political dimension also helps us understand him, for we forget that the Founding Fathers were politicians. It made sense for Adams to move from the sphere of private law to that of public or constitutional law. The Revolution raised the need to defend existing constitutional arrangements against British innovation, and then to devise new constitutional arrangements incorporating English constitutional principles. Adams's grasp of politics taught him the need to serve his country as a matter of patriotism (what the Romans called *pro patria*). Being a constitution-maker required his talents, abilities, learning, and commitment. And yet, though a distinguished maker and defender of constitutions, he had an intermittent, inconsistent record of success as a politician.

As a politician and officeholder in an evolving American government, Adams was at his best as a politician when he was sure of the institutional context in which he was working and of his place in that context. He was most comfortable as a legislator, a delegate in Congress, and a constitution-maker; he knew what those roles required of him and what he should say and do. By contrast, he felt uncertain of his fit with other public roles that he was asked to assume. Heeding Adams's discomfort with unfamiliar roles helps us to grasp what happened to him after he returned to America, becoming the nation's first vice president in 1789 and its second president in 1797. He found both offices torturous.

As vice president, holding an office created by the Constitution's framers as an afterthought, he had no models to guide him. He suffered public embarrassments, including his doomed 1789 campaign to confer a grand title on the president and his equally self-defeating insistence on lecturing the Senate about European customs and diplomatic etiquette.[13] His efforts made sense to him but offended others. As Adams saw it, he was drawing on his learning and experience to bolster the constitutional system's legitimacy. By contrast, many countrymen found his ideas laughable, even abhorrent, precisely because they were trying to throw off habits inherited from a hidebound, monarchical Europe. Some dismayed observers concluded that, having spent too long abroad, Adams had lost touch with American values, ironically paralleling his doubts about Franklin.

President Adams faced a different problem—the suffocating presence of one precedent and model: George Washington. In 1797, at his inauguration, Adams was painfully sure that the public focused not on his assuming power but on Washington's leaving the public stage. For most of his presidency, he sought to model his conduct on Washington's instead of developing his own style of leadership. He did not realize what later presidents came to understand—that being president meant melding your own personality with the presidency's powers and responsibilities, fitting the office to yourself and yourself to the office. Washington achieved those goals; his version of the presidency partook of his chilly formality and rigorous self-restraint—qualities alien to Adams's personality. In trying to be a second President Washington instead of President Adams, he tried to be someone he was not.

Further, Adams kept the members of Washington's cabinet in office—worrying that, if he named his own heads of departments, he might be seen as criticizing Washington. His decision, however, saddled him with advisers who neither shared his views nor respected him. They were loyal to Washington, their former leader, or to Hamilton, their intellectual and political chief—not to Adams. Only in the last year of his term did he take charge of his presidency. He did so too late to win a second term in 1800. Nonetheless, in his last year in office he helped to prevent a war with France; appointed the greatest chief justice in American history, John Marshall; and managed an orderly transition of power to his victorious rival and successor, Thomas Jefferson.

Adams shouldered political responsibilities with which he was comfortable or struggled to cope with political roles in which he was uncomfortable as a man of ideas, an active participant in the Enlightenment's intellectual world. The Enlightenment was a complex mix of kinds of thought—some divided by national context and origin, others sorted into conservative versus radical camps.[14] Adams fit within Britain's conservative, affirming version of the Enlightenment.[15]

Adams found it natural to approach political problems by reference to the life of the mind. Throughout his career, he found comfort in studying enduring arguments about human nature, society, politics, and government, and grounding his political and constitutional labors on that study. Applying his learning to politics, governance, and constitutionalism moved Adams to eloquent enthusiasm; in 1780, he wrote to Abigail:

> I could fill Volumes with Descriptions of Temples and Palaces, Paintings, Sculptures, Tapestry, Porcelaine, &c. &c. &c.—if I could

have time. But I could not do this without neglecting my duty. The Science of Government it is my Duty to study, more than all other Sciences: the Art of Legislation and Administration and Negotiation, ought to take Place, indeed to exclude in a manner all other Arts. I must study Politicks and War that my sons may have liberty to study Mathematicks and Philosophy. My sons ought to study Mathematicks and Philosophy, Geography, natural History, Naval Architecture, navigation, Commerce and Agriculture, in order to give their Children a right to study Painting, Poetry, Musick, Architecture, Statuary, Tapestry and Porcelaine.[16]

For Adams, immersion in the record of human political experiments brought intellectual and psychological benefits, uniting realms of thought and feeling that earlier biographers have sought to distinguish. Adams considered Solon and Lycurgus, Aristotle and Cicero, Sir Edward Coke and James Harrington, as deceased colleagues, fellow laborers in a great enterprise—"the divine science of politicks"—and he passionately identified with that enterprise.[17]

More than two centuries before Adams's birth, another diplomat and author described what politics meant to him in ways resonating with Adams's feelings. In 1513, Niccolò Machiavelli sketched for his friend Francesco Vettori how study consoled him while he languished in exile from Florence:

When evening comes, I return home and enter my study; on the threshold I take off my workday clothes, covered with mud and dirt, and put on the garments of court and palace. Fitted out appropriately, I step inside the venerable courts of the ancients, where, solicitously received by them, I nourish myself on that food that alone is mine and for which I was born; where I am unashamed to converse with them and to question them about the motives for their actions, and they, out of their human kindness, answer me. And for four hours at a time I feel no boredom, I forget all my troubles, I do not dread poverty, and I am not terrified by death. I absorb myself into them completely.[18]

Adams had an instinctive sympathy with Machiavelli's feelings. In a 1790 letter to the travel writer Alexander Jardine (who had praised his *Defence of the Constitutions of Government*), Adams declared, "I know not how it is, but mankind have an aversion to the study of the science of government. Is it because the subject is dry? To me, no romance is more entertaining."[19] Like Machiavelli, Adams derived delight and consolation from studying politics. Like Machiavelli, Adams moved between his "workday" world and "the venerable courts of the ancients." Like Machiavelli, Adams deemed himself fit to enter that intellectual realm because he was confident that they would deem him qualified to enter their world, and because they would "solicitously receive" him to "converse with them." Like Machiavelli, Adams worked hard to understand and to convey the political and historical lessons that the ancients had to teach.[20]

Seeking to explain and justify the Western world's wisdom, reveling in the hard intellectual work that such pursuits required, Adams took his constitutional and political thought personally. His ideas about politics were integral to his sense of who he was, and he took as personal affronts challenges to the ideas that he worked so hard to distill and express.[21] Thus, he upbraided such adversaries as Thomas Paine, Franklin, and Jefferson for ignoring the lessons of history as he understood them. By preferring a simple constitution and spurning ideas of checks and balances and separation of powers, Adams charged, Franklin and Paine were rejecting humanity's amassed wisdom about what a sound constitution should be, endangering the liberties that a sound constitution would protect. By embracing the French Revolution while ignoring the obstacles to sound political building in its path, Adams insisted, Paine and Jefferson were flying in the face of human experience. The positions that Adams took were personal *and* intellectual, reflecting his deep investment in decades of study and reflection. For Adams, each realm of thought, feeling, and experience was linked to and reinforced the other.

Hovering over the other contexts shaping John Adams are his views of slavery and race and those focusing on the question of who get to be citizens and Americans. Most scholars have thought past these issues, assuming that slavery and race were not important components of life in Massachusetts or in New England, and that they therefore did not affect John Adams. We forget that race-based slavery pervaded all the colonies of British North America, and that slavery did not start to erode until in the 1780s Massachusetts courts found it a violation of the state's 1780 constitution.[22] For Adams, slavery was a constant of human society and civilization. And though he may not have been a conscious believer in white supremacy espousing a racist point of view, he nonetheless understood that only white New Englanders and Americans could possess political and legal rights, by default, as white. Only now are we learning to pay attention to this aspect of his thought.[23]

This description of Adams's intertwined personal, political, and intellectual commitments applies equally to his contemporaries. Like him, most of them were quarrelsome, insecure, dogmatic, fearful, and optimistic. Because the American experiment's future was neither clear nor preordained, ordinary and elite Americans clashed bitterly over its nature and destiny. Their battles over politics and ideas had three causes. Like Adams, they all had high stakes in that political experiment's outcome. Creating a new government for a new nation was their time's great challenge, attracting its best and brightest minds, with the prize of fame as the reward for being right. That challenge was more than local and personal; they had all come to believe what Alexander Hamilton argued in *The Federalist No. 1*, that not just America's but humanity's future was at stake.[24]

The best setting for studying the conflicts dividing Americans in the revolutionary and early national periods is that of constitutional creation: devising and putting into effect constitutional frameworks, and authorizing, structuring, and limiting political conflict in a new, independent nation. Although they all wanted a constitution shaping a constitutional system, they differed about what it should be and how it should work.

Adams sought to preserve Anglo-American common-law constitutionalism, in particular its commitment to separation of powers and checks and balances. He spoke out against seductive but dangerous temptations to innovation and simplification.[25]

His congressional adversary John Dickinson of Pennsylvania (later of Delaware) championed a version of constitutionalism imbued with the Quaker faith, promoting peaceful dissent as the best way to preserve rights and liberties.[26]

Thomas Paine of Pennsylvania proposed a competing model of constitutionalism, grounded in popular government and embracing simplicity of constitutional ideas and structures. Benjamin Franklin leaned toward Paine's constitutional vision.[27]

James Madison of Virginia advocated a form of constitutionalism emphasizing the balance between state sovereignty and national supremacy within a federal system, a concept that Adams never fully understood.[28]

Thomas Jefferson of Virginia shared Madison's concern with federalism, but his constitutional vision differed from Madison's (and Adams's) and approached that of Paine and Franklin. Like them, he sought to promote the international democratic revolution ignited by the American Revolution, a point that Adams disputed from the 1790s to their deaths in 1826.[29]

Alexander Hamilton and John Jay of New York offered a nationalist constitutionalism empowering a supreme general government both to restrain states' political powers and to create a great commercial republic for a union that could stand the test of time.[30]

Virginians George Washington and John Marshall shared Hamilton's views, but they were more willing to weave federalism into American nationalism than he was.[31] Their nationalism was flavored with their attachment to Virginia, just as Adams's ideas about politics and government evidenced the impress of New England values and customs.

Competition among these versions of constitutionalism persisted from the 1770s to the 1820s and beyond.[32] The American constitutionalism emerging from that era blended elements from all these versions, but arguments over its content and evolution remained bitter and divisive. If Adams was more intemperate about such matters than others were, it was a difference of degree, not of kind. Not only was each man wedded to his constitutional vision, but each was sure that only his vision's victory would ensure the success of the American republic.

All these men had to operate on two levels equally necessary to constitutional creation. One level was that of principle. The other level was that of practicality, on-the-ground bickering over allocating resources and protecting interests.[33] Constitutional and political tests facing Americans in this era made both levels crucial to the task of constitutional creation. Within a generation, Americans moved from political theorizing to diagnose their former government's flaws; to drawing on history and law to create options for a new form of government; to testing and administering that new form of government—all while trying to remain committed to the idea of a united nation.

The demands of politics in the era of John Adams required a special kind of politician—not abstract political theorists like Hobbes, Locke, Hume, or Rousseau, or practical politicians who ran a government mechanically with no thought for the future. Rather, the time demanded *thinking politicians*, who worked primarily in the practical realm of politics yet who also saw and acted on the larger significance and effects of what they were doing.[34] In the political and constitutional battles of the nation's founding, we see thinking politicians at work.

This book tells the story of one such thinking politician.

Chapter One

"Something should be said of my origin"

From Braintree to Harvard (1735–1755)

John Adams found his family's history fascinating. Certain that his role in creating a new nation was the centerpiece of his life and legacy, he also treasured his past for its usefulness in reminding himself and in edifying his descendants about who he was and what he valued. Beginning his autobiography with an account of his family history, he wrote, "The Customs of Biography require that something should be said of my origin."[1]

Braintree, Massachusetts, Adams's birthplace, was a farming village ten miles south of Boston and thirty miles north of Plymouth.[2] The first English settlers arrived in the area in 1625 and incorporated the town of Braintree in 1640. In 1632 or 1633, Henry Adams arrived, accompanied by his wife, eight sons, and a daughter. This first American Adams, known as Henry Adams of Braintree, was from the English village of Braintree in the county of Essex; he came to New England as part of a company of emigrants led by Rev. Thomas Hooker, the Puritan clergyman who founded the colony of Connecticut.

Henry Adams of Braintree, a maltster (brewer) and a farmer, died in 1646. In 1817, John Adams erected a large granite tombstone in the Hancock Cemetery of the village of Quincy (which had absorbed the town of Braintree), to honor his first American ancestor for "[taking] his flight from the Dragon persecution." This inscription voices a theme of Adams's politics: his admiration for the seventeenth-century Englishmen who resisted political tyranny and religious persecution.[3]

Our John Adams belonged to the fifth generation of Adamses in America descended from Henry Adams of Braintree. Most of them, like him, were independent farmers who plied trades to eke out a living beyond what farming could provide. Among the Adams family's fourth American generation was Deacon John Adams; he was born in 1691, one of ten children. Besides his descent from Henry Adams of Braintree, he counted among his ancestors the Pilgrim couple John and Priscilla Alden. Like his predecessors, Deacon John Adams farmed for part of the year. When the weather prevented farming, he worked as a cordwainer, a shoemaker specializing in fine, soft leather shoes and other high-quality footwear. Cordwainers were a cut above ordinary shoemakers, who though independent tradesmen were near the bottom of colonial New England's social and economic hierarchy.[4]

Deacon John Adams commanded his neighbors' esteem, holding many local offices: tithingman, constable, selectman, tax collector, and lieutenant of the town's militia. Finally, he was a longtime deacon of Braintree's Congregational church—a trusted secular official who helped to administer the church. His son John recalled him as "the honestest Man I ever knew. In Wisdom, Piety, Benevolence and Charity In proportion to his Education and Sphere of Life, I have never seen his Superiour."[5] Adams added: "He had a good education, though not at college, and was a very capable and useful man. . . . [He was] a man of strict piety and great integrity, much esteemed and beloved, wherever he was known, which was not far, his sphere of life being not very extensive."[6]

In 1720, Deacon John Adams bought a saltbox house in Braintree. A structure built at the end of the seventeenth century, with a low, sloping roof pitched toward its back, this house stood by the road connecting Boston to Plymouth. Over the ensuing years he added to the six acres of land that he acquired with the house—a pattern of land acquisition that shaped his son's economic priorities. Deacon John Adams farmed most of his 188 acres, but he also had an orchard, a salt marsh, a meadow, and woodland.

Having achieved financial stability, the deacon sought a wife. In October 1734, he married Susanna Boylston. The groom was forty-three, and his bride was twenty-five; such an age difference between spouses was common in colonial and revolutionary America. It was the first marriage for both of them, though we do not know why Deacon John Adams did not marry until his early forties.[7] Susanna Boylston was the daughter of an eminent minister who belonged to a prominent Boston medical family; she was an energetic woman of convinced opinions who was not shy about expressing them, even arguing with her husband.

John Adams, their first child, was born in an upper-story room of the saltbox house on October 19 O.S. (October 30 N.S.), 1735, a year after his parents' marriage. He was the oldest of three sons; Peter Boylston Adams followed in 1738 and Elihu Adams in 1741. As the eldest son, John became the focus of his parents' ambitions; his father intended him to enter the clergy after a good education, as the deacon's older brother Joseph had done.[8] Peter and Elihu became farmers, like their father, with the minimal schooling needed to practice that calling. Elihu also emulated his father in becoming an officer of the militia. Taking part in the first months of the American Revolution, he died in 1775 at thirty-four, of dysentery contracted in a Continental army camp. Peter Boylston Adams also entered the militia, serving during the Revolution, and returned to farming after the war; he died in 1823, three years before his celebrated brother.

Little is known of John Adams's childhood beyond the anecdotes that he preserved in his diary and autobiography and told to others, who recounted his stories in their books. In his autobiography, he wrote, "I shall not consume much paper in relating the Anecdotes of my Youth."[9] A healthy, sturdy child, he enjoyed exploring the land surrounding his father's farm and such pursuits as hunting and fishing.

Adams felt love, respect, and admiration for his father. He gave his father's family the credit for his education, suggesting that the source of the Adams passion for knowledge was his father's mother: "From his Mother probably my Father received an Admiration of Learning as he called it, which remained with him, through Life, and which prompted him to his unchangeable determination to give his first son a liberal Education."[10] Susanna Boylston Adams makes few appearances in her son's autobiography beyond his dutiful recording of her family background and upbringing. We should not make too much of Adams's failure to discuss his mother, however; many of his contemporaries, among them Benjamin Franklin, Thomas Jefferson, and James Madison, downplayed their mothers in their autobiographies, while stressing their fathers.

Adams's schooling began with happy years studying his ABCs at a "dame school" near Penn Hill run by Dame Belcher, the mother of another deacon of the town church. Besides his studies, John helped his schoolmistress carry the corn she raised to the local gristmill; Dame Belcher gave John three copper cents after each trip and urged him to save the money "to buy land with."[11] Her advice restated the conventional wisdom of John Adams's world.

Adams discussed Dame Belcher only briefly in his autobiography. By contrast, he focused on his first Latin schoolmaster, Joseph Cleverly. Decades later, he remained dissatisfied with Cleverly's poor schooling. He recalled that his disappointment in Cleverly's lackadaisical teaching threatened to extinguish his interest in schooling. Though as a child he may have preferred outdoor pursuits to being cooped up in a one-room schoolhouse, what dominated his account of his time at Braintree's public Latin school was his unhappiness with Cleverly:

> His inattention to his Schollars was such as gave me a disgust to Schools, to books and to study and I spent my time as idle Children do in making and sailing boats and Ships upon the Ponds and Brooks, in making and flying Kites, in driving hoops, playing

marbles, playing Quoits, Wrestling, Swimming, Skaiting and above all in shooting, to which Diversion I was addicted to a degree of Ardor which I know not that I ever felt for any other Business, Study or Amusement.[12]

Adams rebelled against his teacher, "the most Indolent man I ever knew."

In 1749, John urged his father not to send him to college, because he "did not love books." As he recalled in his autobiography, his startled father asked: "What would you do[,] Child?" John insisted that he wanted to be a farmer like his father. Deacon Adams put his son's choice to a test: "Well I will shew you what it is to be a Farmer. You shall go with me to Penny ferry tomorrow Morning and help me get Thatch." After a day of grueling work, his father asked, "Well John are you satisfied with being a Farmer[?]" A weary John insisted that he liked the farmer's life well; Deacon Adams growled, "Ay, but I don't like it so well. So you shall go to School to day." John reluctantly obeyed. (In another version, which he told in old age, his father put him to work at ditching; at the end of two days, John yielded, telling his father that he would rather return to his Latin grammar than keep digging ditches.)[13]

What was pushing him away from school, Adams realized, was impatience with Cleverly, not distaste for learning. Convinced that Cleverly was wrongly delaying his introduction to mathematics, John decided to teach himself the subject. He found a mathematics textbook "and applyd myself to it at home alone and went through the whole Course, overtook and passed by all the Schollars at School, without any master." But, he realized, he could not share his achievement with his father. Because Deacon John Adams preferred that John study Latin (a subject crucial to admission to Harvard), he was indifferent to John's mathematical studies—and Cleverly's inattention to them.[14]

John appealed again to his father, offering a solution to the problem of his schooling. He asked to be enrolled in a local private school run by Joseph Marsh, promising that, if he could attend Marsh's school, he would devote himself to his studies. It was John Adams's first display of his lawyering ability; he was pleading the case for improving the arrangements for his education, with himself as his client and with his father as judge and jury. Impressed with John's determination to pursue an education, the strength of his case against Cleverly, and the soundness of his proposed remedy, Deacon Adams agreed. The next day, he moved John to Marsh's school, persuading Marsh to accept John as a day scholar instead of insisting that he become a boarding student.[15] Deacon John thus reduced the cost of paying Adams's new teacher. Almost immediately, John's taste for learning and study blossomed, and his academic performance improved.

While studying with Marsh, John acquired a collection of Cicero's *Orationes* in Latin, in which he scribbled with pride of ownership, "John Adams His Book 1749/50." This small leather-bound volume rode in John's pocket as he went to and from Marsh's school; it is the earliest relic of the education of John Adams, the first surviving volume of what became one of the largest and richest private libraries in North America.[16] For the rest of his life, Adams admired and identified himself with the Roman senator, orator, lawyer, and philosopher.[17]

In 1751, with the time to apply to Harvard approaching, Deacon John Adams and his son made an agreement governing John's college studies: John agreed to accept his father's payment of his Harvard tuition as an advance distribution of his whole share of his father's estate. Relieved of the burden of financing his college education, John had only to prove himself worthy of admission to Harvard. After a year of study preparing John for the entrance examination, Marsh declared his pupil ready. John did not feel ready; he felt even worse when Marsh told him that he could not go with him to Cambridge for the examination. For the first time, Adams had to face a critical ordeal all by himself.

John rode on horseback from Braintree to Cambridge. As he recalled in old age, he often felt tempted to return home without facing the test, but he feared disappointing his father and his teacher more than he did taking the examination. Told when he arrived that he would have to translate a passage from Latin, he began to worry about his command of the language. Deducing the reasons for Adams's nervousness, a tutor, Joseph Mayhew, led him into an office with a dictionary, a grammar, pen, ink, and paper and told him to take whatever time he needed. To his relief, Adams passed the examination, winning a partial scholarship. He took pleasure in sharing the news with Marsh and his parents, who declared themselves "well pleased" with his success.[18]

In 1751, when John Adams began his college studies, Harvard College was the oldest institution of higher learning in British North America. The college sat in the heart of the town of Cambridge; its two modest brick buildings, Harvard Hall (a dormitory and library) and Massachusetts Hall (offices and classrooms), dominated Cambridge's landscape.[19] At the commencement exercises of 1755, Harvard officials recorded Adams as ranking fourteenth of the twenty-five matriculating students, based on "dignity of family"— a discreet term for the college's attention to social hierarchy rather than academic standing.[20]

One problem tugged at John Adams's mind—the conflict between his parents' hopes that he become a minister and his own religious views. Despite their ambitions, he was aware of his theological doubts even before enrolling at Harvard. He had developed an independent cast of mind regarding religion. The fate of his town's minister, Lemuel Briant, also affected him. Veering from the Congregational church's strict Calvinist teachings, in 1749 Briant preached a sermon rejecting such doctrines as original sin and the idea that the Almighty could save an individual by bestowing grace arbitrarily. This sermon was too much for Briant's parishioners. Controversy rocked Braintree, and the parish leaders put Briant on trial for his opinions and what they called his lax conduct as minister. Briant was tried in the largest room of Deacon Adams's house, where John observed at least some of the proceedings. Though the trial found in Briant's favor on many points, he resigned his pulpit. The trial shattered his high-strung nature, contributing to his death in 1754 at the age of thirty-four. The dispute's aftershocks reverberated through the parish. Realizing that his theological views were uncomfortably close to those for which Briant had been tried, John decided to pursue a secular calling instead of the ministry. For the time being, he kept his doubts to himself.[21]

John threw himself into his studies at Harvard. He applied himself to Latin and Greek, and to moral philosophy and natural philosophy (the era's term for science), the latter under the charge of a charismatic, brilliant scholar, John Winthrop Jr., the Hollis Professor of Mathematics and Natural Philosophy. Winthrop's teaching catalyzed Adams's interest in science, which persisted long after his graduation.[22] Adams exploited the college's library, reading far beyond the assigned texts.

At Harvard, traditions enforcing the rigors of college life persisted beside curricular innovations. The college's rules set a demanding schedule. Students began at dawn, attended regular prayer sessions, and had little time for meals during hours of study. Adams endured these rules without complaint; he also did not take part in the pranks with which students vexed professors and administrators. His time at Harvard confirmed his enthusiasm for deep, wide-ranging reading and study.[23]

In 1753, Adams began keeping a diary in a paper-backed booklet. In his time, it was natural for a college student to keep a diary to examine his life. Previous generations of New Englanders had used diaries as tools of self-examination within the context of Calvinist Protestantism; their efforts at self-evaluation had a theological purpose.[24] Adams's diary was something new; it recorded his self-examination by reference not to a standard dictated by an external context of religious beliefs but rather by his own standard of self-improvement. Though virtue preoccupied him, the values animating his concerns were moral, not theological; inner-directed, not tradition-directed.[25]

Adams used his diary irregularly. Recording a few lines each day, but not always, he noted the weather and sometimes added details of his studies and of his social encounters. Though riddled with gaps, Adams's first experiment with diary keeping was a significant event in his life and in his education. He returned to his diary after his graduation from Harvard, a natural occasion for self-assessment. He recorded notes of his study of law, drafts of essays legal and moral and of letters, and extensive and passionate self-reproaches. He continued his diary through the last year of his second term as vice president. He poured out his heart to his diary, tried out new ways of speaking and writing and new personal and professional roles, and arraigned himself before the bar of his conscience.

John Adams had laid the foundations of his education. Beyond Latin and Greek, the ancient world's history and literature, and natural philosophy and natural history, among its components were the histories of his ancestors' lives in New England Puritan communities and their commitment to learning and study; his father's example and his insistence on John's securing a good education; his antipathy to indolence and his admiration for effective teaching; his hunger for reading; and his decision not to pursue a career in the ministry.

Almost before John could grasp the fact, his college days were coming to an end. In July 1755, he received his bachelor of arts degree. Graduating with distinction, he played a prominent role in the college's commencement exercises. He was chosen as one of four or five seniors (his designated role was "senior sophister") to conduct a formal disputation in Latin, with each disputant addressing a question previously assigned to him. He met the challenge ably and finished the process of commencement as a hero to his family and his neighbors in Braintree. And yet, the nineteen-year-old college graduate had no idea what he should do with his life.

Chapter Two

"It is my Destiny to dig Treasures with my own fingers"

Law and Marriage (1755–1765)

One close observer of Harvard's 1755 commencement exercises was Rev. Thaddeus Maccarty of Worcester. His purpose was to recruit a Latin schoolmaster for his town, and he liked what he saw of the young orator from Braintree. When Maccarty approached John Adams and sketched the terms he was offering on Worcester's behalf, Adams accepted. He would have an occupation, a source of income, and, most important, a respectable time to ponder his choice of career. After spending the summer after graduation with his family, he made the horseback journey of about sixty miles from Braintree to Worcester in one day.

Adams established himself in temporary lodgings with the town's physician, Nahum Willard. He explored Dr. Willard's medical library to satisfy his eager curiosity about books and to test his interest in medicine as a career. Willard was the first of Adams's temporary landlords during his service as schoolmaster. As was the custom, Adams was a boarder, moving from one house to another for a few months at a time, always paying the same rent, for which the town reimbursed him.

Having established himself, Adams suffered the emotional letdown that so often besets new college graduates embarking on the world. Worcester seemed to him an intellectual wasteland, deeply disappointing by contrast with the educational and cultural excitement of Harvard College and Cambridge. The leading town in central Massachusetts, Worcester was forty miles west of Boston and thirty-eight miles east of Springfield. In 1755, with a population of about fifteen hundred, it was little more than a frontier village. Though he appreciated the town's friendliness, Adams felt gloom and frustration, confiding his sour feelings to his diary.

Adams was discontented with Worcester and with school-mastering, which he saw as drudgery mixed with boredom. He had about a dozen young students, whom he was to teach reading, writing, arithmetic, and Latin, with an infusion of religious and moral values. Sometimes he had to use corporal punishment to discipline them.

In September 1755, within weeks of his arrival, he wrote to his friends Nathan Webb and Richard Cranch, depicting his situation in mock-epic terms borrowed from John Milton. He used this satirical tone to cloak his feelings, but the satire could not conceal that he was bored, lonely, and unhappy. He described himself as "the gloomy Paedagogue" and a "haughty Monarch," his workplace as "a school of affliction," and his pupils as "a large number of little runtlings, just capable of lisping A.B.C. and troubling the Master." Though a neighbor reassured him that his teaching would help to make his pupils "Plants of Renown and Cedars of Lebanon," he complained, "I am certain that keeping this school any length of Time would make a base weed and ignoble shrub of me."[1] He begged his friends to write.

In his next letter to Webb, Adams pondered government and politics in ways foreshadowing his later career.[2] Beginning with a pious recognition that "all that part of Creation that lies within our observation is liable to Change," he shifted to the rise and fall of such empires as Rome and Carthage. Then he focused on Great Britain, "the greatest Nation upon the Globe," which had amassed a world-spanning empire.[3] The year 1755 was the first year of its latest, most terrible imperial war. Would the British Empire, he asked, suffer a decline similar to those of Rome, Carthage, and other ancient empires? In that case, might America supplant Britain as the center of the world's greatest empire? "Soon after the Reformation a few people came over into this new world for Concience sake. Perhaps this (apparently) trivial incident, may transfer the great seat of Empire into America. It looks likely to me." He mused on the possibilities of American growth and the need to preserve union among the colonies—for he saw disunion as the leading threat to this happy American future. He explained half seriously that he had fallen prey to his townsmen's obsession with politics, provoked by news of the French and Indian War:

> Be not surprised that I am turn'd Politician. This whole town is immers'd in Politicks. The interests of Nations, and all the dira of War, make the subject of every Conversation. I set and hear, and after having been led thro' a maze of sage observations, I some times retire, and by laying things together, form some reflections pleasing to myself. The produce of one of these reveries, You have read above.

He closed with another plea to write soon and often.[4]

Adams's reasoning in this letter tracked the political thought of Benjamin Franklin—an ironic parallel, given the tension between them as diplomats decades later. In the 1750s, Franklin enthusiastically advocated British imperial greatness. As a colonial lobbyist in London seeking advancement in the empire's administration, he promoted an American role within the empire. He hoped that, just as the emperor Constantine had transferred his government from Rome to Constantinople, a future sovereign might shift the British Empire's capital from England to America—perhaps to Philadelphia.[5]

Adams's letters and diary entries display his fascination with human nature, spurring him to observe his neighbors and his pupils and to record his observations, developing his eye for reading people.

In his diary on March 15, 1756, he pictured himself presiding over his schoolroom as if it were the world in miniature and he was "some Dictator at the head of a commonwealth." He imagined his pupils' futures, which he thought he could predict based on observing their behavior:

> In this little State I can discover all the great Genius's, all the surprizing actions and revolutions of the great World in miniature. I have severall renowned Generalls but 3 feet high, and several deep-projecting Politicians in peticoats. I have others catching and dissecting Flies, accumulating remarkable pebbles, cockle shells &c., with as ardent Curiosity as any Virtuoso in the royal society. Some rattle and Thunder out A, B, C, with as much Fire and impetuosity, as Alexander fought, and very often sit down and cry as heartily, upon being out spelt, as Cesar did, when at Alexanders sepulchre he recollected that the Macedonian Hero had conquered the World before his Age. At one Table sits Mr. Insipid foppling and fluttering, spinning his whirligig, or playing with his fingers as gaily and wittily as any frenchified coxcomb brandishes his Cane or rattles his snuff box. At another sitts the polemical Divine, plodding and wrangling in his mind about Adam's fall in which we sinned all as his primmer has it. In short my little school like the great World, is made up of Kings, Politicians, Divines, L.L.D.s, Fops, Buffoons, Fidlers, Sychophants, Fools, Coxcombs, chimney sweepers, and every other Character drawn in History or seen in the World.[6]

This letter drew on a literary device central to Thomas Gray's poem "Elegy Written in a Country Churchyard" (1751); Gray sketched people buried there, mapping types of humanity and meditating on fate and destiny. Adams also was doing what all good teachers do—taking responsibility for his students. Getting acquainted with them, he expressed with humor, warmth, and understanding the intimacy between teacher and student that often develops. Pursuing this kind of writing refined Adams's knowledge of human traits, abilities, and frailties—including his own.

As schoolmaster, Adams was a figure of some importance in Worcester. Though he was paid little more than a daily laborer, his Harvard degree and his reputation as a learned young man made him a respected figure in the town and a regular part of its social life. Each evening, he recorded conversations in his diary, penned character sketches of his neighbors, and examined himself. On February 16, 1756, he recorded his wistful ambitions:

> Oh! that I could wear out of my mind every mean and base affectation, conquer my natural Pride and Self Conceit, expect no more defference from my fellows than I deserve, acquire that meekness, and humility, which are the sure marks and Characters of a great and generous Soul, and subdue every unworthy Passion and treat all men as I wish to be treated by all. How happy should I then be, in the favour and good will of all honest men, and the sure prospect of a happy immortality![7]

Adams regularly subjected himself to self-exhortation and self-reproach. For example, on April 22, 1756, he wrote, "My Brains seem constantly in as great Confusion, and wild disorder, as Miltons Chaos. They are numb, dead. I have never any bright, refulgent Ideas. Every Thing appears in my mind, dim and obscure like objects seen thro' a dirty glass or roiled water."[8]

Scrutinizing and judging himself in his diary spurred his efforts to refine his behavior and induced him to plumb his mind and heart to decide what he should make of himself. He sought to identify the kind of ambition that he should pursue, the kind that would enable him to choose a career in which he could soar. He tried to distinguish between the self-doubt that he should heed and that he should discard.

The choices facing him, he wrote in his autobiography, were "Divinity, Law, or Physick."[9] The ordeal of Reverend Briant and Adams's recognition of his own heterodox opinions had already canceled any inclination by Adams to become a clergyman. Even so, some of his diary entries read like sermons, suggesting that he was still experimenting with the voice of a clergyman.

As for medicine, he recalled in his autobiography that, in Dr. Willard's library, "I read a good deal in these [medical] Books and entertained many thoughts of Becoming a Physician and a Surgeon."[10] Though he abandoned the idea of a medical career, his interest in medicine may help to explain why he later numbered among his friends such doctors as Joseph Warren, Benjamin Rush, and Benjamin Waterhouse.

Attending a local court of justice began to focus his attention on the law. Adams saw the law as a way to develop his gifts of reasoning, writing, and oratory. He recognized the law's historical character and its centrality to the politics of Massachusetts and of the British Empire. Many of his college classmates and some of his professors had urged him to become a lawyer, citing his skills in speaking and in argument. One obstacle facing Adams was the legal profession's problematic status in Massachusetts. Lawyers were not popular; too many people, including his father, regarded them as sources of contention, whereas New England communities prized consensus.[11] Then as now, it was conventional wisdom to doubt lawyers' ethics. These challenges attracted Adams to the law; they were obstacles that he wanted to overcome and that he believed he could overcome. Finally, Adams's reverence for Cicero induced him to see himself as following in Cicero's footsteps; he recalled that Cicero also was a self-made man who had had to struggle to build his career.[12]

On August 21, 1756, his decision made, Adams signed a contract with Worcester's only lawyer, James Putnam, who pledged to supervise Adams's legal studies for two years. In return, Adams would pay him $100 plus room and board (which would never exceed the town's allowance to Adams for such costs as schoolmaster). Teaching school by day, Adams devoted himself to the law at night.

Adams studied law in the traditional way. First, he read such standard treatises as the works of the seventeenth-century English jurist Sir Edward Coke, the great symbol of the common law. Adams also studied such jurisprudential writers as Hugo Grotius and Samuel Pufendorf, experts on civil law, natural law, and the law of nations. He pored over the legal compendium promulgated by the Byzantine emperor Justinian, valued by Anglo-American lawyers for its analysis of the law of real property, of wills, and of inheritance—the major subjects that Adams would encounter as a practicing attorney.[13]

In Putnam's chambers, Adams immersed himself in the other half of legal training—painstaking transcribing of legal documents, which furthered Putnam's law business while teaching Adams the grinding details of a lawyer's daily work. Copying documents was of special importance in training an eighteenth-century American lawyer. Filing and litigating depended on mastery of the "forms of action at common law," the legal categories into which the law sorted lawsuits. The precision in legal thinking required of lawyers by the forms of action required the wording of legal documents to fit the accepted forms of action; a misplaced or omitted word could invalidate a lawsuit or a defense to it.[14]

When Adams had no pleadings to copy, he read legal treatises, commentaries, form books, and judicial reports. This reading plunged the young law student into the intricate web of doctrines and rules making up the common law. American colonists inherited the common law from England, modifying it to suit their simpler social structures and different needs. American lawyers suffered from the scarcity of law books. Lawyers might need to consult everything from landmark legal treatises and commentaries to form books for a backwoods sheriff or local judge. Because books were scarce and expensive, their owners preserved them with care and vigilance. Lawyers also safeguarded notes of precedents and leading cases, though generous practitioners shared those notes with favored younger members of the bar. Reports of English cases were hard to find in America, and there were no authoritative reports of colonial cases.[15]

Modern law students are used to well-stocked law libraries and rich online databases, but their counterparts in eighteenth-century Massachusetts had to persuade senior attorneys to grant them access to printed volumes and privately compiled case reports. Lawyers made commonplace books, into which they copied extracts from treatises and cases. Adams used parts of at least four volumes of his manuscript diary for common-placing.[16] He also tried to acquire law books for himself, to build a law library that would be an invaluable resource for his practice—a habit dovetailing with his lifelong hunger for books.

As Adams read and copied, he realized to his dismay that his legal education was really self-education. Putnam was a passive mentor; the man who was supposed to supervise his legal studies had little time or inclination to examine him or to discuss the treatises that he was reading and the documents that he was copying. Not only did Adams have to teach himself the law—after two years of self-guided study, he had to figure out how to become a lawyer without Putnam's aid.

Adams's disillusionment with Putnam was so complete that he did not ask Putnam for the customary letter of recommendation from an attorney supervising an aspiring lawyer's studies. Nor did he get himself sworn in at the bar of the Worcester Inferior Pleas Court, the locus of Putnam's practice; Putnam had done nothing to get Adams sworn in there. More important, Adams worried that taking that step on his own would generate suspicious questions about his putative mentor's indifference to him, casting doubt on his candidacy for the bar.

Having returned to Braintree to live with his family, Adams nerved himself to approach established attorneys to forge a network of connections to support his quest to join the bar. The most important was Jeremiah Gridley; others included James Otis, Benjamin Prat, and Oxenbridge Thacher.[17] To ensure that he could answer the questions that Gridley and the others might pose to test his learning, he studied at Harvard College's library. In his diary for October 5, 1758, he recorded his ambitions:

> Let me read with Attention, Deliberation, Distinction. . . . Let me be able to draw the True Character both of the Text of Justinian,

and of the Notes of his Commentator, when I have finished the Book. Few of my Contemporary Beginners, in the Study of the Law, have the Resolution, to aim at much Knowledge in the Civil Law. Let me therefore distinguish myself from them, by the Study of the Civil Law, in its native languages, those of Greece and Rome. I shall gain the Consideration and perhaps favour of Mr. Gridley and Mr. Pratt by this means.[18]

Then he rode to Boston to attend court and to seek out sponsors.

On October 25, 1758, Adams finally got to meet with Gridley in his Boston law office; he was so struck by their meeting that he recorded its details in his diary and later (in slightly different form) in his autobiography.[19] To Adams, Gridley appeared imposing and authoritative; he was fifty-six, about a decade younger than Adams's father. Like many of the province's lawyers, Gridley was an alumnus of Harvard College. By this point in his career, he was Massachusetts's most distinguished lawyer, having trained such leading lights as James Otis and William Cushing, as well as Prat and Thacher.

Gridley questioned Adams closely about his studies, giving him some uncomfortable moments until the younger man dragged forward his latest reading in Latin, which mollified the older man. Then Gridley offered Adams sage counsel about beginning the practice of law. He advised him to pursue the study of the law rather than the gain of it, and not to marry too early. He also pledged to sponsor Adams's admission to the bar of Suffolk County, which included Braintree and, more important for Adams's ambitions, Boston, the fount of provincial legal business.

After thanking Gridley earnestly, the aspiring law student sought out the others on his list. Thacher was cooler to Adams than Gridley had been, but promised his support. Prat refused to support Adams, reproving him for not having a letter from Putnam and for not having got himself sworn in at Worcester, for then he would have been entitled to automatic admission at the bar of Suffolk County. Buoyed by Gridley's and Thacher's promises of support and cowed by Prat's refusal, Adams met with Otis, who was reassuring and supportive.

On November 6, 1758, John Adams sat in the courthouse in Boston, waiting nervously to put himself forward to seek admission to the bar, uncomfortable at the absence of anyone who might sponsor him. At what Adams remembered as the last possible moment, Gridley entered the court. Gridley praised Adams's legal knowledge, his assiduous study with Putnam and on his own, and his fitness to be admitted to the bar. To Adams's relief, the committee immediately admitted him to practice. Then, as was the custom, he shared a bowl of punch with the committee, Gridley, and the other senior members of the bar present for the event.[20] Adams always venerated Gridley, grateful for his patronage and his advice. When Gridley died in 1766, Adams absorbed much of his practice and bought books from his library.

Adams began legal practice in Braintree. Soon after his admission to practice, he took his first case—and it ended badly. It was a dispute between two neighbors of the Adamses, Luke Lambert and Joseph Field. Lambert's horse broke into Field's field, and Lambert entered the field without Field's permission to secure the horse; Field wanted to sue Lambert for damages for trespass. Adams's mother was nagging him to begin practicing law, and Field kept insisting that Adams take his case. He finally gave in, partly because of his fear that his neighbors and potential clients might think him incapable of legal practice if he declined the case. Drafting his declaration (the document beginning the lawsuit), Adams made a small but telling error in pleading. Citing that error, the court found for Lambert and against Field.

In a diary entry written between filing his declaration and having it disallowed, Adams, consumed with worry, reproached himself for his haste, for his failure to avoid an avoidable mistake, and for that mistake's likely damage to his career. He blamed his mother and Field for pushing him to take a case before he felt ready, and Putnam for not having trained him properly. Most of all, he blamed himself for his "Precipitation":[21]

> I this Evening delivered to Mr. Field, a Declaration in Trespass for a Rescue. I was obliged to finish it, without sufficient examination. If it should escape an Abatement, it is quite indigested, and unclerklike. I am ashamed of it, and concerned for it. If my first Writt should be abated, if I should throw a large Bill of Costs on my first Client, my Character and Business will suffer greatly. It will be said, I dont understand my Business. No one will trust his Interest in my hands. I never Saw a Writt, on that Law of the Province. I was perplexed, and am very anxious about it. Now I feel the Dissadvantages of Putnams Insociability, and neglect of me. Had he given me now and then a few Hints concerning Practice, I should be able to judge better at this Hour than I can now. I have Reason to complain of him.

Adams contemplated his future:

> But, it is my Destiny to dig Treasures with my own fingers. No Body will lend me or sell me a Pick axe. How this first Undertaking will terminate, I know not. I hope the Dispute will be settled between them, or submitted, and so my Writt never come to an Examination. But if it should I must take the Consequences. I must assume a Resolution, to bear without freting.[22]

Adams learned his lesson and gained ground as a lawyer. He established a grueling seven-year plan of self-directed study to remedy gaps in his learning. In that way, he told himself, he would match such exemplary practitioners as Otis in legal learning and in skill arguing before a jury—though again he reproved himself for having to subject himself to more academic self-discipline. He also recognized that lawyers had to make themselves known to their neighbors. For the next two years, he followed a pattern defined by three things: close study of legal authorities; moping about his failures to meet his own high standards; and forays into

Braintree's social world. As he tried to keep himself moving forward, dreams of ambition and glory tormented him—and he reproached himself for not achieving his goals. Writing in his diary on November 14, 1760, after his twenty-fifth birthday, he took stock of himself:

> Another Year is now gone and upon Recollection, I find I have executed none of my Plans of study. I cannot Satisfy my self that I am much more knowing either from Books, or Men, from this Chamber, or the World, than I was at least a Year ago. . . . Most of my Time has been spent in Rambling and Dissipation. Riding, and Walking, Smoking Pipes and Spending Evenings, consume a vast Proportion of my Time, and the Cares and Anxieties of Business, damp my Ardor and scatter my attention. But I must stay more at home—and commit more to Writing. A Pen is certainly an excellent Instrument, to fix a Mans Attention and to inflame his Ambition. I am therefore beginning a new literary Year, with the 26th. of my life.[23]

Beside his efforts to educate himself and to circulate in society seeking clients, Adams pursued a new idea. Hoping to rise by choosing a sound cause, he launched a campaign for temperance, seeking to reduce the number of licensed inns in Braintree. In early 1761, the town's selectmen gave him a victory, voting to permit only three such inns. More important to his professional self-image was his campaign against self-taught practitioners known as "pettifoggers."[24] His goals were to define new professional standards for the bar and to devise ways to enforce them. Having fought hard to become a lawyer and to establish his practice, he saw pettifoggers as untrained individuals unscrupulous enough to prey on naive clients. Pompous local dignitaries armed with just a battered sheriff's manual held themselves out as lawyers, though they could only draft an elementary will, draw up a simple deed to sell a piece of land, or file a basic lawsuit. The provincial bar had no power to enforce standards or to drive untrained practitioners from the courts.

To Adams, pettifoggers were threats not just to the elite bar. Without sophisticated legal knowledge, they misled clients and then denied responsibility for their plight. Such conduct confirmed ordinary people's low opinions of all lawyers and promoted disrespect for the law. Adams encouraged his colleagues to close ranks against pettifoggers. He also sought to raise the bar's standards by organizing and taking part in such professional activities as reading circles. His zeal made him few friends in Braintree or Boston, yet it established him as a valued member of the bar, raising his profile as an able, industrious lawyer.

On May 25, 1761, John Adams's father died, a few months past his seventieth birthday. In his autobiography, Adams recorded his love and admiration for Deacon John Adams and his sense of obligation to him. He reported that his father was one of "Seventeen Aged People in Our Neighborhood" carried off by a violent fever, "a kind of Influenza." The same fever threatened his mother's life, but, being younger and stronger, she recovered. On reading the older man's will, Adams discovered that his father had left him a house and barn, amounting to one-third of his real estate, as well as one-third of his personal estate. This house, a second saltbox house resembling his birthplace, would be his home for the next twenty-five years. This new bequest surprised Adams because his father's will silently set aside their agreement under which his college tuition was to be his total inheritance.[25]

After two years of difficulty, Adams's legal practice bloomed; the growth of his business confirmed his success as a skilled advocate. A diary entry for August 1, 1761, weeks after his father's death, shows how comfortable he had become with his work as a lawyer. His sketch of an argument to a jury shows his legal mind in full flower—his learning, his gift for a well-turned phrase, and his ability to explain complex issues. Reading it, we enter the intellectual world of an eighteenth-century lawyer preoccupied with the English constitution.[26]

Adams first stated the lawsuit's origins and facts, blending legal detail with the fervent, ingratiating rhetoric of a counsel's opening address to a jury:

> Daniel Prat vs. Thos. Colson.—This Action was brot by Plaintiff
> vs. Colson as Administrator, on the Estate of Mr. Bolter, for
> Non-Performance of a Covenant of Indenture. Prat was a poor,
> fatherless Child (and) his Mother Unable to provide for him,
> bound him an Apprentice to Mr. Bolter. He was then under 10
> Years of Age, and so was bound for Eleven Years, and some odd
> Months. In Consideration of this very long and unusual Term of
> Apprenticeship his Master convenanted [that is, made a binding
> agreement] to teach him to read, write and Cypher, and to teach
> him the Trade of a Weaver. But we complain that he never taught us
> either to read, write or Cypher, or to weave. Call the Proof.

Then he addressed the relationship between the law and the facts.
Significantly, his argument invoked the core moral principles of the
unwritten British constitution, in a lawsuit by an apprentice against
his master for violating the terms of his apprenticeship:

> The Law, Gentlemen, is extremely tender and indulgent to such
> Actions as these. For such is the Benignity and Humanity of the
> English Constitution that all the weak, and helpless, and friendless
> Part of our Species are taken under its Peculiar Care and Protection.
> Women, Children, and Especially Widows and fatherless Children,
> have always, from the Compassion of the Law peculiar Priviledges
> and Indulgences allowed them.
> Therefore as a poor, fatherless, and friendless Child the Law
> would allow great Indulgence and Lenity to this Plaintiff.

Adams's focus on education resonated with his lifelong preoccupation with education and learning, drawing tight the link between education and legal principle:

> But he is to be favored for Another Reason. Because the English
> Law greatly favours Education. In every English Country, some sort
> of Education, some Acquaintance with Letters, is necessary, that a
> Man may fill any station whatever. (In) the Countries of slavery,
> and Romish superstition, the Laity must not learn to read, lest they
> should detect the gross Impostures of the Priesthood, and shake off

the Yoke of Bondage. But in Protestant Countries and especially in England and its Colonies, Freedom of Enquiry is allowed to be not only the Priviledge but the Duty of every Individual. We know it to be our Duty, to read, examine and judge for ourselves, even of ourselves what is right. No Priest nor Pope has any Right to say what I shall believe, and I will not believe one Word they say, if I think it is not founded in Reason and in Revelation. Now how can I judge what My Bible justifies unless I can read my Bible.

Adams concluded his argument with an analogy that jurors would find familiar. He invoked not just the idea of elections but the need for the voter to use reading to inform himself to cast an effective vote. Adams focused on reading also for studying the Bible, the almanac (useful for weather), and newspapers:

The English Constitution is founded, tis bottomed And grounded on the Knowledge and good sense of the People. The very Ground of our Liberties, is the freedom of Elections. Every Man has in Politicks as well as Religion, a Right to think and speak and Act for himself. No man either King or Subject, Clergyman or Layman has any Right to dictate to me the Person I shall choose for my Legislator and Ruler. I must judge for myself, but how can I judge, how can any Man judge, unless his Mind has been opened and enlarged by Reading. A Man who can read, will find in his Bible, in the common sermon Books that common People have by them and even in the Almanack and News Papers, Rules and observations that will enlarge his Range of Thought, and enable him the better to judge who has and who has not that Integrity of Heart, and that Compass of Knowledge and Understanding, which form the Statesman.

Adams practiced law from 1758 through 1774, when his increasing involvement in colonial resistance to Britain cut into his time. Thereafter he handled cases intermittently, between bouts of service in the First and Second Continental Congresses, until 1777, when his first diplomatic mission ended his legal career. Though he briefly considered returning to law practice after the end of his diplomatic career in 1788 and again after he left the presidency in 1801, he never did.

By the early 1760s, Adams was a skilled trial lawyer. Central to his success as a practitioner were his mastery of the law's intricate technicalities—specifically, the knotty system of pleading and procedure governing all lawsuits—and his gift for explaining complex legal concepts and rules to the ordinary farmers who served on a typical jury.

Adams's practice ranged through all levels of courts in Massachusetts—the major trial courts, the Inferior and Superior Courts of Common Pleas, and such specialized courts as the Vice Admiralty Court (a court handling claims regarding shipping). He regularly appeared at courts in Braintree and in Boston; he also "rode circuit" throughout the province, sometimes as far north as Maine, stopping in towns and villages to appear in court cases or to handle such discrete legal matters as drafting a will. While riding circuit, he would meet with clients.

Adams's diverse caseload showed a full range of legal issues and a client list spanning all levels of society. Mostly, he represented individual clients, but he also handled actions for villages and towns. His client list ranged from ordinary men and women up to such grand figures as John Hancock and former royal governor Francis Bernard. Many of his cases focused on issues of debtor and creditor, the bread and butter of lawyers' practice. He also handled criminal cases, including murder, rape, larceny, assault, and counterfeiting, as well as tarring and feathering, mobbing, and rioting. Though slavery was a relatively minor part of the economy of colonial Massachusetts, Adams's surviving legal papers show that he appeared in some cases in which slaves sought their freedom, on the side of the slave seeking freedom. He insisted that juries never kept anyone in slavery—but in one case, *Newport v. Billing* (No. 39), the jury did so hold. These cases, which arose after 1766, were based on precedent and the facts more than on generalized principles of the rights of man or ideas of the Enlightenment. They never mentioned or discussed race or the relationship between slavery and race.[27]

Adams practiced by himself. There were no law firms as we understand them, though he often joined with another lawyer to handle a specific case, as in the Boston Massacre cases in 1770. Lawyers in Adams's time gave one another remarkable collegiality and moral support. They lent books and entered appearances in a given court when a fellow lawyer could not attend a court session. (Entering an appearance kept a case alive by confirming one's presence in court and readiness to go to law, avoiding a default judgment against one's client.)

We do not know how lucrative Adams's law practice was because his account books have not survived. He benefited more from quantity of business than from any individual fee. In part, as with Jefferson's Virginia in the same period, Massachusetts statutes limited the fees that lawyers could charge.[28] Adams's income came in small payments of twelve or sixteen shillings per legal filing, lawsuit commenced, or lawsuit settled, rather than from any large fees.

Adams's practice was typical of any major lawyer in colonial America—but it matters that he was a Massachusetts lawyer. Ranking with New York, South Carolina, and Pennsylvania, Massachusetts was a sophisticated jurisdiction. Adams's approach to studying law as an intellectual discipline, spurred by his own inclination and by Gridley's counsel, may have ensured his success in so demanding a practice environment.[29]

While practicing law and mastering his profession, Adams continued to indulge his taste for writing, publishing in Boston's newspapers. The heated politics of Boston and of Massachusetts became a focus for him, but at first he decided not to take sides. Instead, he stepped outside factional lines, so that he could freely mock both sides. The dispute that he was watching paralleled those raging in other colonies between backers of a royal governor and supporters of the faction opposing that governor, each side led by prominent local families. In Massachusetts, supporters of Governor Francis Bernard, Lieutenant Governor Thomas Hutchinson, and their allies confronted supporters of James Otis Jr. and his allies.

Under the pen name "Humphrey Ploughjogger," a humble farmer writing phonetically and plainly, Adams mocked the bitter personal tone of the disputes raging in the newspapers. Sometimes, "Ploughjogger" mocked the physical appearance of people of African descent—our first evidence of Adams's less than enlightened view of people of African ancestry.[30] Not content with "Humphrey Ploughjogger," Adams created another persona for himself—a gentleman who wrote learned, condescending essays as "U."[31] At one point Adams pitted "Humphrey Ploughjogger" and "U." against each other. These essays revealed Adams's remarkable ability to create two opposite characters and to maintain the quarrel between them. Adams published three essays as "Ploughjogger" in 1763; a fourth in 1765 in the midst of the Stamp Act controversy; and two more in 1767 targeting his personal friend, political adversary, and legal competitor Jonathan Sewall, who wrote for the newspapers as "J."[32] After 1767, "Humphrey Ploughjogger" vanished from Adams's repertoire. His 1765 essay series "A Dissertation on the Canon and Feudal Law" signaled the more serious tone of his polemical writing during the 1760s and 1770s.

Having established himself as a lawyer, Adams was ready for the next major step in his life—marriage. In describing his life as a boy and a young man, he regularly referred to his attraction to girls and later to women. Regularly, he reproved himself in his diary for wasting time in "gallanting the Girls" or in paying attention to "the Girls." He also remembered Gridley's advice against marrying too early—a mistake that the older man warned would be fatal to a lawyer's career. And yet, from time to time, Adams was tempted.

For example, in 1759 the vivacious Hannah Quincy preoccupied him to such an extent that he recorded in his diary a flirtatious dialogue in which she pelted him with questions about how he, an industrious lawyer, would see relations between himself and his wife. Could she interrupt his train of thought with impunity? Would he rather study his books or spend time with her?[33] Growing impatient with Adams's uncertainty and diffidence about making a match,

Hannah Quincy married the physician Bela Lincoln, who shared her eagerness to marry and start a family. At first so melancholy that he gave up tea because it reminded him of his pleasant hours with Hannah, Adams recovered his balance, urging himself to pursue his ambitions.[34]

At this time, Adams knew only slightly the woman who would become his wife, and she was not the usual kind of young woman whom he gallanted. Abigail Smith was the second of four daughters of Rev. William Smith and Elizabeth Quincy Smith.[35] The family had its roots in Weymouth, a farming village near Braintree and about fourteen miles southeast of Boston, where Reverend Smith had his church. Born on November 22, 1744, about nine years after John, Abigail was close to her mother's mother, Elizabeth Quincy of the powerful, august Quincy family. Elizabeth Quincy was a formidable woman whom her granddaughter admired and emulated in her intelligence, her self-taught learning, and her spirited character.

Abigail's family believed that young women needed little learning beyond reading, writing, and arithmetic; thus, in Abigail's view, they neglected her schooling. Further, their concern for Abigail's fragile health induced them to keep her at home rather than to send her to another town to one of the few schools open to female students; they feared with reason that she might fall prey to one of the waves of disease sweeping through small towns. Nonetheless, Abigail found ways to satisfy her hunger for learning. In this effort, her Grandmother Quincy played a leading role, as did her sisters and friends. Abigail became a tireless reader and writer, using letter writing to foster her education and to examine herself. Abigail had no other way to further her education than to read whatever books came to hand. Her family saw her as a younger daughter destined for marriage. Thus, she tagged along with her older sister, Mary, and Mary's beau Richard Cranch, a friend of John Adams.

Abigail first met John when she was fifteen and he was twenty-four; he had called at Reverend Smith's parsonage as part of his effort to make himself known in the town to advance his law practice.

Unimpressed by Reverend Smith's parade of learning or his quirky behavior, which he mocked in his diary, Adams also did not take to the wit of the minister's two older daughters, Mary and Abigail, especially when they aimed that wit at him. They targeted his vanity and stiffness, traits for which he reproached himself, though he resented others mocking his faults.

John and Abigail gradually changed their views of each other. He saw her wit as a desirable quality, reflecting her brilliant mind. He also realized that she was intellectually curious. These aspects of her appealed to him, though most New England men would not have found them attractive. She was his intellectual equal, just as devoted to reading and writing. Soon he was lending her books, and they were exchanging bantering letters—though she was more careful, and he was more exuberant and reckless, about the proprieties governing their correspondence. For example, on February 14, 1763, he joked about what might have happened had the weather not prevented his visit:

> Accidents are often more Friendly to us, than our own Prudence. I intended to have been at Weymouth Yesterday, but a storm prevented.—Cruel, Yet perhaps blessed storm!—Cruel for detaining me from so much friendly, social Company, and perhaps blessed to you, or me or both, for keeping me at <u>my Distance</u>. For every experimental Phylosopher knows, that the steel and the Magnet or the Glass and feather will not fly together with more Celerity, than somebody And somebody.[36]

Unsure about Abigail's attraction to the self-conscious young lawyer, her parents were skeptical of his profession and critical of his lineage. By contrast, Abigail was a parson's daughter and a member of the Quincy family—qualities as close to aristocracy in colonial New England as imaginable. Also, Reverend Smith and his wife saw Abigail as too young for marriage, not having reached her twentieth year. Gradually, the younger couple wore down her parents' doubts.[37]

In early 1764, an epidemic of smallpox struck Boston. Aware that his trips to Boston on legal business exposed him to the danger of infection, John decided to get himself inoculated—a controversial medical practice and a major undertaking for the patient. Inoculation was risker than vaccination, which was devised years later. The doctor exposed Adams to smallpox, and he contracted a mild version of it, which would then immunize him. An inoculated person might die from the disease, and he had to be isolated to prevent him from exposing others to infection. Abigail was determined to be inoculated as well, but at nineteen she was still under the control of her parents, who refused permission, fearing for her health.

Enduring his inoculation, which included enforced isolation for weeks and a bland, insipid diet, John wrote often to Abigail. He sustained himself with thoughts of her even as doctor's rules forbade him to see her, and he wrote to reassure her of his good health by showing his good spirits. He ensured that his letters to her did not carry infection by smoking them with his cigar, a step repeated at the Smith parsonage before Abigail was allowed to open them. In return, she wrote to entertain him and to prevent his succumbing to boredom, occasionally enclosing tobacco that he might use in smoking his future letters to her.

Their exchanges of letters during the two months of his quarantine were more frequent than all their previous correspondence— more than twenty between April 7 and May 9, 1764. In these letters, they ventured freer expressions of their love and affection, and their occasional vexation with each other. The forced separation, the first of many in their relationship, fostered and deepened their feelings for each other. To reassure Abigail and ease her anxiety about his health and his likelihood of surviving the inoculation, John sent letters teeming with anecdotes and local news, and with accounts of the hospital where he resided and of the doctors' treatment of those being inoculated. Abigail sent letters filled with chatty accounts of her relatives but also took pains to express tenderness and concern for him: "Let her who tenderly cares for you both in Sickness and

Health, intreet you to be careful of that Health upon which depends the Happiness of your a. Smith."[38] She also commented on the similarities and differences of men and women. On April 16, she wrote boldly of her lack of restraint in writing to him: "Dont you think me a Courageous Being? Courage is a laudable, a Glorious Virtue in your Sex, why not in mine? (For my part, I think you ought to applaud me for mine.)"[39]

In early May 1764, they exchanged letters cataloging each other's faults. Abigail reproved John for haughtiness and stiffness, and he scolded her for such pretended defects (virtues, in his eyes) as her habits of reading, thinking, and writing, which she pursued instead of the card playing with which young women occupied their time. He added that she tended to hang her head like a bulrush, that she was not a good singer, and that she was "parrot-toed."[40] Both welcomed his release from quarantine following his inoculation.[41]

On October 25, 1764, after three years of courtship, John and Abigail married. The wedding took place in the parsonage at Weymouth; Reverend Smith performed the ceremony. Three weeks before the wedding, as they arranged the practical details of forming their new household, Abigail wrote, "The cart you mentiond came yesterday, by which I sent as many things as the horse would draw[;] the rest of my things will be ready the Monday after you return from Taunton. And—then Sir if you please you may take me."[42] This flirtatious invitation helped to set the tone for a marriage of fifty-four years, buttressed by a correspondence written with wit, affection, and candor—a marriage crucial to their education about themselves and each other.

Chapter Three

"Britain and America are staring at each other"

Revolutionary Advocate (1761–1774)

On New Year's Day 1766, John Adams wrote in his diary: "We are now upon the Beginning of a Year of greater Expectation than any, that has passed before it. This Year brings Ruin or Salvation to the British Colonies. The Eyes of all America, are fixed on the Parliament. In short, Britain and America are staring at each other.—And they will probably stare more and more for sometime."[1]

Adams's prophecy came true, though he could not have foreseen how true. Anyone trying to predict British North America's future on New Year's Day 1766 would have been shocked by the ensuing events—the first phase of the American Revolution. Indeed, as Adams insisted to Thomas Jefferson and other correspondents when he was an old man, the period between 1760 and 1775 *was* the American Revolution.[2]

Basking in the triumph of the Treaty of Paris of 1763, the British Empire had just won the most prolonged and difficult colonial war of the eighteenth century. Known in America as the French and Indian War and in Europe as the Seven Years' War, the conflict began in the forests of British North America. It raged for nine years across three continents and on the high seas, testing the British and the French empires almost to their financial and administrative breaking points.[3]

As the war raged, British North Americans sought to prove their value to the British Empire. They saw themselves as the happiest and most loyal of all King George III's subjects. They were committed to take up arms in the cause of British liberty against the decadence and tyranny that they associated with France, to counter the dangers that France and its Native American allies posed to them and to the empire.[4] Americans welcomed the British victory in that war. Few foresaw that the war's consequences would generate a frightening disruption of relations between Britain and British North America.

Resistance to British policy beginning in 1765 transformed the lives of all Americans. It not only created new forms of government and new alliances and enmities—for individuals like Adams, it created new ways of thinking, new opportunities, and new career paths.[5] The clash spurred Adams to master the American view of the constitutional and legal doctrines framing the dispute, which he expounded in page after page of intricate argument. He was educating himself to become a revolutionary advocate; he also sought to teach Americans to do the same. For the rest of his life, he thought, wrote, and talked about the Revolution. He deemed himself well qualified to do so, for in 1761, he witnessed what he later insisted was the Revolution's birth.

For Adams, the Revolution was born in a Boston courtroom. As a young lawyer, he observed and took careful notes of court sessions. In February 1761, therefore, he was at his place in the Massachusetts Superior Court in Boston's Town House, pen in hand, following the argument in *Petition of Lechmere*. In an 1817 letter to his former law clerk William Tudor, Adams wryly offered to give a talented painter a sketch of the scene. Conveying the event's drama, Adams was not only describing the scene but reliving it.

In the elegant courtroom sat the five judges of the Massachusetts Superior Court, Lieutenant Governor Thomas Hutchinson presiding. Gathered before them were the lawyers of Boston and of Middlesex County, clad in the legal profession's black robes and powdered wigs. Standing before the judges were the lawyers on both sides of *Petition of Lechmere.* Jeremiah Gridley appeared for the Crown; Oxenbridge Thacher and James Otis Jr. represented Boston merchants opposing the Crown. Adams added a word portrait of himself:

> One circumstance more. Samuel Quincy and John Adams had been admitted Barristers at that Term. John was the youngest he should be painted looking like a short thick fat Archbishop of Canterbury seated at the table, with a pen in his hand, lost in admiration, now & then minuting *those despicable notes which you know that Jonathan Williams Austin, your fellow student in my Office, stole from my desk and printed in the Massachusetts Spy, with two or three bombastic expressions interpolated by himself; and which your Pupil, Judge Minot has printed in his history.*[6]

Petition of Lechmere focused on a controversial British tool of customs enforcement. A writ of assistance was an unrestricted search warrant having force for up to six months after the death of the monarch reigning when it was issued. The writ granted customs officials the power to search anywhere they wished and to seize anything they deemed evidence or contraband (unlawful property, such as smuggled goods). British officials charged with enforcing customs laws and with combating smuggling prized writs of assistance. Not just smugglers but American merchants of all kinds detested these writs as violating their understandings of English constitutional and legal doctrines; the traditional view was that a search warrant must specify the place to be searched and the person or things to be seized, which these writs did not do.[7]

Why was *Petition of Lechmere* before the court? In 1760, King George II had died; the writs issued in his name were due to expire six months after his death, and British customs officials sought to renew them. Arguing for their renewal, Gridley invoked an act of Parliament authorizing the Exchequer in Britain to issue such writs and later parliamentary acts authorizing colonial courts to issue them.

Given Gridley's central place in Adams's understanding of the law, he naturally admired Gridley's "characteristic learning, ingenuity, and dignity." Adams also praised Thacher for "the softness of manners, the ingenuity and cool reasoning, which were remarkable in his amiable character."[8] Otis dazzled him. Adams had once been ambivalent about Otis—grateful that he had supported Adams's candidacy for the bar, yet disliking his fondness for the pettifoggers whom Adams was striving to exclude from the courts. In this case, however, Otis inspired Adams, with an impact still powerful after fifty-six years: "But Otis was a flame of fire! With a promptitude of Classical Allusions, a depth of research, a rapid summary of historical events & dates, a profusion of Legal Authorities, a prophetic glance of his eyes into futurity, and a rapid torrent of impetuous Eloquence he hurried away all before him."[9]

Otis based his argument on a startling claim—that writs of assistance violated Englishmen's constitutional rights, whether they lived in England or in British North America. Though Parliament might have authorized writs of assistance, Otis insisted that the statute had violated basic principles of English liberty; no statute enacted by Parliament could violate those principles. His argument was radical because it asserted a higher standard of constitutionality than Parliament's enactment of a law, though Otis also invoked authorities justifying such an argument.

Otis's argument, made with passion and skill, was political as well as constitutional and legal. He sought to box Hutchinson into a dangerous choice between two unpalatable options—refusing to renew the writs, thereby giving victory to Boston's merchants and defeat to the Crown, or renewing the writs, thereby alienating himself from the people and merchants of Boston and Massachusetts. Recognizing Otis's trap, Hutchinson used delay to escape it.[10] As presiding judge, he adjourned the court, citing the need to secure information from Britain whether the Exchequer was authorizing colonial authorities to issue writs of assistance. Months later, confirmation in hand, Hutchinson led the court in authorizing the writs' renewal.

Petition of Lechmere was entwined with the political rivalry between Otis and Hutchinson and their families, which in turn was entangled with the factionalism besetting colonial Massachusetts politics. Hutchinson belonged to a set of families aligned with the colony's royal governor; Otis belonged to a competing set of families, ranged against the royal governor and his local allies.

Questions of office, power, and political advancement fed this political enmity. James Otis Sr., the attorney's father, had expected to become chief justice of the Massachusetts Superior Court, having secured promises from two previous royal governors that he would be named to that office, once it fell vacant. When Chief Justice Samuel Sewall died in 1760, however, the governor, Sir Francis Bernard, not only had not made any such promise to Otis Sr.—he did not know that his predecessors had done so. Instead, Bernard named Thomas Hutchinson to the post. Hutchinson was not a lawyer and had no legal training, but Bernard knew him to be a friend of the Crown. The political shock waves triggered by Bernard's inadvertent snub to Otis Sr. roiled the colony's elites, spicing with resentment the hostility between Hutchinson and the Otises.[11]

Petition of Lechmere raised a substantive constitutional and legal issue—that of contrasting English and American understandings of constitutional rights. Did that issue have the larger consequences identified by Adams in his letter to Tudor? He wrote:

> Every man of a crowded audience appeared to me to go away, as I did, ready to take arms against writs of assistance. Then and there was the first scene of the first act of opposition to the arbitrary claims of Great Britain. Then and there the child Independence was born. In fifteen years, namely in 1776, he grew up to manhood, and declared himself free.[12]

This letter and Adams's minutes of the case have helped to create a vivid mythology of the Revolution's birth in that Boston courtroom, making Otis the magician who called the spirit of revolution and independence into being. In 1761, however, nobody except a few worried British colonial administrators saw independence as an American goal.

Was Adams engaging in "historical revisionism" in telling this dramatic story of the birth of independence in 1761? Was Adams seeking to win for Massachusetts the leading role in giving rise to the Revolution? Virginians insist that a dispute arising there in the late 1750s and early 1760s was the first open battle between the colonies and the mother country. The "Parsons' Cause" controversy raised issues about the Church of England's entitlement to tax revenues to support its churches and ministers. Such southern revolutionaries as the attorney Patrick Henry responded by challenging British authority.[13] Competition for the honor of beginning the Revolution has pitted the "Parsons' Cause" against *Petition of Lechmere*.[14]

What Adams wrote is not what later critics ascribe to him. Adams identified what was born in 1761 as the "child Independence." According to him, that "child" grew up in the fifteen years between *Petition of Lechmere* and the Declaration of Independence. Thus, his claim differs starkly from the claim for which he has been arraigned as a mythmaker. Over time, the issues first raised in 1761 developed to pose irresolvable questions about the British constitutional framework, helping to force Americans to the brink of independence by 1776. But in 1761 that result was by no means predictable.

The French and Indian War's ending in 1763 briefly abated the urgency of the British need for colonial tax revenues, the catalyst of the writs of assistance case. And yet the war's debts survived the war. In 1764, Britain renewed its demands for colonial revenue, igniting a new dispute with its colonies. The issues surrounding taxation alarmed such attorneys as John Adams, for they threatened the colonists' English constitutional rights as they understood them.

British politicians believed that they had fought the war mostly to protect their American colonies against French expansion. Because Britain had borne the burdens of fighting the war and of paying for it, the mother country begrudged the costs of a war fought mostly for the colonists' benefit. Therefore, the king's ministers agreed, the colonists ought to assume their fair share of the financial burden of defending the empire and protecting territories won from France.[15]

Americans denied that the victory of 1763 was imperial alone. Rather, they insisted, the British ought to share credit with the American militias, who had fought and died alongside British regulars.[16] Because the victory was a joint effort, the colonists had proved their role in securing the victory and should not be taxed to pay for it. This claim did not convince the British, who listened to British officers and soldiers who mocked American militias as untrained, cowardly, and useless. Convinced of their case for taxation and of the emptiness of American arguments against it, the king's ministers were ready to impose new taxes on the colonies by acts of Parliament to save the empire's finances.

In 1764, Great Britain announced that it would levy taxes and the colonists would pay them. This plan was new to the Americans, though other subjects in the empire had long shouldered the burden of paying for British regulars stationed in their midst.[17] As a first step, Chancellor of the Exchequer George Grenville seized the opportunity presented by the expiration in 1763 of the Molasses Act of 1733 to build American taxation into a new statute. The old law, taxing molasses (an ingredient of rum derived from making refined sugar), had been enacted to prevent the colonists from smuggling molasses from non-British Caribbean colonies. The 1733 statute never worked because it set the tax too high and customs enforcement was unreliable and corrupt. Grenville's act would cut the tax rate in half while intensifying enforcement; he hoped that these changes would make the new statute enforceable and palatable.[18] The new American Revenue Act was nicknamed the Sugar Act.

Despite Grenville's hopes, some Americans found the Sugar Act problematic. In May 1764, the Boston town meeting adopted instructions (drafted by John's second cousin Samuel Adams) to its representatives in the colonial legislature, the Massachusetts General Court. The instructions attacked the Sugar Act as a dangerous precursor of new taxes: "If Taxes are laid upon us in any Shape without ever having a Legal Representation where they are laid, are we not reduced from the Character of Free Subjects to the miserable State of Tributary Slaves—[?]"[19]

These instructions stressed a central point of dispute between the colonies and Britain—the link between representation and taxation. The colonists insisted that a vital rule of the unwritten British constitution was "No taxation without representation." British subjects could be taxed only by a legislature in which they were represented by representatives whom they could elect. Because Americans could not vote for members of Parliament, they could not be taxed by Parliament. By contrast, neither the king's ministers nor Parliament saw any constitutional problem with Britain taxing the colonists, nor did they see that the colonists might have genuine objections to such taxes for reasons beyond mere unwillingness to pay.

To justify "no taxation without representation," the colonists invoked a great English precedent. In 1629, Charles I dissolved Parliament; for years thereafter, he justified imposing new taxes on his subjects by his sole authority as monarch.[20] His efforts provoked a civil war, which in 1649 cost him his throne and his head. A long process of redefining the relationship between governors and governed culminated in the Glorious Revolution of 1688–89, in which King William III and Queen Mary acknowledged that they owed their thrones to Parliament and the English people.[21] In the 1760s, Americans argued bitterly, Parliament had decided that "no taxation without representation" was good enough for the mother country but not for American subjects. Seeing British taxes imposed on them as unconstitutional, Americans were determined to reject them.

British authorities brushed aside the issue of representation. Fed up with American efforts to evade customs duties by smuggling, British officials dismissed American constitutional arguments against parliamentary taxation as excuses for smuggling.[22] Also, by pushing their arguments for "no taxation without representation," the colonists unwittingly spotlighted the defects of representation in Britain—which were extensive. Few Englishmen voted in parliamentary elections, property qualifications for voting were too high, and district and borough lines had not been redrawn for centuries. Cities arising after the drawing of those lines (such as Birmingham and Manchester) went unrepresented. Some places having representation (such as Old Sarum) had dwindled away, but the owner of that land still had the right to elect members of the House of Commons representing an unpopulated region. Heeding American arguments about representation of the colonists in Parliament would open up a Pandora's box of defective representation in Britain.[23]

Instead, the British rejected the American case for representation. Each member of Parliament, this argument ran, represented the whole British people, not just his constituents; thus, he had to consider the interests of all the king's subjects. With this duty of virtual representation governing members of Parliament, British advocates concluded, there was no need for actual representation. Most Americans were unconvinced.[24]

Beyond issues of taxation and representation, whose vision of the unwritten English constitution would govern the American colonists?[25] Britain had an unwritten constitution—comprising statutory law, common law, customary law, and such documents of constitutional and legal importance as the Magna Carta.[26] The problem was that an unwritten constitution could have multiple, contradictory meanings, depending on who was interpreting it and for what purpose. Two such conceptions arose in the controversy between the colonies and Britain.

British authorities envisioned an unwritten constitution enshrining the supremacy of Parliament. Because in the seventeenth century Parliament had defended Englishmen's rights against Kings James I, Charles I, Charles II, and James II, Parliament deserved to reign supreme. In particular, because the colonies were founded on territories conquered by Britain, the colonists had only those constitutional rights that Parliament chose to recognize.

By contrast, Americans believed that the unwritten British constitution's central principle was restraint on power from whatever source. Power lacking restraint was arbitrary, which violated the constitution. Thus, to Americans, British claims of parliamentary supremacy over the colonies were unconstitutional. Further, Americans argued, their territories had not been conquered. Rather, they had been vacant; Americans had occupied them and created colonies without the mother country's aid. Thus, American subjects had the same rights, privileges, and immunities that subjects in the mother country had. This vision of the English constitution was central to John Adams's thinking. (Both arguments conveniently omitted Native Americans.)

These two models of the English constitution clashed in an intermittent but increasingly bitter argument that culminated with the declaration of American independence in 1776. In a world of law, one conception had to prevail—but which? The English constitutional system had no final judge acceptable to both sides who could issue an authoritative decision resolving the dispute. By 1776, the lack of such a final judge would shatter the British Empire.[27]

In 1764, the Sugar Act came too swiftly for Americans to organize resistance, but Parliament hinted that Britain might impose other taxes.[28] Americans therefore were ready for the Stamp Act of 1765. The Stamp Act imposed on Americans a form of taxation already used in the mother country. All paper goods—court filings, newspapers, pamphlets, and playing cards—had to bear a stamp symbolizing the tax paid.[29]

Seeing the dangers posed by the Sugar Act and the Stamp Act, Adams had begun to prepare himself to argue for the American cause. In the summer of 1765, as the Stamp Act was moving through Parliament, and as Abigail was enduring the ordeal of childbirth for the first time, giving birth to their daughter Abigail (Nabby), John was downstairs in his law office in his Braintree house's front parlor, writing on the constitutional dimensions of the Stamp Act controversy. In his autobiography he modestly called it "a Speculation or rather a Rhapsody."[30]

Adams was a member of the Sodality, a legal reading and debating society organized by Jeremiah Gridley. The Sodality's purpose was to assemble lawyers to discuss recent books of interest and to debate legal responses to public issues. Adams presented his essay on the Stamp Act to the Sodality. Praising his work, the group urged him to publish it. "A Dissertation on the Canon and Feudal Law" first saw print as a series of four articles in the *Boston Gazette*; reprinted in London, the series appeared as a small book in 1768.[31]

Adams began by tracing the dangers to liberty posed in medieval England by the union of canon law (doctrines of church law promulgated by the Roman Catholic Church) and feudal law (legal doctrines giving shape to feudalism). That episode of English history ended happily, he wrote, for England rejected canon and feudal law. Then Adams likened past to present. He warned that British policy was risking bringing tyranny to America, just as canon law and feudal law had tyrannized England.

Adams declared that the unwritten British constitution had to mean the same thing in the colonies that it meant in the mother country. There could not be one constitution for Britain and another for America, one set of rights for subjects in Britain and a narrower set of rights for subjects in America. Further, he insisted, the unwritten core principle of the British constitution was restraint on arbitrary power; Parliament's claimed power to legislate for the colonies exemplified arbitrary power. Adams warned that now was the time to resist such unconstitutional measures.

The "Dissertation," Adams's first major publication, won him more chances to defend the cause with his pen. In the fall of 1765, Braintree's town meeting asked Adams to draft instructions for the town's representatives to the Massachusetts General Court. Adams prepared a powerful, eloquent draft declaring the town's opposition to the Stamp Act:

> We further recommend the most clear and explicit Assertion and Vindication of our Rights and Liberties, to be entered on the Public Records; that the World may know, in the present and all future

Generations, that we have a clear Knowledge and a just Sense of them, and, with Submission to Divine Providence, that we never can be Slaves.[32]

On September 24, the town meeting adopted his draft. Printed in the newspapers, these instructions circulated through the province; at least forty other towns adopted them.

The "Dissertation" and the "Braintree Instructions" signaled Adams's debut as an advocate of resistance to British policies. His gifts for expounding learned legal and constitutional arguments enabled him to take the place of James Otis Jr. Otis was slowly descending into madness, which sidelined him from the dispute with Britain by the end of the 1760s and led to his death in 1783.[33] For the next few years, Adams wrote essays for Boston newspapers, making the colonists' case and refuting defenders of the British position.[34]

Samuel Adams practiced a different kind of leadership in the same cause. Older than his cousin John by eight years, Samuel was one of the first popular leaders of colonial resistance. Working naturally and easily with such groups as the Sons of Liberty, he focused on mustering the people to resistance.[35] John found Samuel's preference for radical, bottom-up activism disturbing. He also was wary of Samuel's leanings toward American independence, a step that he deemed unwarranted. For John Adams, the conflict with the mother country was a sad, bitter family quarrel—but he had no desire to break up the family. He preferred to address the dispute through the constitutional means that he saw as the strongest basis for the colonists' position. He had little liking for or understanding of such things as organizing the Sons of Liberty and orchestrating public displays of opposition to British governance. Seeking resolution of the dispute between the colonies and Britain that would preserve the empire, Adams still considered himself an Englishman writing and arguing in defense of English rights.

Adams chose a limited role in the movement opposing British policies. He would write polemics advancing the Americans' constitutional case, but that was all. Beyond his skepticism of the radicals' position, he had a more practical reason for limiting his participation. He had a growing family to support; in 1767, Abigail had given birth to their second child and first son, John Quincy, and Adams needed to devote himself to his law practice.

Adams owned a farm adjoining his house in Braintree, and he dreamed of returning to farming to support himself and his family—avoiding politics, the law, and other sources of contention. Though he loved the study of law and was an expert trial lawyer, he increasingly saw legal practice as a means to an end—supporting his family—and not as a career commanding his devotion. Though recognizing the need to ride circuit to sustain his law practice, he begrudged the time with his family that he lost in journeying from town to town, pursuing clients and cases.

In early 1770, however, Adams's legal practice brought him the most important cases of his career *and* plunged him anew into politics. The long-term cause was the growing hostility between Bostonians and British troops sent to occupy the town in October 1768. Bostonians hated the presence of British regulars; they saw their town as under siege. British troops saw Bostonians as uncouth, rebellious colonials. The longer British forces occupied Boston, the more the hostility between soldiers and townspeople escalated.[36]

On February 22, 1770, an argument erupted between Ebenezer Richardson, a pro-British Bostonian, and some of his neighbors, who suspected him of being a Crown informer. When the war of words boiled over, a mob pelted Richardson, his wife, and their house with garbage, stones, and clubs and then began to break the house's windows. Window glass was a luxury; this kind of vengeance was destined to provoke Richardson's wrath. Threatening the rioting townsmen with a musket, Richardson fired point-blank at them, seriously wounding the teenage Samuel Gore and mortally wounding Christopher Seider, eleven years old. Curiosity had drawn both victims to the wrong place at the worst time. Seider's funeral became an occasion for public displays of mourning and of anger against the British.[37]

On March 5, 1770, a cold night on a snow-blanketed Boston street, a sentry got into an argument with an apprentice. A crowd soon gathered at the corner of King Street and Royal Exchange Street, before the Custom House. After listening to the argument, the angry Bostonians began pelting the sentry with snowballs. Soon they were throwing not just snowballs but snowballs packed around stones, stones lacking a snowy coat, and other dangerous missiles. The beleaguered sentry rang the bell hanging from his sentry box.

Answering the bell's summons, Captain Thomas Preston marched a squad from the Twenty-Ninth (Worcestershire) Regiment of Foot into the square. Taking up a position between the sentry box and the crowd, the soldiers stood with bayonets fixed and muskets loaded. Jeering at them and daring them to fire was a raucous crowd including roustabouts, apprentices, and sailors. One was Crispus Attucks, a large, strongly built African American sailor in his late forties, a leader of the sailors on the Boston docks.

Walking between the lines of soldiers and townsmen with his sword drawn, seeking to keep the squad calm in the face of an angry mob, Preston repeatedly ordered his men not to fire, while he tried to persuade the rioters to disperse. The crowd knew that usually soldiers had no authority to fire on civilians, but they forgot or did not know that soldiers could fire if they justifiably believed themselves in danger.

Suddenly Private Hugh Montgomery was hit by a white object (a snowball or a piece of wood) thrown by someone in the crowd. He lost his balance but regained his footing; raising his musket, he accidentally discharged it. His shot turned the tense standoff into a slaughter. Convinced that they were under attack and that they could shoot in self-defense, the soldiers fired into the crowd, without any order from Preston. Seeing dead and wounded men falling, and hearing the roar of muskets, the crowd fled the scene.

Attucks and four others were killed outright or mortally wounded; it is unclear whether the soldiers were aiming at specific men or whether they just fired into the crowd. Two victims, Attucks and Samuel Gray, were leaders of the crowd; some witnesses testified that soldiers had aimed at them. Six others fell wounded but did not die. Two victims had had the bad luck to be drawn to the scene by curiosity. One of them, Patrick Carr, declared on his deathbed that the soldiers had fired in self-defense and that he did not blame them for what had happened. Other Bostonians were not so forgiving.

Angry townsmen dubbed the event the "Boston Massacre."[38] An engraving by the silversmith and Son of Liberty Paul Revere did much to define Bostonians' and posterity's views of the incident. It shows Preston and his men, their faces grim; the soldiers fire into the crowd, at their sword-pointing captain's command. Revere depicts the Bostonians as innocent, horrified, well-dressed white gentlemen (the engraving omits Crispus Attucks). Revere did not show the projectiles that the crowd threw. Revere also showed a musket firing at the crowd from a window overlooking the scene in a building labeled "Butcher's Hall;" supposedly that shot was fired by a Bostonian pro-British customs official. This aspect of Revere's image may have no basis in fact, but it suggested the Richardson incident of the previous month.[39]

Indicted for murder, the British soldiers and Captain Preston desperately sought counsel. Adams made no entries in his diary about the matter at the time; our only source is his autobiography, written more than three decades later. That account illustrates Adams's tendency in recollection decades after an event to present his memories as perhaps more vivid, and giving himself a more dramatic role, than the evidence might warrant.

As Adams recalled the matter, James Forrest, a Boston merchant known as the "Irish infant," tearfully approached him on the soldiers' behalf. Forrest beseeched Adams to take the soldiers' case, reporting that no other lawyer would do so. Even Robert Auchmuty and Josiah Quincy Jr. would act as counsel only if Adams joined them. Stunned by Forrest's report, Adams recalled, he agreed to represent the soldiers:

> I had no hesitation in answering that Council [Counsel] ought to be the very last thing that an accused Person should want in a free Country. That the Bar ought in my opinion to be independent and impartial at all Times And in every Circumstance. And that Persons whose Lives were at Stake ought to have the Council they preferred: But he must be sensible this would be as important a Cause as ever was tryed in any Court or Country of the World: and that every Lawyer must hold himself responsible not only to his Country, but to the highest and most infallible of all Trybunals for the Part he should Act. He must therefore expect from me no Art or Address, No Sophistry or Prevarication in such a Cause; nor any thing more than Fact, Evidence and Law would justify. Captain Preston he said requested and desired no more: and that he had such an Opinion, from all he had heard from all Parties of me, that he could chearfully trust his Life with me.[40]

Three years after the Boston Massacre, writing in his diary on March 5, 1773, Adams reflected: "The Part I took in Defence of Captn. Preston and the Soldiers, procured me Anxiety, and Obloquy enough. It was, however, one of the most gallant, generous, manly and disinterested Actions of my whole Life, and one of the best Pieces of service I ever rendered my Country."[41]

Adams insisted in his autobiography that he was paid only eighteen guineas, a small fee for so burdensome and politically charged a case. Contemporary accountings of the trial's costs show, however, that Adams received closer to forty-two guineas (a third of the fees paid to the three main defense counsel). Some scholars suggest that Adams also received nonmonetary compensation for this case—support for his candidacy for one of the four Boston seats in the Massachusetts General Court.[42]

Recalling that he put before Abigail the question of representing the soldiers, the possible threat to his law practice, and his obligation to provide legal counsel, he recorded her response: "That excellent lady, who has always encouraged me, burst into a flood of Tears, but said that she was very sensible of all the Danger to her and to our Children as well as to me, but she thought I had done as I ought, she was very willing to share in all that was to come and place her trust in Providence."[43]

Radical opponents of British policy knew that Adams and Quincy could be trusted to show that Boston was a town of law, and that the soldiers would get a fair trial with such able lawyers representing them. In sum, the evidence suggests that Adams's worries that his part in the trial would damage his legal career or his social and political standing had no basis. Adams was lead defense counsel, with Quincy supporting him. Auchmuty was retained by Captain Preston but was not active at his trial. Assisting Crown authorities in the prosecution was Robert Treat Paine, named by the town of Boston to ensure that Crown authorities would bring a vigorous case against the soldiers.

All spring and summer, Boston waited tensely for the trials to begin. Two baseless rumors circulated then—that Bostonians would invade the jail, capture Preston, and hang him; and that Governor Hutchinson and his allies were seeking a royal pardon for Preston and his men. Preston's trial took place in October, and the trial of the soldiers was held in November.

Adams and Quincy made sure to choose jurors not from Boston itself but from nearby towns whose residents were unfamiliar with Boston's conditions—unfamiliar specifically with the kinds of people thronging the docks, from where the soldiers' attackers came. Furthermore, in both trials, Adams focused the jurors' attention on the events of March 5, steering them away from thinking about the occupation of Boston.

At trial, Adams used two tactics that worked brilliantly. First, he put the British government on trial, arguing that because an army was a poor instrument to enforce law and order, imperial authorities had put the soldiers in an impossible position: "Soldiers quartered in a populous town, will always occasion two mobs, where they prevent one.—They are wretched conservators of the peace!" Second, he also put on trial the Bostonians assembled on March 5, bluntly and repeatedly calling them a "mob." In his learned closing argument, featuring quotations from the Italian legal reformer Marquis Cesare di Beccaria, the medieval English jurist Sir John Fortescue, and the seventeenth-century republican writer Algernon Sidney, Adams stressed the crowd's mob-like character. Focusing on Attucks, he played what modern polemicists term the "race card," calling Attucks "a stout Molatto fellow, whose very looks, was enough to terrify any person." Here, though Adams might have been expressing his own racial views, it was just as likely that he was appealing to what he knew would be the jurors' views and, like any good trial lawyer, making common cause with them. Urging the jurors to imagine themselves in the soldiers' place, Adams said that his clients confronted a hostile mob, willing to kill them and terrifying them with shrieks "almost as terrible as an Indian yell." Thus, the soldiers acted in self-defense, and the jurors should acquit them of murder.[44] This argument's impact on the jury was especially great coming from a known advocate of the American cause.

Adams restrained Quincy from probing what he deemed irrelevant issues concerning the antagonism between the townspeople and British forces. Though some scholars have questioned Adams's legal ethics in restraining Quincy (at one point Adams threatened to resign from the case if Quincy persisted), Adams reined in Quincy because he was confident that it was not necessary to pursue his line of argument, for Adams's tactics would secure the soldiers' acquittal. Adams was fully in line with the era's ethical rules guiding a criminal defense counsel.[45] (Adams and Quincy may have had a further advantage over the prosecution because the prosecutors may not have had their hearts in the case.)[46] Toward the end of his closing argument, Adams returned to the reasonable legal tone dominating his case, urging the jurors to focus on the facts of March 5 as proved at trial: "Facts are stubborn things; and whatever may be our wishes, our inclinations, or the dictates of our passions, they cannot alter the state of facts and evidence."[47]

The jury acquitted Captain Preston on all charges. The jury also acquitted six of the eight soldiers in their trial for multiple counts of murder. The jurors convicted two soldiers of the lesser crime of manslaughter, saving them from the gallows but requiring them to be branded on their thumbs with the letter M.[48]

In 1771, after the Boston Massacre trials, Adams fell ill—the first sign of a pattern of illness following stressful public action that recurred throughout his career. The Boston Massacre trials were the likeliest source of his exhaustion, but he also had allowed himself to be drawn into politics, having been elected to the Massachusetts General Court's lower house. Further, Susanna, the daughter whose birth had been a source of happiness and of worry to her parents, died, aged thirteen months. Soon after, Abigail gave birth to a second son, whom they named Charles, but the pregnancy was difficult for her. These private and public sources of stress proved too much for John. He moved Abigail and the children back to Braintree, while spending long hours in his Boston office to catch up with his work and to have a place where he could be on his own. In 1772, Abigail gave birth to a third son, Thomas Boylston Adams.

In January 1773, Adams again took a leading role in politics behind the scenes. The occasion was the address to the Massachusetts General Court by the new governor, Thomas Hutchinson. The first American-born royal governor of an American colony, Hutchinson should have been a model for ambitious countrymen seeking to advance themselves. Instead, he was a focus of suspicion and resentment as a too-eager advocate of the British cause. Now Hutchinson decided to begin his governorship by challenging his fellow subjects' resistance to British policy. In his opening address to the General Court, like a monarch's speech from the throne opening a session of Parliament, Hutchinson defended parliamentary supremacy. After fruitless appeals to British authorities for aid, Hutchinson decided that he would make the case for the British position himself, believing that his duty as governor compelled him to do so.

Hutchinson's challenge generated not one response but two. The leadership of the legislature's lower house enlisted John Adams to prepare a response to the governor's address more learned and legal than the "popular" response prepared by a legislative committee led by Samuel Adams. Hutchinson answered both replies. Another committee (again aided by John Adams) prepared a second response. The exchanges filled a pamphlet of 126 pages, which circulated throughout Massachusetts and attracted newspaper coverage in other colonies.

Adams was sure that his was the sound constitutional position. Further, he was confident that Hutchinson had injured himself politically in the people's eyes by making such a vehement pro-British case, and in the eyes of his backers in London by being too confrontational.[49] Even so, he grumbled in his diary that he needed to focus on his law practice and his family, not on further controversies. It was a typical Adams complaint, resisting temptation to congratulate himself and reminding himself of his obligations.

The House elected Adams to the governor's council, but Hutchinson vetoed his election. In Adams's eyes, the Hutchinson-Oliver alliance sought to control the privileges of office-holding in Massachusetts, standing against their friends and neighbors. They were upholding the British cause at the expense of American rights under the British constitution.

For Adams, the contest between Britain and America focused on Massachusetts. He did not yet grasp that the controversy with Britain was American, not just a matter for Massachusetts or for New England. One reason that Adams failed at first to see the full scope of the dispute with Britain was the difficulty of communication between colonies.[50] Most advocates of the American cause had only a sketchy sense of events outside their native colony.[51] Not until the First Continental Congress in 1774 could advocates of the American position understand what these disputes meant to colonists elsewhere in British North America. In this provincial myopia, Adams was not alone. Most Americans saw the relationship between their own "country" and Britain as more direct and immediate than those with fellow colonies.[52]

One controversy stressing the dispute's local character but also carrying imperial consequences was that over judicial independence in Massachusetts.[53] Should judges appointed by the king depend on the colonial legislature for their pay, or should they be paid by the Crown? In the Boston town meeting in December 1772, a leading figure of the community, Colonel William Brattle, stunned Bostonians by advocating Crown salaries for superior court judges. In January and February 1773, at the same time as the dispute between the Massachusetts General Court and Governor Hutchinson, Brattle and Adams fought in a series of signed essays in the *Boston Gazette*. Adams won plaudits for his vigorous, learned, and effective argument that the colony ought to pay its own judges. If the Crown were to pay superior court judges, Adams insisted, royal salaries for those judges might put them under the Crown's thumb.

Adams's essays are also noteworthy as an early appearance of what became his rhetorical style in larger projects of political and constitutional argument. Adams would structure his writing by basing it on another text—in this case, Brattle's essays. Adams would argue to that text like a lawyer cross-examining a witness, point by point and assertion by assertion. So close was his attention to his adversary's text that someone not familiar with both sides of the argument might have trouble following Adams through the thicket of assertion and response, claim and refutation. In such later works as his 1775 *Novanglus* essays, his 1787 *Defence of the Constitutions*, his 1791 *Discourses on Davila*, and his 1809–11 essays for the *Boston Patriot*, he used the same style of argument.

The years 1772–73 brought the most dramatic confrontation yet between the colonists and Britain. The king's ministers reconsidered their approach to raising revenue from and reinforcing British authority over the colonies. Spurring these efforts were the fiscal ills of the British East India Company, a monopoly controlling Britain's tea trade with its Asian colonies, including among its shareholders leading British politicians. To save the company from bankruptcy, the ministry devised a plan that, they hoped, would bring the company short-term help and also might defuse colonial resistance to British taxation. Parliament repealed all British taxes on the colonies except a three-penny tax on tea. The company planned to ship large quantities of tea to American ports, setting its price low enough to cover the tea tax, so that the taxed cut-rate tea would cost less than tea once did. They expected Americans to buy the tea at the bargain price, paying the tax without raising constitutional difficulties.

To King George's ministers, the tea plan seemed brilliant in three ways. First, the East India Company would receive a badly needed infusion of cash from sales of cut-rate tea. Second, bolstering the company's finances would save influential politicians' investments in the company. Third, Americans paying the tea tax as part of the reduced price of tea would undermine American objections to British taxation.[54]

Americans rejected the tea policy from the moment they heard of it and readied themselves to resist the ministry's plan. Insisting that buying cut-rate tea would mean accepting an unconstitutional tax, they decided not to buy. Further, they resented the British attempt to bail out a corrupt, insolvent corporation holding a monopoly of the tea trade, especially by having Americans bear the burden of that bailout while sacrificing their constitutional rights. In three cities to which the tea ships sailed, American resistance prevented landing of the tea. In Boston, Governor Hutchinson, determined to support the ministry, ordered the tea ships to dock. On December 5, 1773, Abigail Adams reported to her friend Mercy Otis Warren: "The tea that bainful weed, is arrived. . . . The proceedings of our Citizens have been United, Spirited and firm. The Flame is kindeled and like Lightening it catches from Soul to Soul."[55]

Eleven days later, on December 16, 1773, a stormy meeting of the Sons of Liberty at Old North Church, chaired by Samuel

Adams, vented public outrage at the tea ships in Boston harbor. At the meeting's close, nearly two hundred men costumed as Native American warriors headed to the harbor and swarmed aboard the tea ships. A locksmith accompanying the mock Indians broke each lock securing the ships' holds; the demonstrators seized 342 crates of tea, worth about £10,000, and tossed them into Boston Harbor, breaking the crates open with their hatchets to ensure that salt water would soak the tea and ruin it. The locksmith then repaired the locks on the holds, dramatizing the raiders' respect for lawful property and their issue only with unconstitutional property. When the raiders found that one of them had pocketed tea for his own use, they stripped him naked, tossed into the harbor the tea they found on him and his clothing, and made him walk home in the freezing cold. The "destruction of the tea" was an effective act of political theater. (Bostonians at the time called the event the "destruction of the tea"; the name "Boston Tea Party" did not arise until more than sixty years later, a product of battles over how history should recall the Revolution.)[56]

The night after the destruction of the tea, John Adams recorded in his diary his praise of an act dramatizing colonial resistance to unconstitutional British taxes:

> This is the most magnificent Movement of all. There is a Dignity, a Majesty, a Sublimity, in this last Effort of the Patriots, that I greatly admire. The People should never rise, without doing something to be remembered—something notable And striking. This Destruction of the Tea is so bold, so daring, so firm, intrepid and inflexible, and it must have so important Consequences, and so lasting, that I cant but consider it as an Epocha in History.[57]

The tea crisis helped to end Hutchinson's political career. It followed hard on the heels of the leak in June 1773 of letters among Hutchinson, the previous governor (Francis Bernard), and British authorities. In one letter, Hutchinson suggested the "Abridgment of what are called English liberties." His effectiveness destroyed by the revelation of his letters and by the destruction of the tea, Hutchinson left Massachusetts for England on June 1, 1774. He never returned. Adams paid little attention to the fall of the man whom he had seen as the incarnation of the crisis with Britain. He knew that the British government would not take the tea's destruction lightly.[58]

When in early 1774 Lord North and his cabinet learned of the events in Boston, they decided to make an example of Massachusetts, which they scorned as a rebellious colony needing sharp measures to bring it to heel.[59] Parliament enacted a set of statutes to punish Boston and Massachusetts for destroying company property and resisting the Tea Act: they were called the Coercive Acts; Americans renamed them the Intolerable Acts.

The Massachusetts Government Act revoked Massachusetts's royal charter and limited the calling of town meetings to one per year per town. The Boston Port Act closed the port of Boston until Massachusetts reimbursed the East India Company for the value of the destroyed tea and until King George III was satisfied that order had been restored in Massachusetts. The Administration of Justice Act gave the royal governor of Massachusetts sole, unreviewable discretion to transfer to Britain any British official in Massachusetts accused of a crime there, if he found that the official could not get a fair trial in Massachusetts. The Quartering Act required American householders to house British soldiers on demand from British authorities. Because this measure applied not just to Massachusetts but to all of British North America, it evoked general alarm.

Americans lumped together with the Intolerable Acts the British North America (Quebec) Act. This measure extended the province of Quebec to include lands west of the American colonies, blocking American investors and speculators from buying those lands. It also guaranteed religious freedom to Catholics; deleted from oaths of citizenship in Quebec the requirement to support Protestant Christianity; restored French civil law in Quebec (except that British common law still covered public-law questions); and allowed Catholic churches to impose tithes on their parishioners.

New Englanders, always fearing Catholicism, saw this statute as threatening English and American liberties.[60]

In enacting the Coercive Acts, the British overplayed their hand. Previously, Americans who wanted to stay out of the fight with Britain could ignore conflicts between Britain and Massachusetts. The Coercive Acts made that position untenable. Instead, they inspired an American backlash threatening Britain's authority over the mainland colonies of British North America. Every colony except Georgia (too far away and too poor to act) chose delegates to the first intercolonial meeting since the Stamp Act Congress of 1765.[61]

On June 17, 1774, the Massachusetts General Court chose five delegates to what we call the First Continental Congress. James Bowdoin, a wealthy and politically active merchant, refused to serve, but Thomas Cushing, Samuel Adams, John Adams, and Robert Treat Paine accepted. Except for Samuel Adams, known as a leader of the radicals and the Sons of Liberty, they were politically moderate to conservative. All were graduates of Harvard College; Cushing, John Adams, and Robert Treat Paine were lawyers.[62]

Adams accepted his election with mixed feelings. He was reluctant to leave his family, uncertain about the new political world he was about to enter, and unsure whether he was up to the challenge of representing Massachusetts in the first American assembly. For eight years, he had been immersed in formulating arguments against unconstitutional British measures. He had learned much, and he had sought to teach much. Now a new world was opening before him, and he was ambivalent about taking the next step. He was about to enter a new level of political thought and action—a dawning world of American politics, in which he would have to take the measure of fellow colonists from New Hampshire to South Carolina while they were taking his measure. He would have to learn how to work with them in common cause.

On June 20, 1774, he confided to his diary his curiosity and apprehension:

> There is a new, and a grand Scene open before me—a Congress.
>
> This will be an assembly of the wisest Men upon the Continent, who are Americans in Principle, i.e. against the Taxation of Americans, by Authority of Parliament.
>
> I feel myself unequal to this Business. A more extensive Knowledge of the Realm, the Colonies, and of Commerce, as well as of Law and Policy, is necessary, than I am Master of.
>
> What can be done? Will it be expedient to propose an Annual Congress of Committees? to Petition.—Will it do to petition at all?—to the K [King]? to the L [Lords]? to the C [Commons]?
>
> What will such Consultations avail? Deliberations alone will not do. We must petition, or recommend to the Assemblies to petition, or [unfinished sentence]
>
> The Ideas of the People, are as various, as their Faces. One thinks, no more petitions, former having been neglected and despized. Some are for Resolves—Spirited Resolves—and some are for bolder Councils.
>
> I will keep an exact Diary, of my journey, as well as a Journal of the Proceedings of the Congress.[63]

Chapter Four

"We must for the future stand upon our own Leggs or fall"

Continental Congress and Independence (1774–1777)

In August 1774, a carriage bearing the Massachusetts delegates to the First Continental Congress rattled to Philadelphia; John Adams and his colleagues were unsure what to expect when they arrived. Previous intercolonial gatherings had been like meetings of diplomats from rival nations.[1] In 1774, by contrast, the delegates representing twelve of the thirteen colonies of British North America were hoping to work together as members of an American union, in the first truly American political institution. In the process, they were about to invent American politics, a shared political enterprise held together by a common vision of American goals, principles, and interests that would devise an American national identity. The delegates to the First Continental Congress were about to begin learning how to be Americans, how to work together as Americans, and how to define what it meant to be American.[2]

The Massachusetts delegates decided to be cooperative and collegial; they wanted to counter the prevailing image of Massachusetts as a hotbed of dissension and rebellion. They decided to hold back, to listen rather than talk, to consider other delegates' proposals for action rather than demand action themselves. They recognized that the Congress would be riven by faction, and they did not want to add to it. Early in the proceedings, for example, two conservative delegates—John Jay of New York and John Rutledge of South Carolina—sought to find a fault line that would divide their colleagues and frustrate the Congress's work. When Massachusetts delegate Thomas Cushing offered a motion that the Congress open its daily sessions with prayer, Rutledge and Jay objected that the delegates were so religiously diverse that they could not agree on a clergyman to lead them in prayer. In response, Samuel Adams assured his colleagues that he could listen to a prayer offered by any good clergyman who was a friend to his country. He then suggested Rev. Jacob Duché of Philadelphia, one of the highest-toned Anglican ministers in the city. Jay and Rutledge were nonplussed: for a Congregationalist to propose that an Anglican minster lead the delegates in prayer was astonishingly broad-minded. Samuel Adams's astute move finished the attempt by Jay and Rutledge to divide the delegates by religion.[3]

Remaining circumspect in the debates, John Adams let others carry the ideological and rhetorical weight in discussing British policy and what action Congress should take against it. He also recorded his observations of people from other regions and other colonies. Other politicians at the Congress were similarly curious. Each colony's delegates sought enlightenment—and entertainment—in scrutinizing traits and peculiarities of dress, habit, religion, and speech displayed by fellow politicians from elsewhere. Adams filled his diary and his letters to Abigail with vivid descriptions of politicians he had met, of the cities he had seen, of the dinners he had attended, and of the taverns he had visited. He promised Abigail that he would show her his diary when he returned, but, even as he protested that he had too little time to write, he dashed off a letter to describe what he was experiencing: "There is in the Congress a Collection of the greatest Men upon this Continent, in Point of Abilities, Virtues and Fortunes. The Magnanimity, and public Spirit, which I see here, makes me blush for the sordid venal Herd, which I have seen in my own province." He bubbled over with enthusiasm for what he was experiencing and what he was seeing—like a man from the country visiting the big city for the first time. At the same time, he shared with Abigail the arguments and difficulties that he had to face—for example, how to decide how voting would take place in Congress, whether by colonies, by population, or by some other form of representation. His willingness to bring her into these arguments testified to his appreciation of Abigail's intelligence and political understanding and his sense of her as an intellectual partner.[4]

The First Continental Congress devised a coordinated American strategy to respond to the Intolerable Acts. That strategy's center-piece was the Association, an array of committees in each colony organized to enforce American boycotting of British trade—the method that had persuaded Parliament to repeal the Stamp Act in 1766. Recognizing the need to devise a continuing American polit-ical and governmental apparatus to respond to future developments, the delegates scheduled a second Continental Congress to convene six months after the adjournment of the first.

Americans had not waited for the calling of the Second Continental Congress to debate and devise policies binding the colonies. Instead, reactions to the First Congress's measures and to the controversies swirling around them dominated American newspapers. Thus, in the late fall of 1774, after Adams's return from Philadelphia, a writer using the pen name *Massachusettensis* began publishing in the *Massachusetts Gazette, and the Boston Post-Boy and Advertiser* a series of essays defending the British position. The man behind *Massachusettensis* was Daniel Leonard, a lawyer from Taunton five years Adams's junior. Leonard had supported the co-lonial position until Hutchinson had converted him to the British cause. It was only decades later that Adams learned that his antago-nist had been Leonard. At the time, he made a mistaken deduction—that *Massachusettensis* was his friend and antagonist Jonathan Sewall.

Concerned lest *Massachusettensis* win adherents to the British cause, Adams decided to respond.

From January through April 1775, Adams published twelve scholarly, hard-hitting essays, using the pen name *Novanglus*. These essays set forth his most thorough statement of the American position on the constitutional dispute with Britain.[5] Demonstrating his mastery of the Americans' evolving constitutional and legal arguments, *Novanglus* also showed a profound grasp of the intellectual and moral significance of the quarrel between Britain and its colonies: "It is in vain to expect or hope to carry on a government, against the universal bent and genius of the people, we may whimper and whine as much as we will, but nature made it impossible, when she made men."[6] *Novanglus* finds few readers today because of its argument's intricacy and its point-by-point response to *Massachusettensis*. In their rhetorical and argumentative density, the *Novanglus* essays exemplified Adams's legal training. Like other lawyers of his time, Adams used an argumentative style too prolix and tangled for those not immersed in the dispute. His essays were so effective in presenting their case, however, that they confirmed him as a leading advocate of the colonial cause.

Between the end of the First Continental Congress in October 1774 and the convening of the Second in May 1775, Adams returned to his law practice and to his family. Even so, the experience of stepping onto the American political stage made him restless. Though he was the leading lawyer in Massachusetts, he realized that now he was more interested in politics than in his law practice. As he had jokingly written in 1755, he was becoming a politician—now an American politician, though careful always to represent Massachusetts and its interests.

In December 1774, the Massachusetts Provincial Congress—a body standing outside the colony's established political structure but with the same membership as the lower house of the General Court—elected John Adams as one of the colony's delegates to the impending Second Continental Congress. This new meeting was to determine the effects of the policies adopted by the First Continental Congress and to assess what future actions might be needed.

By 1774, most of Massachusetts except a small area around Boston was hostile to royal authority. On April 18, 1775, the province's military governor, General Thomas Gage, ordered British soldiers to seize caches of weapons and munitions in town arsenals near Boston; they also were to arrest Samuel Adams and John Hancock, whom Gage saw as leaders of American resistance. Gage was trying not to crush revolutionary sentiment but rather to prevent it from overwhelming the province.[7]

Colonists learned of the British plans, and a group of riders devoted to the patriot cause fanned out into the countryside to inform the people. Paul Revere, William Dawes, Samuel Prescott, and others roused the countryside and warned Hancock and Adams so that they avoided capture. Though captured by British forces, Revere misled and distracted them as they questioned him, causing a crucial delay in carrying out Gage's orders. The next morning, when British regulars marched into Lexington, they found the town's militia turned out. The "minutemen"—so called for their ability to be ready for action in one minute—meant only to offer a show of resistance, a performance of their duty to defend the town's arsenal. Once that show was done, they planned to retire in good order, not provoking the regulars. In that tense moment of confrontation, however, a shot rang out; nobody has determined who fired it. The regulars assumed that the Americans had fired on them, and they fired back into the retreating minutemen, killing eight and wounding ten more. As the British soldiers seized the town's arsenal and its contents, riders and ringing church bells spread news of the skirmish at Lexington through the area. By the time British forces arrived at Concord (their next target, six miles from Lexington), seized caches of weapons and ammunition, and sought to cross the Old North Bridge, a formidable force of colonial militiamen barred their way. Another moment of silent tension ended when the British soldiers fired on the militia. To their surprise and alarm, the colonists fired back. That exchange of fire was the first colonial military resistance to British forces. Stunned, the British retreated, enduring withering fire from colonial militiamen all along the road back to Boston. By the end of the retreat, 73 British soldiers had been killed, 174 had been wounded, and 26 were missing; American casualties were 49 killed, 41 wounded, and 5 missing. News of the battles moved swiftly down North America's eastern coast, reaching Philadelphia within a week.[8]

For Adams, the news from Massachusetts was shattering. He worried because his wife and children were living in Braintree, near the likely theaters of war, as British soldiers faced Massachusetts militiamen. The news of bloodshed put an end to Adams's hopes of healing the breach between the colonies and Britain. As a result, Adams abandoned his former skepticism and became one of independence's most insistent advocates in Congress.

Abigail's anguished report of the Battle of Bunker Hill strengthened his resolve even as it moved him to sorrow:

> The Day; perhaps the decisive Day is come on which the fate of America depends. My bursting Heart must find vent at my pen. I have just heard that our dear Friend Dr. Warren is no more but fell gloriously fighting for his Country—saying better to die honourably in the field than ignominiously hang upon the Gallows. Great is our Loss. He has distinguished himself in every engagement, by his courage and fortitude, by animating the Soldiers and leading them on by his own example. A particuliar account of these dreadful, but I hope Glorious Days will be transmitted you, no doubt in the exactest manner.[9]

Furious that his colleagues were still debating as his countrymen were dying in the cause, Adams recognized that embracing independence was only the beginning. Even if the colonies declared independence and formed an American union, Adams asked himself, could they resist Britain's determination to maintain its authority over the colonies and the power that London would bring to bear?

War would force American subjects of George III to choose the land of their children, neighbors, and friends over their king and their homeland across the ocean. How many would make that choice, and at what cost? As Adams knew, no colony in the history of the Western world had won independence from its mother country. He asked himself what would make such a revolution a success.

One practical dimension of the problem was that of organizing American forces to resist the British. In June, when Congress created the Continental army, it chose Virginia delegate George Washington to command it. In his *Autobiography*, written decades later, Adams claimed that he had been responsible for the choice of Washington. Further, he insisted, he had been instrumental in rallying New England delegates behind Washington's candidacy, helping to frustrate the military ambitions of his Massachusetts colleague John Hancock, the Second Continental Congress's president. Some scholars charge Adams with exaggerating his claims, as the only evidence for his version of events is his uncorroborated *Autobiography*. Yet again this controversy suggests a pattern guiding assessment of Adams's reminiscences of his role in turning points of the Revolution and the creation of the new nation. Though perhaps we should be skeptical of his asserted central role in such events, we can trust his accounts of his arguments and thinking at such junctures.[10] However it happened, Congress chose Washington. Accepting his appointment as the army's commander in chief, he took his leave of Congress and, having bought supplies (including five military textbooks to guide him), journeyed northward, to Cambridge, to take command of the Continental army.

Even with American forces in the field, many of Adams's colleagues still were not ready for the ultimate step of declaring independence. Instead, igniting Adams's baffled fury, they made a last-ditch effort to seek King George III's intervention in the controversy between his ministry and the colonies. After considerable debate, on July 5, 1775, Congress adopted a petition addressed to the king. This "Olive Branch Petition" was a last conciliatory request to George

III by the delegates in Congress in their private capacity as leading colonists of British North America. Thus, the petition makes no reference to Congress.[11] Petitioning the king was a practice deeply rooted in English constitutional and political argument; it was an exercise of a constitutional right held by all English subjects. The right of petition was a means to focus the monarch's attention on problems afflicting some of his subjects, who hoped that he would answer their petition by doing justice among all his subjects.

The mindset from which the Olive Branch Petition grew had found powerful form in "The Idea of a Patriot King," a 1738 essay by the political essayist Henry St. John, Viscount Bolingbroke (a writer whose works Adams read and reread).[12] Using Bolingbroke's theory, the delegates addressed George III as a patriot king not allied with any faction but duty-bound to consider impartially the whole realm's interests, and required by that duty to hear and mediate conflicting claims from all his subjects. Adams had studied Bolingbroke's writings with care and sympathy, but he doubted the Olive Branch Petition's chances. In his view, the American blood shed at Lexington and Concord meant that the time for arguments and petitions was over.

Congress used a draft prepared by John Dickinson of Pennsylvania, a noted attorney and politician who had won fame in 1767–68 for his influential defense of the American cause, *Letters from a Farmer in Pennsylvania*.[13] Though he admired Dickinson's *Letters*, Adams was skeptical of, even hostile to, the Olive Branch Petition. Outvoted in Congress by those who wanted to make one last appeal, Adams at first kept his doubts to himself and signed the petition. Even so, as the petition's engrossed copies traveled to England for presentation to George III, Adams stewed over his opposition to the measure and decided to vent his feelings.

On July 24, 1775, Adams wrote letters to Abigail and to his longtime friend and political ally James Warren. Writing to Warren, he mocked the petition, deriding Dickinson as "a certain great Fortune and piddling Genius . . . [who] has given a silly cast to our whole

Doings"—though he was careful not to mention Dickinson's name. To warn Warren not to circulate his letter, he began with the phrase "In Confidence." Warren never got the letter, however.[14]

Like many contemporaries, Adams aired his feelings in private letters, hoping that those letters would stay confidential. Unfortunately for Adams, his private opinion became disastrously public. Adams prepared a bundle of letters—those he had written to Warren and to Abigail and a letter from Virginia delegate Benjamin Harrison to George Washington—and entrusted them to Benjamin Hichborn, a young Massachusetts law clerk who had begged for the assignment of delivering the letters to prove himself a loyal supporter of the Revolution. As Hichborn tried to cross Narragansett Bay, however, the British captured him and the bundle of letters. Draper's *Massachusetts Gazette* published the letters on August 17, 1775; those letters also saw print in London that September.

The publication of Adams's letters, with his quotable strictures on Dickinson, made his words common knowledge. Insulted, Dickinson and his allies in Congress ostracized Adams for weeks. The resulting political difficulties plaguing Adams induced him to mock himself in later years as "obnoxious, suspected, and unpopular."[15] The reality was mixed. True, Adams had a reputation for being contentious—one reason he had reined himself in during the First Continental Congress in 1774. Even so, he had established himself as an able, tireless advocate with extensive knowledge of the British constitution. His colleagues in Congress respected him because of his energy and his willingness to serve on dozens of committees; they valued his capacity for hard legislative work. Whatever resentment turned some against him, he was prepared to survive it and to put it behind him. Only later did he brood on his unpopularity.

For Adams, the American crisis had troubling effects on the rule of law, which as a man of law he sought to uphold. During a visit home in 1775, he had an encounter that he recorded in his *Autobiography*. This incident posed in dramatic terms the conflict between how he saw the Revolution and how some of his neighbors understood the matter:

> I met a Man who had sometimes been my Client, and sometimes I had been against him. He, though a common Horse jockey, was sometimes in the right, and I had commonly been successfull in his favour in our Courts of Law. He was always in the Law, and had been sued in many Actions, at almost every Court. As soon as he saw me, he came up to me, and his first Salutation to me was "Oh! Mr. Adams what great Things have you and your Colleagues done for Us! We can never be gratefull enough to you. There are no Courts of Justice now in this Province, and I hope there never will be another!" . . . Is this the Object for which I have been contending? said I to myself, for I rode along without any Answer to this Wretch. Are these the Sentiments of such People? And how many of them are there in the Country? Half the Nation for what I know: for half the Nation are Debtors if not more, and these have been in all Countries, the Sentiments of Debtors.[16]

Adams also found himself pondering in the context of the Revolution the claims of those who were not debtors. On March 31, 1776, Abigail wrote a lively letter, giving him advice about framing new codes of laws:

> I long to hear that you have declared an independancy—and by the way in the new Code of Laws which I suppose it will be necessary for you to make I desire you would Remember the Ladies, and be more generous and favourable to them than your ancestors. Do not put such unlimited power into the hands of the Husbands. Remember all Men would be tyrants if they could. If perticuliar care and attention is not paid to the Laidies we are determined to foment a Rebelion, and will not hold ourselves bound by any Laws in which we have no voice, or Representation.[17]

Adams at first answered Abigail's suggestion with heavy-handed humor. On April 14, he told her of his surprise that, beyond apprentices revolting against their masters, students against their teachers and professors, "Indians [against] their Guardians," and slaves against their masters, "another Tribe more numerous and powerfull than all the rest were grown discontented." Joking that men's privileges were not absolute, he added: "Depend upon it, We know better than to repeal our Masculine systems. Altho they are in full Force, you know they are little more than Theory. We dare not exert our Power in its full Latitude. We are obliged to go fair, and softly, and in Practice you know We are the subjects. We have only the Name of Masters." He concluded by blaming the British for inciting such a rebellion.[18]

This exchange has become famous in the history of American feminist thought; later critics credit Abigail's far-sightedness and criticize John's sexist inability to follow her. Even so, it is rarely noted that Abigail's letter had at least a brief impact on John's thinking. On May 26, 1776, in a letter to his friend and political ally James Sullivan, Adams sought to counter some of Sullivan's ideas about voting and representation: "Whence arises the Right of the Men to govern Women, without their Consent?"[19]

Abigail's correspondence with John reminded him of how much he missed his family, of how ardently he wanted to return to them, and of how the competing pressures of serving in Congress and helping to run a revolution kept him in Philadelphia. Writing to her on April 15, 1776, he explained the importance of the work he was doing and how his family should see it:

I will not bear the Reproaches of my Children. I will tell them that I studied and laboured to procure a free Constitution of Government for them to solace themselves under, and if they do not prefer this to ample Fortune, to Ease and Elegance, they are not my Children, and I care not what becomes of them. They shall live upon thin Diet, wear mean Cloaths, and work hard, with Chearfull

Hearts and free Spirits or they may be the Children of the Earth or of no one, for me.[20]

Beginning in the fall of 1775, John Adams turned his attention to restoring "a free Constitution of Government" for the colonies. He was responding to a growing atmosphere of domestic crisis. In late 1775 and early 1776, royal governors fled their colonial posts, often after dissolving colonial legislatures. The collapse of these governments left a void of legitimacy in the colonies. Because Americans stressed legitimacy as a constitutional value, they saw the lack of legitimate government as a serious issue. Mere power was not enough; for a government to have authority—lawful power—it had to have both actual power and a source of legitimacy justifying its power. True, the dissolved colonial legislatures had reassembled as provincial congresses and conventions, seeking to preserve continuity of governance and responsiveness to the crises of the Revolution, but even so, they knew that they lacked legitimacy. They were self-appointed legislative bodies; they had not been elected to perform the tasks they were undertaking, and they were not governed by any authoritative constitutional rules beyond those in the obsolete colonial charters.

Frantic to restore legitimate government, many American politicians turned for advice to John Adams, whom they regarded as an expert constitutional thinker. Such politicians as James Warren of Massachusetts, William Hooper and John Penn of North Carolina, Jonathan Dickinson Sergeant of New Jersey, and Richard Henry Lee and George Wythe of Virginia beseeched him for advice. Hoping to provide a solution, he devoted himself to the question for months, sending out letter after letter. As the requests for advice kept pouring in, Adams tired of copying and recopying the same letter. He had to publish. In April 1776, he penned an anonymous pamphlet, "Thoughts on Government."

Eager to share his labors with Abigail, Adams sent her a copy of his pamphlet. In her response, Abigail pretended that she did not know who had written the pamphlet but hinted that she deduced the author's identity, was pleased with the pamphlet, and understood his main point:

> I this day Received yours of the 20 of April accompanied with a Letter upon Goverment. Upon reading it I some how or other felt an uncommon affection for it; I could not help thinking it was a near relation of a very intimate Friend of mine. If I am mistaken in its descent, I know it has a near affinity to the Sentiments of that person, and tho I cannot pretend to be an adept in the art of Goverment; yet it looks rational that a Goverment of Good Laws well administerd should carry with them the fairest prospect of happiness to a community, as well as to individuals.[21]

Adams offered in "Thoughts on Government" a terse, eloquent manual for devising state constitutions.[22] Extolling "the divine science of politicks" and counseling that "good government, is an empire of Laws,"[23] Adams argued that republican government was the only way for Americans to preserve their liberties. To this end, he prescribed a design for a written constitution creating a legislature having two houses, balanced by an independent governor with ample powers. Acknowledging that different colonies might have different political values, he made his proposals in "Thoughts on Government" adaptable to different colonies. Those that were less democratic (for Adams, less like the New England colonies) could tailor his suggestions to their situation—for example, having the governor elected by the legislature instead of by the people. At the pamphlet's close, Adams sought to present the quest for legitimate constitutional government within a larger perspective framed by the context of the Age of Enlightenment:

> You and I, my dear Friend, have been sent into life, at a time when the greatest law-givers of antiquity would have wished to have

lived. How few of the human race have ever enjoyed an opportunity of making an election of government more than of air, soil, or
climate, for themselves or their children. When! Before the present
epocha, had three millions of people full power and a fair opportunity to form and establish the wisest and happiest government that
human wisdom can contrive.[24]

"Thoughts on Government" answered the calls of Adams's
contemporaries for advice about creating legitimate government.
It also presented Adams's response to a rival model of constitutional government presented by Thomas Paine in *Common Sense*,
published in January 1776. Paine's eloquent pamphlet made a powerful case for American independence. It rejected monarchy as il-
legitimate, severing the last tie linking the colonists to the mother
country, their loyalty to the British Crown. Paine also assailed the
folly of empire and justified the practicalities of independence. He
demonstrated how absurd it was for a continent to be ruled by an
island; insisted that the colonies could and should claim and win
their independence; and argued that, because liberty itself was at
risk, an independent America was liberty's only refuge in the world.
Finally, he offered a sketch of what he endorsed as the basic forms
of American government at the state level and at the interstate level.

Though Adams admired Paine's case for American independence, he scorned the last part of *Common Sense* presenting Paine's
prescription for new forms of American government. Paine rejected
checks and balances and separation of powers as mystifications
imposed by aristocrats and lawyers on the people; he argued that
the people never would violate their own liberties. The core of his
design for government was a one-house assembly, which could
create executive and judicial institutions when necessary. Adams
dismissed Paine's arguments as contrary to the lessons of history and
human nature. Writing to Abigail on March 19, 1776, he observed
of *Common Sense*, "This Writer has a better Hand at pulling down
than building. . . . [He] seems to have very inadequate Ideas of what

is proper and necessary to be done, in order to form Constitutions for single Colonies, as well as a great Model of Union for the whole." Indeed, John assured Abigail, "It has been very generally propagated through the Continent that I wrote this Pamphlet. But altho I could not have written any Thing in so manly and striking a style, I flatter myself I should have made a more respectable Figure as an Architect, if I had undertaken such a Work."[25]

Adams recalled in his autobiography that he and Paine argued vehemently, face to face, about the conflict between *Common Sense* and "Thoughts on Government." According to Adams, Paine denounced him for publishing "Thoughts on Government" precisely because it clashed with Paine's views in *Common Sense*.[26] This would be only the first of several conflicts between the two men.

Ironically, Adams's and Paine's ideas about new forms of government did coincide on one point. Despite Adams's comment to Abigail to the contrary, the prescriptions for *American* government in both pamphlets paralleled each other. Both *Common Sense* and "Thoughts on Government" proposed an American Congress as the sole institution of a new government for the United States, with power to deal only with affairs of the entire alliance. Neither Paine nor Adams considered whether such a government should have power over individual Americans or power to check the states. In other words, neither man saw the need to explore issues of federalism, let alone its significance for the American constitutional experiment. Further, neither Paine nor Adams discussed the relevance of or need for checks and balances or separation of powers at the national or American level. That issue did not arise until the late 1780s, when the effort to ratify the US Constitution as a successor to the Articles of Confederation became the dominant American political issue. By that time, Adams insisted that separation of powers and checks and balances were indispensably necessary ingredients of all successful constitutional governments at all levels. Paine remained convinced that such things were devices deliberately adopted to render constitutional government too complicated for ordinary people to understand.

In May 1776, as "Thoughts on Government" circulated beyond Philadelphia and Boston, Adams continued to focus on the constitutional and political dimensions of independence. Dominating his thinking were political ideas rooted in Anglo-American constitutionalism as informed by classical political thought going back to Aristotle and Polybius. Adams persisted in connecting the challenge of independence to previous experiments in politics and government.

On occasion, as in "Thoughts on Government," he seemed to endorse what later generations have called American exceptionalism, the idea that Americans were different from other peoples in ways that mattered for their experiments in government. Adams, however, was more realistic than devotees of American exceptionalism. Adams argued only for an exceptionalism of *opportunity*—a chance granted to Americans by historical circumstances to create good governments that might become blessings to the rest of the world. Adams never held the view that Americans were inherently different from other peoples—inherently innocent, pure, or uncorrupted; he rejected that view all his life. Instead, he maintained, Americans were subject to the same internal and external forces shaping and corrupting human nature throughout history; he insisted that they still had to guard against falling prey to these dangers.[27]

In May 1776, deciding that he had to build on the foundation that he had laid in "Thoughts on Government," Adams again took up his pen, but this time as a legislative draftsman. First, he framed a resolution authorizing the colonies to form new state constitutions, which the Second Continental Congress adopted on May 10, 1776. Then he added a preamble, which Congress adopted on May 15. Adams's preamble offered a powerful argument justifying the resolution's response to the hostile actions of King George III and Great Britain against the colonies, putting the blame on the king for driving the American colonies to independence:

Whereas his Britannic Majesty, in conjunction with the Lords and Commons of Great-Britain, has, by a late Act of Parliament, excluded the inhabitants of these United Colonies from the protection of his crown; and whereas no answer whatever to the humble petition of the Colonies, for redress of grievances and reconciliation with Great-Britain, has been or is likely to be given, but the whole force of that kingdom, aided by foreign mercenaries, is to be exerted for the destruction of the good people of these Colonies; and whereas it appears absolutely irreconcileable to reason and good conscience for the people of these Colonies now to take the oaths and affirmations necessary for the support of any government under the crown of Great-Britain, and it is necessary that the exercise of every kind of authority under the said Crown should be totally suppressed, and all the powers of government exerted under the authority of the people of the Colonies, for the preservation of internal peace, virtue, and good order, as well as for the defence of their lives, liberties, and properties, against the hostile invasions and cruel depredations of their enemies: Therefore,

Resolved, That it be recommended to the respective assemblies and conventions of the United Colonies, where no government sufficient to the exigencies of their affairs hath been hitherto established, to adopt such government as shall, in the opinion of the Representatives of the People, best conduce to the happiness and safety of their constituents in particular, and America in general.[28]

Adams was deeply proud of the preamble, though its lawyerly tone did not make it as inspiring as the Declaration of Independence that Jefferson drafted two months later. The conservative James Duane of New York got Adams's point; he attacked the preamble as "a Machine for the fabrication of Independence." Adams responded (or so he recorded for posterity), "I thought it was Independence itself: but We must have it with more formality yet."[29]

Duane was right, as Adams knew. Congress's authorization for states to create new governments to replace their old colonial charters did not just restore legitimate government for the American states. Congress's action abrogated kingly authority, partly by turning colonies into states, partly by authorizing the Americans to frame and adopt new forms of government for them. These new forms of government were to be created by and responsible to the people of each state, rather than to the Crown, and they would have no reason to look to the Crown for anything. Congress's action echoed Adams's suggestion in *Thoughts on Government* that legal writs and subpoenas run in the name of the states and their people rather than in the name of the king; that proposal also abrogated royal authority. The congressional resolution not only launched what Adams later called "an age of revolutions and constitutions" but also became part of the experiments in government that it called into being. Various states incorporated the text of Congress's May 1776 resolution and its preamble into their new state constitutions, justifying their framing and adoption.[30]

As the debate on independence spread throughout the thirteen colonies, local and provincial congresses adopted resolutions begging, even demanding, that Congress act on the issue. Congress monitored the growing pressure for independence while trying to not get too far ahead of the sentiments of ordinary Americans.[31] Adams also monitored public opinion, while discussing with like-minded colleagues the need to prepare for independence. On June 2, 1776, answering Henry Knox, a fellow Massachusetts citizen and artilleryman in the field with General Washington, Adams wrote: "We must for the future Stand upon our own Leggs or fall."[32] Finally, on June 8, 1776, Richard Henry Lee of Virginia returned to Congress and proposed three resolutions approved by the Virginia convention and ordered by that convention to be recommended to Congress. The first demanded American independence from Great Britain; the second demanded the framing and adoption of articles of union to unite the colonies to enable them to resist Britain; and the third demanded that Congress seek diplomatic alliances with powerful European countries (such alliances, the Virginians hoped, would secure diplomatic support for the American bid for independence, as well as arms, supplies, and funding).

Seizing on Lee's resolutions, Congress opened the question of independence for full debate. Until this time, various colonies had been hesitant to make common cause with New England; they had argued that the colonial brawl with Great Britain was a matter peculiar to Massachusetts. Virginia's resolutions, combined with the delegates' recognition that Britain was bent on subduing all the mainland American colonies by force, made it imperative for Congress to debate independence and the related matters that Lee had raised.

Congress recognized that some formal statement issued under its authority would be needed to end the American constitutional argument with Great Britain and to explain the case for independence to the colonists, to European nations, and to posterity. Congress therefore named a committee to draft such a declaration. Its members included Thomas Jefferson of Virginia, who replaced Lee (who, as the resolutions' proposer, would have been a member of the committee); Benjamin Franklin of Pennsylvania (the most eminent American in the Western world and a key advocate of independence); Philip Livingston of New York (representing a crucial colony from the mid-Atlantic region); and Roger Sherman of Connecticut (a senior figure in American politics and one of the most respected members of Congress). As a leading advocate of independence, John Adams was a natural choice for the committee.

By this point, Adams and Jefferson had come to know each other as fellow delegates, lawyers, and intellectuals. Long after the fact, Adams wrote in his *Autobiography* an account of his early impressions of Jefferson:

> Mr. Jefferson had been now about a Year a Member of Congress, but had attended his Duty in the House but a very small part of the time and when there had never spoken in public: and during the whole Time I satt with him in Congress, I never heard him utter three Sentences together. . . . It will naturally be enquired, how it happened that he was appointed on a Committee of such importance. There were more reasons than one. Mr. Jefferson had the Reputation of a masterly Pen. He had been chosen a Delegate in

Virginia, in consequence of a very handsome public Paper which he had written for the House of Burgesses, which had given him the Character of a fine Writer. Another reason was that Mr. Richard Henry Lee was not beloved by the most of his Colleagues from Virginia and Mr. Jefferson was sett up to rival and supplant him. This could be done only by the Pen, for Mr. Jefferson could stand no competition with him or any one else in Elocution and public debate.[33]

In an 1822 letter to Timothy Pickering, Adams noted that Jefferson was "so prompt, frank, explicit, and decisive upon committees and in conversation . . . that he soon seized upon my heart."[34] Though this friendship was one of the longest and richest in American history, the two men were notably different from each other; they embodied contrasts of build, temperament, and oratory. Jefferson was tall and lanky, whereas Adams was short and stocky. Jefferson was not given to public speaking, whereas Adams was a skilled and frequent orator. Jefferson was a law-office lawyer whose preferred tasks were research and drafting; Adams was a skilled trial lawyer. They used these differences to complement each other in Congress and in later shared responsibilities, forming an able, mutually trusting partnership.

Within the drafting committee, wrangling began over who would draft the Declaration. We have two versions of the final decision—Adams's version, given in letters and in his *Autobiography*, and Jefferson's version, given in his *Autobiography*. Adams claimed that he had persuaded Jefferson to draft the Declaration; Jefferson insisted that the entire committee urged him to do it. Whichever version was correct, the reasons that Adams gave to justify his view that Jefferson should be the draftsman probably represent the arguments that Adams made:

> Mr. Jefferson desired me to . . . make the Draught. This I declined and gave several reasons for declining. 1. That he was a Virginian and I a Massachusettensian. 2. that he was a southern Man and I a

northern one. 3. That I had been so obnoxious for my early and constant Zeal in promoting the Measure, that any draught of mine, would undergo a more severe Scrutiny and Criticism in Congress, than one of his composition. 4thly and lastly and that would be reason enough if there were no other, I had a great Opinion of the Elegance of his pen and none at all of my own. I therefore insisted that no hesitation should be made on his part. He accordingly took the Minutes and in a day or two produced to me his Draught.[35]

Once Jefferson finished his draft, Adams became Congress's leading advocate both for independence and for Jefferson's Declaration; Jefferson later gratefully recalled that Adams was "our Colossus on the floor."[36] Congress cut about a fourth of Jefferson's draft and in the process greatly improved it in cogency, force, and logical consistency.[37] On July 2, 1776, Congress adopted Lee's resolutions. Two days later, after considerable debate, the body adopted its revised version of Jefferson's draft Declaration. On the night of July 2–3, 1776, exalted by his victory, Adams wrote two letters to Abigail, pouring out a flood of emotions inspired by the events of the day. In his second letter, he declared his faith that the colonies ultimately would win independence:

> You will think me transported with Enthusiasm but I am not.—I am well aware of the Toil and Blood and Treasure, that it will cost Us to maintain this Declaration, and support and defend these States.—Yet through all the Gloom I can see the Rays of ravishing Light and Glory. I can see that the End is more than worth all the Means. And that Posterity will tryumph in that Days Transaction, even altho We should rue it, which I trust in God We shall not.[38]

Adams soon became one of the Continental Congress's workhorses, serving on many committees and chairing dozens. In particular, he worked with Benjamin Franklin, John Dickinson, Robert Morris, and Benjamin Harrison V to frame a Model Treaty for the new nation to propose to future allies and trading partners. This plan distilled the idealism that Adams hoped would guide American foreign relations, seeking the goal of free and reciprocal trade among the signing nations while avoiding American entanglement in European affairs. Adams's work on the Model Treaty focused on the concluding part of a four-part design to secure the legitimacy of the United States as a new nation within the context of the law of nations. The first part was to encourage the creation of state constitutions; the second was to invent a way of organizing the states as an American Union (which resulted in the Articles of Confederation); the third was to issue a declaration of American independence; and the fourth was to devise a plan for making treaties with other nations (the Model Treaty). The purpose of Adams's plan was to usher the United States into the Atlantic World as a full-fledged member of the community of nations.[39] Meanwhile, Adams wrote home to describe to Abigail some of the work that he faced in Congress, including such matters as designing the Great Seal for the United States.[40]

In the fall of 1776, Adams traveled with Franklin and Edward Rutledge of South Carolina to Staten Island in New York, to represent Congress in talks with the British naval commander, Admiral Lord Richard Howe. Hoping to hear that Howe was prepared to negotiate a peaceful settlement of the dispute with the mother country, including perhaps recognition of American independence, Adams and his colleagues were disappointed to learn that Howe had neither official permission nor personal inclination to consider independence or to recognize Congress. The talks broke off and never resumed.

On the way to this conference with Howe, when the American delegates reached Brunswick, New Jersey, they discovered that the inns were so full that Franklin and Adams had to share a tiny room and a bed that almost filled it. The room had one small window, which was open. Adams arose to close it, fearing the effects of the night air. He recalled:

Oh! says Franklin dont shut the Window. We shall be suffocated. I answered I was afraid of the Evening Air. Dr. Franklin replied, the

Air within this C[h]amber will soon be, and indeed is now worse than that without Doors: come! Open the Window and come to bed, and I will convince you: I believe you are not acquainted with my Theory of Colds. Opening the Window and leaping into Bed, I said I had read his Letters to Dr. Cooper in which he had advanced, that, that Nobody ever got cold by going into a cold Church, or any other cold Air: but the Theory was so little consistent with my experience, that I thought it a Paradox: However I had so much curiosity to hear his reasons, that I would run the risque of a cold. The Doctor then began an harangue, upon Air and cold and Respiration and Perspiration, with which I was so much amused that I soon fell asleep, and left him and his Philosophy together.

Adams continued with a sketch of what he dimly remembered Franklin's theory to be, as well as his continuing skepticism about it, but he also noted that Franklin, like him, soon drifted off to sleep in midharangue.[41]

Some aspects of Congress filled Adams with hope, but often he nearly boiled over with exasperation at Congress's slow, uncertain pace. Having stomached congressional dilatoriness for nearly three years, Adams found his patience on the verge of snapping. He concluded that his colleagues seemed warlike, timorous, daring, and disorganized, all at once; they breathed fire against Britain while failing to take the actions needed to organize and direct American war efforts. Sometimes, also, Adams shared the impatience of some delegates in Congress with the war's slow progress and the caution of General Washington, the Continental army's commander in chief. Always, just under the surface of his thoughts was his desire to withdraw from Congress and return to Braintree and his family. In April 1777, he exploded to Abigail:

Is it not intollerable, that the opening Spring, which I should enjoy with my Wife and Children upon my little Farm, should pass away, and laugh at me, for labouring, Day after Day, and Month after Month, in a Conclave, Where neither Taste, nor Fancy, nor Reason, nor Passion, nor Appetite can be gratified?

Posterity! You will never know, how much it cost the present Generation, to preserve your Freedom! I hope you will make a good Use of it. If you do not, I shall repent in Heaven, that I ever took half the Pains to preserve it.[42]

That spring, Abigail had had to write a gentle reproof to John for having sent a bundle of letters home but omitting one for his youngest son, Thomas Boylston Adams: "It would have grieved you if you had seen your youngest Son stand by his Mamma and when she deliverd out to the others their Letters, he inquired for one, but none appearing he stood in silent grief with the Tears running down his face, nor could he be pacified till I gave him one of mine.— Pappa does not Love him he says so well as he does Brothers."[43] No sooner did John receive this letter than he wrote a special one to "Mr Thomas Adams Braintree":

My dear Son Thomas
The only Reason why I omitted to write you when I wrote to your Brothers, was because I thought you was as yet too young to be able to read Writing, not because I had less Affection for you than for them: for you may rely upon it, you have as great a share in your Fathers Esteem and Affection as any of his Children.

I hope you will be good and learn to read and write well, and then I shall take a Pride and Pleasure in your constant Correspondence. Give my Love to your Mamma, your worthy Sister, and Brothers, and to all the rest of the Family.

Pray, when you write me a Letter, let me know how many Calves are raising, how many Ducks and Geese, and how the Garden looks. I long to take a Walk with you to see them, and the green Meadows and Pastures. I am your Father,
John Adams[44]

In the first half of 1777, Abigail not only had to run the family farm and take care of four children but also was pregnant for the sixth time. She tried to keep John reassured about her health, as when she began one letter on July 2: "I sit down to write you a few lines this morning as I am loth the post should go, without telling you that I am well, as usual. Suppose you will be more anxious for me this month than common."[45] A week later, however, she had to report:

> I sit down to write you this post, and from my present feelings tis the last I shall be able to write for some time if I should do well. I have been very unwell for this week past, with some complaints that have been new to me, tho I hope not dangerous.
>
> I was last night taken with a shaking fit, and am very apprehensive that a life was lost. As I have no reason to day to think otherways; what may be the consequences to me, Heaven only knows. I know not of any injury to myself, nor any thing which could occasion what I fear.
>
> I would not Have you too much allarmd. I keep up some Spirits yet, tho I would have you prepaird for any Event that may happen.
>
> I can add no more than that I am in every Situation unfeignedly Yours, Yours.[46]

From Philadelphia, John wrote, mingling empathy, anguish, and concern: "Oh that I could be near, to say a few kind Words, or shew a few Kind Looks, or do a few kind Actions. Oh that I could take from my dearest, a share of her Distress, or relieve her of the whole."[47] John was no stranger to hearing of his wife's and family's travails when he was far from home and unable to help—but the potential loss of the baby, ending their last attempt to have a child, brought things home to him in a particularly devastating way.

On July 16, Abigail wrote to John to convey the sad news that, although she survived the delivery of the child on July 11, Elizabeth was indeed stillborn. Abigail wrote that she had set her heart upon a second daughter, and that their daughter Abigail was deeply distraught, but she also assured him that she was recovering from the heartbreak of this loss: "So short sighted and so little a way can we look into futurity that we ought patiently to submit to the dispensation of Heaven." She wanted him to know that she was recovering her strength: "I However feel myself weakend by this exertion, yet I could not refrain [from] the temptation of writing with my own Hand to you."[48]

When John received the news of Elizabeth's stillbirth, after having written three letters expressing anxious hopes for the safe birth of a daughter, he wrote to express gratitude for Abigail's good health and sorrow for Elizabeth:

> Is it not unaccountable, that one should feel so strong an Affection for an Infant, that one has never seen, nor shall see? Yet I must confess to you, the Loss of this sweet little Girl, has most tenderly and sensibly affected me. I feel a Grief and Mortification, that is heightened tho it is not wholly occasioned, by my Sympathy with the Mother. My dear little Nabbys Tears are sweetly becoming her generous Tenderness and sensibility of Nature. They are Arguments too of her good sense and Discretion.[49]

The separations of John and Abigail caused them worry and pain. At one point, John wrote sadly, "Poor, unhappy I! who have never an opportunity to share with my Family, their Distresses, nor to contribute in the least degree to relieve them! I suffer more in solitary silence, than I should if I were with them."[50] And yet their ability to express themselves openly and eloquently showed the possibilities of intimacy and trust that they found in the written word, and in fragile envelopes carrying anxiously written pages between Braintree and Philadelphia.[51]

In the meantime, Adams had impressed his colleagues with his careful study of the problems facing the United States, particularly on the world stage.[52] Based on his contributions to congressional debates on European affairs and the challenges facing the new nation, Congress chose him as one of the first diplomats to represent the United States abroad.

Adams accepted the mission, but the news filled him with uneasiness, because he had just managed to return home for some rare time with his wife and children and because the hazards of a transatlantic voyage in time of war alarmed him. Still, driven by his duty to his country, Adams agreed—though he waited a day before writing his letter of acceptance. Then he broke the news to Abigail. After some discussion whether she and the children should accompany him, the couple reached a difficult decision: Abigail and three of their children would remain in Braintree, but John Quincy Adams, ten years old, would go with his father. On February 13, 1778, father and son boarded the frigate *Boston*, which sailed for Europe two days later. For both John and John Quincy, a new stage of their education was beginning.

Chapter Five

"May the Design of my Voyage be answered"

Revolutionary Diplomat, Polemicist, and Constitution-Maker (1778–1783)

For John Adams, the American Revolution fell into three parts. From 1765 to 1774, he emerged as a revolutionary advocate. From 1774 to 1777, he was indispensable as a member of the Continental Congress and as a key participant in the debates on independence. He took pleasure in these efforts. By contrast, he found 1778 to 1783, his time as an American revolutionary diplomat, deeply painful. He savored only one interlude, in 1779, when he returned to Massachusetts and immersed himself in constitution-making. Otherwise, though his efforts helped to secure the Netherlands as an ally for the United States and provided needed funding for the Confederation Congress, his diplomatic service left him sad and bitter—about the French, Congress, and a man whom he had once esteemed, Benjamin Franklin.

Adams's experience of the Revolution abroad vexed him. His quest to redeem himself from attacks aimed at him during that time overshadowed the rest of his life. Spurring his quest for redemption was his anxiety that he would be denied recognition for his diplomatic labors and would be blamed for sins that were not his. Even so, he found that time so painful that, as an old man writing his autobiography decades later, he stopped writing just as he got to the part dealing with his second mission to Europe.

In late 1777, the Continental Congress gave Adams his first diplomatic assignment, hoping not just to benefit from his expertise but also to solve a problem caused by sectional politics. In 1776, Congress had sent Silas Deane of Connecticut, Arthur Lee of Virginia, and Benjamin Franklin of Pennsylvania to France to negotiate a treaty of alliance; instead, the American diplomats exploded in recrimination. Suspicious and distrustful, Lee accused Deane of corruption; when Franklin defended Deane, Lee attacked him as well. These wrangles tracked fault lines dividing sectional groups of delegates in Congress; a dispute at home would have consequences abroad, and a dispute abroad would roil congressional waters at home. Congress had chosen a geographically balanced delegation to accommodate sectional divisions.[1] Thus, after recalling Deane, Congress chose Adams, another New Englander, to replace him.[2]

Congress found it hard to choose individuals to represent the United States abroad. Because it had no way to nurture a pool of diplomats, it had to draw on those who were available and willing to go.[3] Only Franklin, who had been a colonial agent in Britain and a member of the international scientific community, had well-honed diplomatic skills grounded in experience.[4] Further, the states composing the United States viewed one another with suspicion, exacerbating the difficulty of presenting a united front and a coherent diplomatic stance abroad.[5] Those whom Congress sent to Europe were mostly truculent advocates of American interests with scanty diplomatic skills, like Adams, with a few collegial politicians possessing tact, deference, and the ability to keep silent, like Franklin and John Jay.[6]

John rejected Abigail's plea to accompany him to Europe, urging her to consider the voyage's dangers and his desire not to risk her or their children.[7] Boarding the US frigate *Boston* on February 13, 1778, John and John Quincy had to wait two days before the ship sailed. The delay gave John a chance to dash off a loving parting note to Abigail:

> We shall be soon on Board, and may God prosper our Voyage, in every Stage of it, as much as at the Beginning, and send to you, my dear Children and all my Friends, the choicest of Blessings—so Wishes and prays yours, with an Ardour, that neither Absence, nor any other Event can abate,
>   John Adams
>   Johnny sends his Duty to his Mamma and his Love to his sister and Brothers. He behaves like a Man.[8]

The *Boston* endured a harrowing transatlantic voyage of six weeks, during which father and son explored the world of calculus and pored over French books to perfect their command of the language. They also witnessed a naval engagement with a British warship that failed to capture their vessel; they saw a ship's officer die of his wounds, after John Adams had to hold the wounded man in his arms as the ship's surgeon amputated his leg. On March 30, Adams showed his anxiety about the challenge facing him, writing in his diary, "May the Design of my Voyage be answered."[9]

The *Boston* landed at Bordeaux on April 1. After eight days' travel across France, the Adams party reached Passy, just outside Paris, where Franklin opened his home to them. Adams learned that on February 6, a week before he and his son had sailed, Franklin had persuaded the French to recognize US independence and had negotiated a treaty of alliance with France; Franklin had capitalized on the Continental Army's defeat of the British general John Burgoyne at Saratoga in October 1777. Though Adams welcomed Franklin's achievement, the knowledge that Franklin had made his trip to France unnecessary vexed him. No longer having a mission, he worked to establish a role for himself in Paris. He organized the American mission's paperwork and finances,[10] acted as its chronicler to update Congress and the nation on European developments, and provided a needed third vote to break deadlocks between Franklin and Lee, who detested each other.

Adams equated the obligations of a diplomat to his country with those of an attorney to his client—zealous representation. A diplomat, however, differed from a lawyer in two respects. First, diplomacy only sometimes required an adversarial stance; second, diplomatic negotiations, unlike trials, lacked a presiding judge to warn a diplomat to step back. Further, Adams was too aware of the war at home to be comfortable abroad. He knew that his family was living in a nation at war; his anxiety for their safety dramatized for him America's plight. He wrote constantly to Abigail, and she wrote constantly to him, but the difficulties of getting letters across the Atlantic misled each that the other was not writing. For example, Abigail wrote on June 18, 1778:

> At length my anxiety is relieved and the happy happy tidings of your arrival and safety in France has reachd my Ears and blessd my Eyes. By an English paper taken in a prize and carried into Salem, under the Paris News there is mention made of my Dearest Friends arrival at the abode of the venerable Dr. Frankling.—What have I not suffered for this month past? The Fear of your being finally lost daily increased upon my mind, for not the least inteligence could be procured with regard to the Boston save what our Enemies told us that she was taken and carried into England. My anxious Friends by their endeavours to console me plainly discoverd their own fears, upon this occasion, but my joy is great in receiving the constant and repeated congratulations of my Friends, and in seeing the unfeigned joy of the countanances of all I meet. The vessel was in general given up as taken or lost.[11]

Adams worked to make himself an effective diplomat. Exacerbating his insecurities were his awe of Europe and his intimidation at representing the United States in the center of the Western world; work helped to keep those insecurities in check. Even so, though Adams's ability to argue proved of great value when he wrote essays as an advocate for the American cause to influence a European readership, his polemical talents did not include the indirect approach, the soft voice, or a sense of knowing (like a lawyer in court) when to stop arguing.

Though he tried to get used to French habits, modes of conversation, and mores, Adams found that challenge embarrassing. For example, on April 2, 1778, the day after his arrival, he attended a dinner at Bordeaux, where a young, attractive lady asked him through an interpreter, "Mr. Adams, by your Name I conclude you are descended from the first Man and Woman, and probably in your family may be preserved the tradition which may resolve a difficulty which I could never explain. I never could understand how the first Couple found out the Art of lying together?" Stunned, Adams declared, with "Ironical Gravity":

> Madame My Family resembles the first Couple both in the name and in their frailties so much that I have no doubt We are descended from that in Paradise. But the Subject was perfectly understood by Us, whether by tradition I could not tell: I rather thought it was by Instinct, for there was a Physical quality in Us resembling the Power of Electricity or of the Magnet, by which when a Pair approached within a striking distance they flew together like the Needle to the Pole or like two Objects in electric Experiments.

On hearing his answer translated, the young woman answered, "Well I know not how it was, but this I know it is a very happy Shock." In his *Autobiography*, Adams noted that this story was comparatively decent, unlike so many he had heard in France; he warned posterity against importing French manners into America.[12]

As he had when they served in Congress, Adams worked well with Franklin; he acquired his sour view of Franklin only gradually, after his return to diplomatic service in 1780.[13] Nonetheless, Adams never could understand Franklin's forays into French society. Franklin charmed the French aristocracy at dinner parties and soirées, always seeking to further the American cause. The effectiveness of Franklin's indirect strategy escaped Adams.

To get Adams used to diplomacy by other means, and to make him comfortable in French society, Franklin included him in social invitations. At first, Adams appreciated Franklin's generosity and enjoyed himself. Still, partying and consorting with ladies struck the lawyerly diplomat as a poor way to get the French to take their American ally seriously. American fortunes in the war suffered in 1778 and 1779, and the French seemed to him to be too indifferent to the United States to provide necessary support. Adams brooded over what he saw as Franklin's undue deference to the French and his slipshod administration of American affairs.

At first, Adams welcomed the French-American treaty. He spurned rumored British overtures to persuade the United States to make a separate peace, equating "Departing from the Treaty [with] . . . violating the public Faith."[14] And yet his own inclinations and his observation of Franklin's willingness to accommodate the French caused him increasing concern. Bringing a litigator's mindset to diplomacy, Adams wanted to work with the French directly and on paper. Eventually his litigator's approach to Franco-American relations led him to pound the table and to raise his voice—although, during his first mission (1778–79), he confined his doubts about Franklin's style of diplomacy to his diary. For example, Franklin's shaky French surprised him: "Dr. Franklin was reported to speak french very well, but I found . . . that he did not speak it, grammatically, and upon my asking him sometimes whether a Phrase he had used was correct, he acknowledged to me, that he was wholly inattentive to the grammar. His pronunciation too . . . I soon found was very inaccurate, and some Gentlemen of high rank afterwards candidly told me that it was so confused, that it was scarcely possible to understand him."[15]

Adams felt growing skepticism about Franklin and about the French foreign minister, the Comte de Vergennes. Franklin, he complained in his diary, was too lazy, too fond of flattery, insufficiently committed to his diplomatic responsibilities, and too likely to take a pro-French view of the alliance. Adams saw Vergennes as concerned only with French interests, scanting those of the United States. At first, he kept his doubts to himself.

In turn, Vergennes was becoming irked by Adams's insistence that France had to do more to help the United States in the war, such as assigning French vessels to guard American merchant ships crossing the Atlantic. Fueling Vergennes's distrust of Adams were reports from America by Conrad Alexandre Gérard, French minister to the United States, insisting falsely that Adams secretly favored the British. Adams sensed Vergennes's dislike and reciprocated it fully. Further, his background as a New England Protestant predisposed him to share his region's distrust of the Catholic French, though they were allies in the war against Britain.[16] Also, Adams chafed at being overshadowed by Franklin; he found vexing the French tendency to heed Franklin and ignore Adams.[17]

John Adams found himself eclipsed in French perceptions even by an Adams who was not in Europe—his cousin Samuel—and noted his indignation in his diary on February 11, 1779: "It being settled that he was not the famous Adams, the Consequence was plain—he was some Man that nobody had ever heard of before— and therefore a Man of no Consequence—a Cypher. And I am inclined to think that all Parties both in France and England—Whiggs and Tories in England—the Friends of Franklin, Deane and Lee, differing in many other Things agreed in this—that I was not the fameux Adams."[18]

Vergennes's distaste for Adams was not merely personal. Rather, he feared that Adams represented an anti-French party in Congress and that he was scheming to make a separate peace with Britain.[19] At Vergennes's direction, Gérard lobbied Congress to rescind the three-man commission and name Franklin sole American minister to France, an action that they took on September 14, 1778. Ironically, Adams had proposed the same idea to his cousin Samuel five months earlier, hoping to cut the legation's costs. In February

1779, news of Congress's action reached Passy, with no word of Congress's intentions regarding Adams.

Adams found Congress's decision no surprise, but he was irked by its failure to give him a new assignment, to order him home, or to say anything at all about him. Deciding that his presence in France served no purpose, Adams sought permission to return home.[20] He confided his sense of humiliation to Abigail on February 28: "The Scaffold is cutt away, and I am left kicking and sprawling in the Mire, I think. It is hardly a state of Disgrace that I am in but rather of total Neglect and Contempt. The humane People about me, feel for my situation they say: But I feel for my Countrys situation. If I had deserved such Treatment, I should have deserved to be told so at least, and then I should have known my Duty."[21]

Wearying of public service and missing his family, Adams decided that he would retire not only from diplomacy but also from public life. On February 20, 1779, he wrote to Abigail: "The Congress I presume expect that I should come home, and I shall come accordingly. As they have no Business for me in Europe I must contrive to get some for myself at home.—Prepare yourself for removing to Boston into the old House—for there you shall go, and there, I will draw Writs and Deeds, and harrangue jurys and be happy."[22] On February 13, 1779, Abigail wrote John, gently scolding him for his seeming failure to write and explaining that her complaints grew out of her concern for him: "You chide me for my complaints, when in reality I had so little occasion for them. I must intreat you to attribute it to the real cause—an over anxious Solicitude to hear of your welfare, and an ill grounded fear least multiplicity of publick cares, and avocations might render you less attentive to your pen than I could wish."[23] As John wrestled with deciding what to write home, fearing lest British authorities intercept and publish his letters, Abigail struggled with her need to have news of John and her wish to ease his spirits.

Finally, on March 8, 1779, having received congressional permission, he and John Quincy left Paris. From Lorient, they sailed on June 17 aboard the French frigate *Le Sensible*, arriving in Boston on August 3 after a voyage much calmer and easier than their trip to Paris had been. Within a week of his return, Adams plunged again into work—but this time it was work dear to his heart, that of creating a constitution for his home state.[24]

Independence had required the thirteen rebelling states to replace their colonial charters with new constitutions; Adams had spurred this effort with his April 1776 pamphlet *Thoughts on Government* and with the resolution and preamble that he drafted for Congress in May.[25] Massachusetts's search for a new constitution began in the fall of 1776, when the state's legislature asked the town meetings to empower it to write a constitution. The towns rejected the idea; Concord argued that "a Constitution [made and] alterable by the Supreme Legislature is no security at all to the Subject against any Encroachment of the Governing part on any or all of their Rights & privileges."[26] Lexington urged (Pittsfield agreed) that the constitution be framed by a convention and submitted to "the Inhabitants, as Towns, or Societies, to express their Approbation, or the contrary."[27]

On April 4, 1777, the General Court announced that the legislature chosen at the next election would be authorized to frame a new constitution, ignoring Concord's recommendation; the legislature agreed (paralleling Lexington's and Pittsfield's recommendations) that the proposed constitution would go to the town meetings for acceptance or rejection. In the spring of 1778, the legislature sent its proposed constitution to the towns. The voters rejected it by better than a four to one margin, 9,972 to 2,083. The townspeople complained that the constitution did not sufficiently protect individual rights; that its system of separation of powers and checks and balances was grossly inadequate; that its plan for legislative representation favored the state's eastern counties at the western counties' expense; and that the legislature's framing of the constitution did not respect the people's right to exercise the constituent power—the power to make and adopt a constitution.

The General Court started over. Polling the town meetings and finding that townsmen favored a new convention by a vote of more than two to one, in June 1779 the General Court called on each town to elect delegates to a convention. The court announced that the convention would draft a constitution and submit it to the town meetings and that the towns would send the convention their results (each town's report of its decision and opinions on the constitution), setting forth votes on the constitution article by article. In its final session, the convention would decide whether the constitution had been adopted by the required two-thirds vote. Braintree elected John Adams to represent it at the constitutional convention.

In September 1779, the delegates convened in Cambridge; they elected a thirty-member drafting committee, which chose a three-member subcommittee (James Bowdoin, Samuel Adams, and John Adams). That subcommittee assigned the task of drafting a constitution to John Adams. The assignment was a chance to apply his ideas about constitutionalism to creating a constitution for his home state, to reconcile theory and practice. Working through September and October, he presented his *Report of a Constitution* to the convention on November 1.[28]

Adams took up his pen at a pivotal time in the evolution of American constitutionalism. The first wave of state constitution-making in 1776 had produced constitutions exalting the legislature while limiting executive and judicial powers and independence. The early constitution-makers did not sufficiently recognize the need to separate institutions and powers or to create a system of checks and balances. By contrast, New York's 1777 constitution, framed by a committee led by John Jay, signaled a new wave of constitution-making. Its themes were concern for balance among three branches of government (legislative, executive, and judiciary), a powerful governor elected by the people, and a careful arrangement of separation of powers and checks and balances. Adams liked the New York constitution, believing that *Thoughts on Government* had guided its

framing. Now, he would have a chance to bring constitutional creation to new heights.

Adams's draft began, emulating the Virginia constitution of
1776, with a Declaration of Rights of thirty articles, the last of which
became the most famous:

> XXX.—In the government of this Commonwealth, the legislative
> department shall never exercise the executive and judicial powers,
> or either of them: The executive shall never exercise the legislative
> and judicial powers, or either of them: The judicial shall never ex-
> ercise the legislative and executive powers, or either of them: to the
> end it may be a government of laws and not of men.[29]

Adams echoed other states' declarations of rights by phrasing the
provisions of the Massachusetts declaration in "should" language
rather than in the "shall/shall not" language of statutory command.
It codified right principles or right things to guide the citizenry in
assessing the doings of their elected representatives, rather than
presenting judicially enforceable commands and prohibitions regarding individual rights.[30]

In the Frame of Government accompanying the Declaration
of Rights, Adams devised a two-house legislature, the House of
Representatives more numerous than the Senate. This constitution made a considerable advance over its 1778 precursor in its
arrangements for representation of the people throughout the state,
in addressing separation of powers and checks and balances, and in
creating an independent governor elected directly by the people.
One unique aspect of Adams's Frame of Government was chapter
V, which provided for the governance of Harvard College, for the
fostering of literary and other knowledge, and for the promotion of
education.[31]

Reconvening on October 28 and receiving Adams's draft on
November 1, the convention continued its labors until November
17, when it adjourned again, scheduling a new session to meet in

Boston on January 5. On and off the convention worked, submitting the revised draft to the towns on March 2. Though approving Adams's work, the convention made a few changes to it. It subjected the governor's veto to override by a two-thirds vote of both houses of the state legislature—an innovation borrowed from New York's 1777 constitution but one that Adams had criticized because he believed that the governor's veto (like that of the king of Great Britain) should be absolute. The delegates made other revisions to Adams's draft, such as authorizing the militiamen to elect their own officers (instead of having them appointed by the governor); eliminating Adams's proposed term limit for the governor (no more than five one-year terms out of every seven); and loosening his proposed property qualification for legislators to cover personal property as well as land held as freehold (that is, land held without limits on ownership rights).[32]

After the convention submitted the draft constitution to the towns, it adjourned. It reconvened on June 2 and began reviewing the results submitted by the town meetings. Several days of deliberations followed, during which the convention juggled votes to show that all the provisions of the proposed constitution had won the needed two-thirds vote.[33] Finally, on June 16, 1780, the convention announced that, every provision having won approval by a two-thirds majority, the new constitution had been adopted and would take effect as of October 25. Then the convention voted to dissolve.

Adams had had to leave the convention for a new diplomatic mission almost immediately after he presented his draft, but his departure did not end his engagement with the constitution. From an ocean away, he kept watch. Writing a letter full of news about Massachusetts on January 18, 1780, Abigail made sure to inform John that his colleagues missed him and regarded him with esteem:

> The Blocade of the roads has been a sad hinderance to the meeting of the convention, a few only of the near Members could get together, so few that they were obliged to adjourn. Many of them

mourn the absence of one whom water, not snow seperates from them. They are pleased to say that he was more attended to than any other member, and had more weight and influence upon the minds of the convention.[34]

John sent letter after letter to his cousin Samuel inquiring as to the progress of ratification. On February 23, 1780, he wrote: "I hope You will be so good as to inform me of what passes, particularly what progress the Convention makes in the Constitution. I assure You it is more comfortable making Constitutions in the dead of Winter at Cambridge or Boston, than sailing in a leaky Ship, or climbing on foot or upon Mules over the Mountains of Gallicia and the Pyranees."[35]

John wrote Samuel again two years later, eager for news of the workings of the new form of government once it was put into effect:

Pray how does your Constitution work? How does the privy Council play its Part? Are there no Inconveniences found in it? It is the Part which I have been most anxious about, least it should become unpopular and Gentlemen should be averse to serve in it. This Form of Government has a very high Reputation in Europe, and I wish it may be as well approved in Practice as it is in Theory.[36]

The Massachusetts constitution of 1780 won the reputation that it has had ever since, as the most eloquent state constitution framed during the Revolution.[37] The constitution and the process of its framing and adoption influenced all later American efforts at constitution-making—including that, seven years later, to frame a new form of government for the United States. Along with the 1777 constitution of New York, the Massachusetts constitution of 1780 was a leading influence on the US Constitution. It was the highwater mark of Adams's influence on the development of American constitutionalism; he was an "absent framer" whose work shaped what happened in Philadelphia in 1787, even though he was not there.[38]

Adams had intended his return to Massachusetts to end his public service, but his stay at home lasted barely four months. In October 1779, Adams's friend Henry Laurens of South Carolina wrote to him that Congress wanted to send him abroad again. It had named him an American minister plenipotentiary, charging him with negotiating a peace treaty with Great Britain. Laurens assured Adams that his acceptance of this appointment would give great joy to "the true friends of American independence."[39] Writing back almost immediately, Adams expressed ambivalence about the appointment but concluded by accepting the post:

> I have received no Commission, nor Instructions, nor any particular Information of the Plan, but from the Advice and Information from you and Several others of my Friends at Philadelphia, and here, I shall make no Hesitation to say, that notwithstanding the Delicacy, and Danger of this Commission, I suppose, I shall accept it, without Hesitation, and trust Events to Heaven as I have been long used to do.[40]

This time two of his sons, John Quincy and Charles, would accompany him to Europe. Again John rejected Abigail's plea to travel with him with all the children, insisting that the voyage would be too dangerous.[41] Though Abigail allowed John Quincy and Charles to go, she was not shy about expressing her sorrow at their leaving. Writing on November 14, 1779, "Portia" (a pen name that John and Abigail chose to denote her patient, patriotic loyalty, like that of Marcus Brutus's wife) poured out her heart to her "Dearest of Friends":

> My habitation, how disconsolate it looks! My table I set down to it but cannot swallow my food. . . .
> . . . My dear sons I can not think of them without a tear, little do they know the feelings of a Mothers Heart! May they be good and usefull as their Father then will they in some measure reward the anxiety of a Mother. My tenderest Love to them. . . .

God almighty bless and protect my dearest Friend and in his
own time restore him to the affectionate Bosom of
Portia[42]

That day, the Adams party, including Francis Dana, a secretary to
the American legation, sailed for France, again aboard the French
vessel *La Sensible*. Unfortunately, the ship developed a series of leaks
that prevented it from reaching France. Instead, the captain landed
at El Ferrol on Spain's northwest coast. Adams and his party had
to travel overland from El Ferrol over the Pyrenees, reaching Paris
on February 8, 1780. Almost immediately, Adams began a civil yet
testy correspondence with Vergennes about whether, when, and
how he should announce his mission. The French foreign minister
insisted that it would be premature to disclose Adams's mission,
lest the announcement imply that the Americans were ready to
give up. Vergennes also may have been at least as concerned about
Adams engaging in diplomacy out of French control—in particular, he did not want Adams to seek a separate peace. Vergennes
advised Adams to publish a vague statement that his mission had
to do with "the future pacification," a cryptic phrase that Adams
agreed to use.[43]

Adams next sought a French passport from Vergennes so that he
could go to Amsterdam to open negotiations to secure Dutch recog-
nition of the United States, and also to persuade Dutch bankers to
make badly needed loans to prop up the Confederation's finances.
Vergennes stalled on dealing with Adams's request for a week.[44]
Franklin agreed with Vergennes, doubting the effects on European
perceptions of the United States were Adams to go begging to the
Dutch. Despite Vergennes's stubbornness and Franklin's skepticism,
Adams insisted that it was good and necessary to reach out to the
Netherlands for recognition and aid. As the spring and summer of
1780 elapsed, Adams still hoped that his mission to Amsterdam
might bring valuable benefits to the United States—should he ever
get permission to undertake it.

Conflicting news—good fortune for Britain, setbacks for America, setbacks for Britain, good fortune for America—kept Adams and his American correspondents confused and uncertain. Adams's spirts rose and fell with each shift of news. At the same time, his anxieties about the French-American alliance continued to grow. The war's uncertain tidings similarly unsettled Vergennes and the French foreign ministry, making the dialogue between Adams and Vergennes increasingly edgy.

Vergennes finally went around Adams's back to Franklin and to his own minister in the United States, the Chevalier de la Luzerne, Gérard's successor. Vergennes asked Luzerne to induce Congress to instruct Adams to obey Vergennes's "advice and opinion."[45] Also, Vergennes persuaded Franklin to write to Congress that Adams had "given Offence to the Court here."[46] Even so, Vergennes finally agreed to give Adams his passport—whether "to get rid of me," as Adams fretted, or to recognize the inevitable, owing to Congress's insistence that it wanted to open diplomatic and financial communication with the Netherlands.[47]

While awaiting his passport, Adams took up a congenial task—writing to shape European public opinion. His first such work (published in French in November 1780 and in English in January 1781) was his *Translation of Thomas Pownall's "Memorial to the Sovereigns of Europe."* Pownall, a former royal governor of New Jersey and Massachusetts, was a creative imperial statesman with a vision of a transformed British Empire. Adams used Pownall's *Memorial* as a jumping-off point for his own vision of what the United States would become after winning independence, leading the world away from obsessions with imperial glory and dynastic succession to a new, liberal world dominated by commerce. After writing an extended letter to the president of Congress on April 19, 1780, addressing these themes, Adams revised and reworked that text into a pamphlet intended for a European audience.[48]

Adams's second writing project was *Letters from a Distinguished American.* Here, again, he wrote to answer another polemicist—in this case, the Loyalist Joseph Galloway, once of Pennsylvania, who in 1780 published *Cool Thoughts on the Consequences of American Independence*. Adams presented his vision of a future in which a reconciled British Empire and an independent United States could have cordial, prosperous diplomatic and economic relations. He worked with a friend in Britain, Edmund Jennings (who may have been a British spy), to secure the letters' publication in London newspapers, but Jennings got only the first ten letters into print, and the essays appeared two years after Adams wrote them. Jennings also changed the dates of the letters and altered the writer's alleged identity from a Briton disenchanted with the empire's war policy (Adams's original plan) to a "distinguished American." (The essays did not see print in full until 1978.)[49]

Adams's third essay series was the "Replies to Hendrik Calkoen"—twenty-six essays prompted by the meeting between Adams and the prominent Dutch lawyer (whom Adams respectfully called "the giant of the law in Amsterdam"). Fascinated by his country's seventeenth-century revolution from Spain and curious about the similarities and differences between the Dutch and American Revolutions, Calkoen sent Adams a set of queries about the American Revolution. Calkoen used the essays Adams wrote in response as the basis for his lecture on the American Revolution; he also circulated the essays, hoping to induce influential lawyers and bankers in Amsterdam to favor the American cause. Though Adams never recovered his original essays from Calkoen, he used his drafts to reconstruct them and published them in London in 1786; they were reprinted in the United States in 1789. Adams used all three series of essays to practice his own version of diplomacy by other means—seeking to shape public opinion of the American cause and its likelihood of success.[50]

Adams continued to ponder what he should be doing. He preferred to write home to his wife and children, as Abigail loved to write to him—though at certain periods of his time abroad, her letters to him far outstripped in number, length, and emotional openness his letters to her. Their correspondence is replete with lists of letters sent and received, and inquiries after letters apparently not received—a habit common to those exchanging letters across the ocean. Abigail hinted, cajoled, and even begged John to write more often. Overworked, stressed, and feeling pangs of guilt, John answered that he was so busy that he wrote as often as he could, though not as often as he wished. Their friction over correspondence ebbed and flowed, as letters entrusted to the mails did or did not arrive. Keeping track of the frequency of John's letters, Abigail often taxed him with the amount of time elapsing between his missives. She sometimes upbraided her son as well. In December 1778, the eleven-year-old John Quincy sought to intervene in his parents' disputes about who was writing enough, or not enough:

> It is now with Great Pleasure that I now sit down to write to you & many a time since I came here I have done the same though you say in several Letters that . . . you have not rec'd but two or three Letters from My Pappa or me but Pappa rec'd a Letter from Uncle Smith Dated November the 3th in which he says that he had taken a Number of Letters for the family Yours have been pretty lucky but I have not rec'd but 2 Letters from you however My Pappa has rec'd several from you in which you complain'd a great deal of my Pappa's not writing to you but be assured that it is not that for he has wrote a great number of Letters to you.[51]

Abigail struggled to keep the Adams farm going and sought other ways to generate income, asking John to ship her products from Europe that she could resell in America. Both suffered from Congress's slow, inadequate system of paying American diplomats so that they could meet their expenses.[52]

Abigail also served as her husband's eyes and ears for American opinion. While John was in Europe, Abigail was in regular contact with James Lovell, a Massachusetts lawyer, politician, and delegate to the Continental Congress. Lovell gave her news of John (and sometimes of John Quincy); Abigail was hungry for such news and, frustrated by her husband's intermittent, terse letters, was grateful to Lovell for providing information. She conveyed to John whatever useful political news Lovell could share with her.

Lovell also posed a challenge for Abigail, as he was daringly flirtatious with her, even on occasion calling her Portia and skirting the edge of propriety. She valued her connection with him; at times she too was willing to engage in flirting, but she issued coy reproofs when Lovell stepped too close to the line set by eighteenth-century conventions. Ignoring Lovell's seeming overtures to another man's wife, Abigail remained true to her husband, however frustrating she found his absence from home.[53]

On July 27, 1780, John and his sons began the journey by carriage to Amsterdam, passport in hand.[54] Soon after he arrived, on August 10, Adams opened talks with Dutch authorities. In the meantime, he arranged for John Quincy, thirteen, and Charles, ten, to enroll at the University of Leyden. John Quincy took to the plan, but Charles, who at first had welcomed his first trip abroad as an adventure, increasingly suffered from homesickness. John arranged for Charles to return to America; the boy left on August 12, 1781. Writing to inform Abigail of her son's impending return, John noted sadly, "My dear Charles will go home with Maj. Jackson. Put him to school and keep him steady.—He is a delightfull Child, but has too exquisite sensibility for Europe."[55] Meanwhile, in July 1781, John Quincy went to St. Petersburg as secretary and French interpreter for Francis Dana, the new American minister to Russia. The Dana mission was a failure, for Catherine the Great declined to recognize American independence.

In the summer of 1781, as talks with the Dutch dragged on, Adams began to get letters reporting that Vergennes was plotting against him with the aid of American allies in Congress, encouraged in their doings by Franklin. His main sources were his wife, Abigail, and James Lovell. Writing of her sorrow that she could not "protect you from the Slanderous arrow that flieth in Secret," Abigail denounced Franklin's 1780 letter to the president of Congress as "this low this dirty this Infamous t[his] diabolical peice of envy and malice."[56]

In August 1781, Congress recast its approach to the anticipated peace talks with Britain, naming Franklin, Henry Laurens, John Jay, and Thomas Jefferson to serve with Adams. Their decision was the indirect doing of Vergennes through Luzerne; the foreign minister did not want to have to deal with Adams as sole American representative. Adams accepted this arrangement with resignation blended with anger, skeptical of the congressional mandate that the Americans work in concert with France.[57]

Bouts of illness (a product of stress from his diplomatic efforts and from the war's uncertain state) interrupted Adams's grueling negotiations with the Dutch. Word of the great French-American victory at the Battle of Yorktown (in October 1781) and the allies' capture of British general Charles Cornwallis's army spurred the Dutch to endorse the American cause. On April 19, 1782, the Netherlands recognized American independence; the leader of the Dutch government, Stadtholder William V, received Adams's credentials as the first American minister to Holland.[58] Adams also persuaded Dutch bankers to make loans to the United States that bolstered Congress's finances and credit. These talks made Adams what biographer James Grant has dubbed him—America's first "junk bonds promoter."[59] Adams's successful mission to the Netherlands was his first solo diplomatic achievement.

One of the new negotiators, John Jay, arrived in Paris with his wife, Sarah Livingston Jay, on June 23, 1782, fresh from his failed diplomatic mission to Spain. Laurens and Jefferson, the other two new negotiators, were unable to reach Paris. Captured by the British as he made his way to Europe, Laurens spent the rest of the war as a prisoner in the Tower of London. Still prostrated by the death of his wife, Martha, in 1782, Jefferson never began his journey to Europe. The burden of the negotiations fell on Jay and Franklin, as Adams was still in the Netherlands. In October 1782, when at Jay's behest he finally returned to France, Adams was so furious at Franklin for undermining him with Congress that he refused to visit Franklin. Mollifying Adams to prod the work of negotiating peace forward required the intervention of an American merchant, Matthew Ridley. Ridley persuaded Adams that it was better to honor the proprieties, however distasteful, to avoid revealing the strained relations between the American negotiators.[60]

Adams and Jay then began to review the task before them. Jay was a born diplomat, like Franklin. As a descendant of the Huguenots (French Protestants), he resented the persecution of his ancestors by France's Roman Catholics; he thus shared Adams's suspicion of the French. That Jay and Adams were both lawyers and constitution-makers fostered their growing friendship and partnership. Having won Franklin's and Adams's esteem, Jay became the American delegation's core member.[61]

Taking a pivotal step, Jay and Adams decided to ignore Congress's mandate to coordinate with the French, because the French and the Americans had different diplomatic goals. Adams and Jay saw that France gave low priority to American independence. To extract themselves from a difficult, unprofitable war, they would sell out the Americans for a separate peace with Britain. By contrast, independence was the Americans' first priority. If the French were giving greater weight to their own interests than to the American alliance, Jay and Adams decided, the Americans should look out for their country's interests in the same way.

Confronting Franklin, Jay and Adams told him that they were ready to ignore Congress's instructions and negotiate directly with Britain, explaining their reasons. In answer to Franklin's amazed query, "Then you are prepared to break our instructions if you take an independence course now[?]," Jay confirmed that he would do so, shattering his long clay pipe in the fireplace to emphasize his point (according to Jay family tradition).[62] Reluctantly, Franklin accepted their decision. Once the Americans had negotiated the peace treaty with Britain, Franklin took on the delicate task of briefing Vergennes on what the Americans had done without him.[63]

After months of negotiation, the diplomats concluded the Treaty of Paris of 1783, agreed on in preliminary form in November 1782 and achieving final, official status on September 3, 1783.[64] In this treaty, Britain recognized American independence and American fishing rights along the New England coast (a priority for Adams) and ceded all territory between the Allegheny Mountains and the Mississippi River to the United States, doubling its size. The treaty left issues of Loyalist claims for confiscated property in America to future diplomacy, once the American negotiators threatened to seek compensation for Americans' claims for property destroyed by British and Loyalist forces (a priority for Franklin).

The treaty was an American victory, the product of shrewd negotiations by the American diplomats aided by British admission that the war to keep the colonies was failing. One casualty of that failure was Lord North's ministry. In late 1782, losing a vote of confidence in the House of Commons, North and his colleagues resigned. The new ministry, led by the Marquis of Rockingham, told George III that, because the American war was all but lost, it would be best to conclude a peace treaty with the United States and defeat the French later.

The artist Benjamin West was commissioned to mark the treaty's completion by painting a group portrait of the negotiators, but the British diplomats refused to sit for it, and West left the painting unfinished. *The Peacemakers*, an icon of US diplomatic history, captures the Americans' satisfaction and weariness. John Jay stands, ramrod-straight, on the left; a contented Adams sits beside a smiling Franklin on a couch at the painting's center. Henry Laurens, looking anxious, stands next to Franklin; and Franklin's grandson, William Temple Franklin, sits next to his grandfather, holding a pen to show that he was the Americans' secretary. (Actually, Laurens was still in England, and the younger Franklin was not invited to attend the signing ceremony.)[65]

Following completion of the negotiations, Adams brooded over his future. Though eager to return home, he hoped that Congress might name him the first American minister to Great Britain, believing that he had earned the appointment. Adams spent most of 1783 fretting that Congress would not recognize his past services by giving him any new diplomatic assignment. Instead, he feared, those prizes would go to Franklin or to whomever Franklin wanted to have them. Haunted by rumors of congressional schemes against him spurred by French agents and by Franklin, and no longer able to contain himself, Adams began to denounce Franklin in letters home and in conversations.[66] Insisting that only he and Jay deserved principal credit for the treaty, he focused his wrath on Franklin. The New Englanders to whom he unburdened himself shared his views and fed them back to him. Even so, Adams's emotional explosions were inappropriate for a man of his age and standing. Unintentionally, Adams confirmed the doubts that many in Congress held of his judgment and even of his stability. His concern that others take him seriously caused him to behave in a way that made such respect all but impossible.

Each letter Adams wrote defending himself seemed to most in Congress to reinforce the case against him. Finally, Franklin, a seasoned veteran of epistolary politics, fired back—with devastating effect. On July 22, 1783, Franklin wrote to Robert R. Livingston, the Confederation Congress's secretary for foreign affairs, complaining about Adams's lack of discretion: "I am persuaded however, that [Adams] means well for his Country, is always an honest Man and often a Wise One, but sometimes and in some things absolutely out of his Senses."[67] Franklin's comment on Adams was a masterly insult, blending initial approbation with a pointed insinuation of doubt. Franklin's sentence, confirming people's worst doubts about Adams, did more damage to Adams's reputation, then and thereafter, than the most scathing of Adams's letters could inflict on Franklin.

Adams's confidence and reputation never fully recovered from this blow. The contents of Franklin's letter became notorious within Congress and among American politicians, haunting Adams for the rest of his life. Still, Adams's diplomatic service continued, beginning a new chapter in his education, and a new, more troubled, and more frustrating time for him and for his family.

In this saltbox house in Quincy, Massachusetts, John Adams was born on October 19 (O.S.; October 30, N.S.), 1735, the oldest son of Deacon John Adams and Susannah Boylston Adams. *Library of Congress, HABS MASS,11-QUI,6--5*

John Adams attended Harvard College, receiving his bachelor of arts degree in 1755. Though his parents intended him to earn his degree to become a minister, he instead chose the law as a profession. *"A Prospect of the Colledges in Cambridge in New England." Engraving by William Burgis, ca. 1726. Library of Congress, LC-DIG-pga-00404*

Paul Revere's 1770 engraving, from a drawing by Henry Pelham, depicts the "Boston Massacre." On March 5, 1770, an angry dispute between British regulars and Bostonians spun out of control; the regulars fired point-blank into the crowd. In his engraving, Revere made all the townspeople white, omitting Crispus Attucks, the massacre's first victim. Under the print is a poem that begins: "Unhappy Boston! see thy Sons deplore, Thy hallowed Walks besmeared with guiltless Gore." The caption lists the massacre's victims. John Adams was chief defense counsel for the soldiers and their commanding officer, winning an acquittal for all but two soldiers, who were convicted of manslaughter. *Library of Congress, LC-DIG-ppmsca-01657*

This pastel portrait by Benjamin Blyth depicts Abigail Smith Adams in 1766, two years after her marriage to John Adams. *Library of Congress, LC-DIG-hec-13515*

In this iconic engraving, taken from a life-size painting by John Trumbull, the committee of the Second Continental Congress assigned to draft a declaration of independence presents its work to Congress. John Adams stands at the group's center. Trumbull painted this group portrait decades after the event, so that even though he took life portraits of as many participants as possible, they all looked considerably older than they were in 1776. *Library of Congress, LC-DIG-pga-07154*

This satirical engraving shows two men representing Spain and France leading George III by a rope attached to his neck, and Lord Shelburne through a gate formed by spears. From the gate's crossbar tumble the British lion, a crown, and a unicorn—the elements of the British coat of arms. Shelburne (third from right) is followed by a man carrying a scourge with thirteen lashes labeled "America" and dragging a surly Dutchman. Their destination is a building labeled "Inquisition," at the top of a hill on the left. *"Blessed Are the Peacemakers," London, 1783. Library of Congress, LC-USZ62-45467*

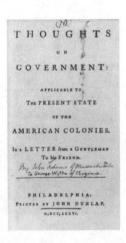

This engraving depicts Benjamin Franklin as the dazzled French saw him, and as he artfully presented himself—as a genial American sage—while he was the first American minister to France. Though at first he admired Franklin, Adams grew to dislike and resent him—feelings that Franklin reciprocated, which complicated their work together during the negotiation of the Treaty of Paris. *French engraving (1778) after life portrait by Joseph Sifrede Duplessis. Library of Congress, LC-DIG-ppmsca-10080*

John Adams's most influential and important publication, "Thoughts on Government" (Philadelphia, 1776), was a how-to manual for writing a new constitution. It had powerful influence on the states in 1776 and thereafter. Adams published the pamphlet anonymously, but his authorship soon leaked out. As a notation on the title page shows, Adams derived this pamphlet from letters he wrote to such colleagues as George Wythe and Richard Henry Lee of Virginia. *Library of Congress, LC-USZ62-64709*

His Excellency JOHN JAY *President of Congress & Minister Plenipotentiary from Congress at Madrid.*
Pub.d May 16.th 1783 by R. Wilkinson N.o 58 Cornhill, London.

Adams's fellow diplomat, the tactful John Jay, became the key member of the team of negotiators who concluded the Treaty of Paris of 1783. Benjamin Franklin and Adams were able to deal with Jay, who held them together to present a united front to Great Britain. Ending the Revolutionary War, the treaty required Britain to recognize US independence and to cede territory that doubled the size of the United States. *John Jay, profile engraving after life drawing by Pierre Eugène Du Simitière. Library of Congress, LC-USZ62-45481*

The émigré American artist John Singleton Copley painted a life-size portrait of John Adams as an American diplomat; Adams likely dressed this way for his first audience with King George III in 1785. Adams referred to the painting as a piece of vanity. *Library of Congress, LC-USZ62-1909*

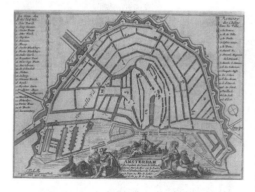

Amsterdam is remarkably unchanged from when John Adams visited the city as first American minister to the Netherlands and persuaded the Dutch to recognize the United States. Adams also talked Dutch bankers into making much-needed loans to the United States to keep the new nation's finances afloat. *"Amsterdam: ville capitale du Comte de Hollande," engraved by Nicolas de Fer, ca. 1695. David Rumsey Map Collection, no.11668083.jp2*

Abigail Adams was often an absentee First Lady, as bouts of illness kept her at the family home in Braintree. She disliked the nation's first and second temporary capitals, New York and Philadelphia, and she loathed the new "federal city," Washington, DC. She hung laundry to dry in the East Room of the Executive Mansion (now the White House). *Portrait by Gilbert Stuart, ca. 1797–1801. Library of Congress, LC-USZ62-25768*

This silhouette, cut from life, shows Washington during his third year as president of the United States. Adams was deeply ambivalent about Washington, during his time as Washington's vice president and then as his successor as president. *Library of Congress, LC-USZ62-137898*

This engraving, framing President John Adams with the flags and arms of
the sixteen American states, suggests the image that most Americans had of
Adams during his presidency. It seems to be inspired by the Copley portrait
of Adams as diplomat, with the central image reversed. *A New Display of the
United States,* 1799. Library of Congress, LC-DIG-ppmsca-15716

Abigail Adams was often an absentee First Lady, as bouts of illness kept her at the family home in Braintree. She disliked the nation's first and second temporary capitals, New York and Philadelphia, and she loathed the new "federal city," Washington, DC. She hung laundry to dry in the East Room of the Executive Mansion (now the White House). *Portrait by Gilbert Stuart, ca. 1797–1801. Library of Congress, LC-USZ62-25768*

The USS *Constitution*, perhaps the most famous ship in American naval history, was one of those built by the federal government during President John Adams's administration, pursuing Adams's lifelong commitment to a strong US Navy. It is still on active duty, anchored in Boston Harbor. *Library of Congress LC-DIG-pga-01152*

The Virginia attorney and veteran of the American Revolution John Marshall first served John Adams as the junior member of the American diplomatic team embroiled in the XYZ Affair. After serving in the US House of Representatives, Marshall was first secretary of war and then secretary of state in Adams's administration. In 1801, Adams named Marshall the fourth chief justice of the United States. Marshall was the greatest chief justice in US history; his appointment was Adams's greatest achievement as president. *Engraving, ca. 1808, of profile life portrait of*

John Marshall by Charles Balthazar Julien Fevrier de Saint-Memin. Library of Congress, LC-USZ62-8499

This engraving, published in 1834, shows the nation's permanent capital, the city of Washington, as John and Abigail Adams knew it in 1800. Its perspective is from the west front of the US Capitol grounds. The engraving depicts the west end of the west grounds and Pennsylvania Avenue, with poplar trees planted in 1803. *Engraving by James Heath, ca. 1800. Library of Congress, LC-USZ62-2125*

A leading physician and a fellow signer of the Declaration of Independence, Benjamin Rush frequently exchanged letters with John Adams. Making his great project the restoration of the friendship between Adams and Jefferson, Rush succeeded in 1812; he died the following year, mourned by both his friends. *Engraving, ca. 1802, after profile life portrait by Charles Balthazar Julien Fevrier de Saint-Memin. Library of Congress, LC-DIG-pga-13208*

When John and Abigail Adams returned from Europe in 1788, they moved into the Vassall-Borland House in Quincy (which had absorbed Braintree). Adams named it Peacefield, to commemorate the peace treaty with Britain that he helped negotiate in 1783 and the peace treaty with France negotiated by his diplomats in 1800. Here John and Abigail lived for the rest of their lives. *Library of Congress, LC-G613-74176*

Hanging on the wall of the dining room of Peacefield is Gilbert Stuart's 1825 portrait of John Adams in his ninetieth year. This powerful likeness captures the spirit of John Adams within his aged body. *Library of Congress, LC-G613-77305*

A FOOT-RACE

This engraved cartoon shows the candidates for president in 1824 as competitors in a foot race. John Adams is calling, "Hurrah for our son Jack," whereas others are cheering, "Hurrah for our Jackson!" Contrary to the cartoon, John Adams took great pains not to advocate his son's candidacy, fearing that his political enemies would see him as seeking to establish a monarchy. *Engraving by David Claypoole Johnson. Library of Congress, LC-DIG-ds-05217*

The eastern building of the Library of Congress, originally known as the Annex when it opened in 1939, was renamed the John Adams Building in 1980. Designed in a restrained but detailed art deco style by Pierson & Watson with Alexander Buel Trowbridge as consulting architect, it is Adams's only monument in Washington, DC. *Library of Congress, LC-DIG-ppmsca-37894*

Chapter Six

"Every phenomenon that occurs in the history of government"

American Minister and Constitutional Commentator (1784–1788)

John Adams was ambivalent about what to do after the peace treaty had established American independence. He wanted to return to America; he had even submitted his resignation as a diplomat to the Confederation Congress in December 1782.[1] He could not leave Europe, however, without Congress's authorization, and while he stayed, he let himself speculate about whether Congress would show that it valued his past services by entrusting him with another mission.

Against that background, he and Abigail engaged in a loving war of wills and desires, conducted across the Atlantic. She begged him to return home, and with equal ardor he pleaded with her to join him in London. Though she yielded at last to his entreaties, Abigail at first insisted that it was unwise for her to attempt the journey and far better for John to return to America. Beyond her concerns about the voyage, she cited a new set of worries: What figure would she cut in London by John's side?

> Theory and practise are two very different things; and the object magnifies, as I approach nearer to it. I think if you were abroad in

a private Character, and necessitated to continue there; I should not hesitate so much at comeing to you. But a mere American as I am, unacquainted with the Etiquette of courts, taught to say the thing I mean, and to wear my Heart in my countantance, I am sure I should make an awkward figure. And then it would mortify my pride if I should be thought to disgrace you. Yet strip Royalty of its pomp, and power, and what are its votaries more than their fellow worms? I have so little of the Ape about me; that I have refused every publick invitation to figure in the Gay World, and sequestered myself in this Humble cottage, content with rural Life and my domestick employments in the midst of which; I have sometimes Smiled, upon recollecting that I had the Honour of being allied to an Ambassador[.][2]

While John and Abigail were discussing the question, another family matter intruded itself. Their daughter Abigail (known as Nabby) was being courted by a young man eight years her senior, Royall Tyler. A Harvard graduate and a friend of Francis Dana, Tyler had a reputation as a rake. He had charmed Abigail and persuaded her that he had reformed, but at first John was skeptical and angry that the dissolute Tyler should aspire to his daughter. He soon relented, and Nabby and Tyler became betrothed.

John informed Congress about European affairs, explaining why negotiation of commercial agreements should take place in London and hinting that he should be given that mission.[3] On October 29, 1783, Congress voted to assign new responsibilities to the American peace commissioners. Adams, Franklin, and Jay were to establish diplomatic relations and seek treaties with sixteen major European and North African powers.[4] In 1784, Congress also elected Jay secretary for foreign affairs to succeed Robert R. Livingston and chose Thomas Jefferson to take Jay's place on the negotiating team.

Jefferson arrived in Europe in August 1784. Almost immediately, he and Adams resumed their friendship and political partnership.[5] They commiserated with each other about the difficulties of securing respect for the United States and contending with rapacious European bankers; they also shared European news and whatever American news came to hand. John had one success—he finally persuaded Abigail to come to Europe. Though still hoping that he would come home, she admitted her sadness: "The airy delusive phantom Hope, how has she eluded my prospects. And my expectations of your return from month to month, have vanished." But she also made clear that she wanted nothing more than to be with him, even if it was in Europe:

> You invite me to you, you call me to follow you, the most earnest wish of my soul is to be with you—but you can scarcly form an Idea of the conflict of my mind. It appears to me such an enterprize, the ocean so formidable, the quitting my habitation and my Country, leaving my Children, my Friends, with the Idea that prehaps I may never see them again, without my Husband to console and comfort me under these apprehensions—indeed my dear Friend there are hours when I feel unequal to the trial. But on the other hand I console myself with the Idea of being joyfully and tenderly received by the best of Husbands and Friends, and of meeting a dear and long absent Son. But the difference is; my fears, and anxieties, are present; my hopes, and expectations, distant.[6]

Abigail and Nabby sailed from Boston on June 20, 1784. Writing to her sister, Elizabeth Smith Shaw, Abigail vividly described life at sea:

> It is very difficult to write at sea, in the serenest Weather the vessel rolls; and exceeds the moderate rocking of a cradle, and a calm gives one more motion, than a side wind going at 7 and 8 knots an hour: I am now setting in my *State room*, which is about 8 foot square, with two Cabbins, and a chair, which compleatly fills it, and I write leaning one Arm upon my cabbin, with a peice of Board in my lap, whilst I steady myself by holding my other hand upon the opposite Cabbin; from this you will judge what accommodations we have for writing; the door of my room opens into the Great Cabbin where we set, dine, and the Gentlemen sleep: we cannot Breath with our door shut, so that except when we dress and undress, we

live in common. A sweet Situation for a delicate Lady, but necessity has no law: and we are very fortunate, in our company.[7]

After a turbulent voyage, the Adamses arrived in London on July 21. Two days later, Abigail expressed joy at her arrival and relief that her ordeal of ocean travel was ended:

At length Heaven be praised I am with our daughter safely landed upon the British Shore after a passage of 30 days from Boston to the Downs. We landed at Deal the 20 instant, rejoiced at any rate to set our feet again upon the land. What is past, and what we sufferd by sickness and fatigue, I will think no more of. It is all done away in the joyfull hope of soon holding to my Bosom the dearest best of Friends. . . . . . .I think no inducement less than that of comeing to the tenderest of Friends could ever prevail with me to cross the ocean, nor do I ever wish to try it but once more.[8]

John wrote back immediately: "Your Letter . . . has made me the happiest Man upon Earth. I am twenty Years younger than I was Yesterday."[9] Because he had to travel to Amsterdam to negotiate further loans, John did not reunite with Abigail until August 7; then they traveled to Auteuil, outside Paris.[10]

Seeing his mission as only partial confirmation by Congress of his value as a diplomat, Adams hoped and moped—until he finally received the assignment that he had yearned to get. On February 24, 1785, the Confederation Congress named Adams American minister to Great Britain; the news reached him on May 2.[11] Adams would be the first American to represent his nation before his former monarch—a great honor and an unsettling challenge. At about the same time, Congress named Jefferson to succeed Franklin as American minister to France; Franklin was retiring and returning to Philadelphia.

Before any diplomacy could take place, Adams had first to meet King George III and present his credentials.[12] The audience took place on June 1. In a letter to John Jay that he wrote the day afterward,

Adams reported every detail of the meeting and of his talk with the king, including his own speech to the monarch:

> The Appointment of a Minister from the United States to your Majestys Court, will form an Epocha, in the History of England and of America. I think myself more fortunate, than all my fellow Citizens, in having the distinguish'd Honour, to be the first to Stand in your Majestys Royal Presence, in a diplomatic Character: and I Shall esteem myself the happiest of Men, if I can be instrumental in recommending my Country, more and more to your Majestys Royal Benevolence and of restoring an entire esteem, Confidence and Affection, or in better Words, "the old good Nature and the old good Humour" between People who, tho Seperated by an Ocean and under different Governments have the Same Language, a Similar Religion and kindred Blood.— I beg your Majestys Permission to add, that although I have Sometimes before, been entrusted by my Country it was never in my whole Life in a manner So agreable to myself.[13]

King George's answer showed considerable emotion. After noting how "extraordinary" their meeting was, he thanked Adams for "the language you have now held[, which] is So extreamly proper, and the Feelings you have discovered, So justly adapted to the Occasion." George "receive[d] with Pleasure, the Assurances of the friendly Dispositions of the United States" and expressed happiness that "the Choice has fallen upon you to be [American] Minister." The king added his view that he had "done nothing in the late Contest, but what I thought myself indispensably bound to do by the Duty which I owed to my People." Noting with frankness that he "was the last to consent to the Seperation," he admitted that American independence was now a fact, and expressed his willingness to "meet the Friendship of the United States as an independent Power." Adams's diplomatic words and behavior, the monarch added, persuaded him that he was right to do so.[14]

After that triumph, however, Adams found his mission frustrating and disappointing. Congress instructed him to induce Britain to redress a long list of American grievances—but Adams knew that Britain would not step back from its positions.

Adams was to demand that Britain cede to the United States the western forts and posts specified by the treaty. He was to demand that Britain compensate Americans for property (including slaves) seized during the war. He was to insist that Britain grant the United States "most favored nation" trading status. (The country having that status gets the best trading terms and conditions that the other nation offers—including the lowest tariffs, or exemption from tariffs; the fewest trade barriers; and the highest import quotas—or none.) Finally, he was to require the British to restrain British creditors' demands for payment of debts owed by Americans.[15] The British position on these matters was that, as long as the United States was in violation of provisions of the treaty, Britain need not carry out its duties under the treaty; furthermore, Britain saw no reason to grant the United States "most favored nation" status.

The only diplomatic success that Adams could claim was his negotiation with Prussia in 1785 of a treaty of recognition and commerce. In partnership with Jefferson, he also laid the groundwork for a treaty with Portugal, which was not concluded until 1791. He and Jefferson tried to secure a treaty with Tripoli, but the sultan's envoy demanded tribute that the diplomats could not ensure that the United States would pay.

Meanwhile, private vexations warred with public business for John Adams's attention—in particular, Royall Tyler's conduct as Nabby's fiancé. Tyler sent no answers to Nabby's letters to him, leaving her disappointed and hurt. The reports of Tyler's bad character that Abigail was getting persuaded her to abandon her former high opinion of Tyler, and John was content to go along with her. On her own, Nabby rejected Tyler and ended her engagement to him. She turned instead to the secretary of the American mission in London, Colonel William Stephens Smith, whom she eventually married.

Adams turned to the life of the mind to distract himself, but even there he found new reason for vexation—European disdain for American experiments in government expressed by the theorists of reform known as philosophes.[16] Adams found particularly irksome a 1778 letter that the French economist Anne Robert Jacques Turgot had written the English dissenting clergyman and political activist Richard Price. Adams first read Turgot's letter as an appendix to Price's 1784 pamphlet, *Observations on the American Revolution, and on the Means of Making It a Blessing to the World*, which Price sent to Adams.[17] Thanking Price for the pamphlet,[18] Adams focused on Turgot's letter rather than on Price's text. He found irritating Turgot's insistence that checks and balances and separation of powers were unnecessary and pernicious mystifications, and that the people should concentrate all political authority in one center. Adams covered the pamphlet's margins with testy handwritten comments. Turgot's praise for Pennsylvania's 1776 constitution, which he extolled as Franklin's work, exasperated Adams, because he thought little of Pennsylvania's constitution and doubted Franklin's understanding of constitutional government. At one point, Adams exploded in wrath:

> Is it possible that the writer of this paragraph should have ever read Plato, Livy, Polybius, Machiavel, Sidney, Harrington, or that he should ever have thought of the nature of man or of a society? What does he mean [by] collecting all authority in one center? What does he mean by the center of a nation? Where would he have the legislation placed? Where the execution? Where the decision of controversies? Emptier piece of declamation I never read: it is impossible to give a greater proof of ignorance.[19]

By itself, Turgot's letter might have spurred Adams into writing a work on constitutionalism, but a more urgent stimulus to action was the news from America that arrived in late 1786: political upheavals at home threatened American constitutional stability. The Adamses learned of the outbreak in Massachusetts of Shays's Rebellion.[20] This insurrection by Massachusetts farmers seeking freedom from the crushing burdens of debt and of debt-related litigation closed courts in western Massachusetts and provoked similar outbreaks from the Virginia backcountry to the "independent republic" of Vermont. Shays's Rebellion seemed to threaten the survival of Massachusetts's government—a danger that Adams took personally, both because it was his home state and because he had done so much to frame its constitution.

Disagreeing with the Adamses, Jefferson welcomed Shays's Rebellion as proving the people's commitment to their liberties: "The spirit of resistance to government is so valuable on certain occasions, that I wish it to be always kept alive. It will often be exercised when wrong, but better so than not to be exercised at all. I like a little rebellion now and then. It is like a storm in the Atmosphere."[21]

Rejecting Jefferson's optimism as naive, Adams saw Shays's Rebellion as a challenge to all that he believed about politics, government, and law. If such a rebellion could erupt in a state with a good constitution, he fretted, what would happen in other states? Was this insurrection an American outbreak of internal upheavals that had toppled republican governments throughout history? Were his efforts at constitutional creation for nothing? What effect would such news have on the skeptical monarchs, diplomats, and philosophes of Europe? Would they not dismiss the American Revolution as doomed to failure, and republican constitutional government along with it?

Even after March 1787, when he learned of the defeat in January 1787 of the insurgents by the state's militia (backed up by several hundred Continental soldiers sent by Secretary of War Henry Knox), Adams continued to find Shays's Rebellion alarming. He set to work, pen in hand, books piled around him in his study. His goals were to defend American experiments in government, to prove their value, and to refute arguments at home and abroad against the ideas and principles guaranteeing a constitution's worth.

Adams analyzed a wide range of constitutions ancient, medieval, and modern, American and foreign; his goal was to distill the general principles animating them, his method and research epitomizing the Age of Enlightenment. He titled his vast treatise *A Defence of the Constitutions of Government of the United States.*[22]

At first, Adams quoted extracts from his sources as launchpads for his commentary. As he wrote, however, haste drove him to copy more material from others and to provide less of his own; the result was a sourcebook or casebook of comparative constitutional history. The problem was that the mass of detail in Adams's volumes threatened to obscure the points that he sought to make, in the process fatiguing or alienating potential readers. Adams saw that the way he was writing would damage the project, but his sense of urgency drove his pen, leaving him no time for revision: "The preceding Letters have been produced upon the spur of a particular occasion, which made it necessary to write and publish with precipitation, or it might have been useless to have published at all. The whole has been done in the midst of other occupations, in so much hurry, that scarce a moment could be spared to correct the style, adjust the method, pare off excrescences, or even obliterate repetitions; in all which respects it stands in the need of an apology."[23]

The method that Adams used to compose the *Defence* paralleled that of his earlier large-scale works of constitutional argument. He was so intent on refuting his adversary (or agreeing with his source), sometimes line by line, that he forgot the need to make evident his major themes or to map out his argument.[24]

Adams's goal was not originality or creativity. Rather, in writing or rather compiling his *Defence*, he was seeking to distill the amassed wisdom of the ages about human nature, society, politics, and government.[25] His argument was relatively simple and straightforward. He had two linked purposes, one theoretical and one political. His theoretical purpose was to show that the only republican constitutions having a chance of success were those with separated institutions checking and balancing one another, corresponding to the different levels or orders of society—monarchic, aristocratic, and democratic, or rule by the one, the few, and the many. The

institutions that Adams thought indispensable to a sound republican constitution were a two-house legislature, with an upper house
representing aristocratic elements and a lower house representing
democratic elements, and a powerful, independent chief executive
embodying the monarchic principle. The governor would check and
balance the legislature, as the two legislative houses would check
and balance the executive, and if the governor allied himself with
one house, the other would check and balance that alliance. The
three institutions would share the power to make laws, preserving
liberty by preventing any one institution or any one part of society
from prevailing over the others.

Adams rejected "simple" models of government having only a
one-house legislature, or lacking an independent chief executive, or
embracing both bad ideas (as with Pennsylvania). The history of all
societies, Adams insisted, taught the need to strike a balance in the
structure of government among the three orders of society (the one,
the few, and the many):

> All nations, from the beginning, have been agitated by the same
> passions. The principles developed here will go a great way in
> explaining every phenomenon that occurs in the history of gov-
> ernment. The vegetable and animal kingdoms, and those heav-
> enly bodies whose existence and movements we are as yet only
> permitted faintly to perceive, do not appear to be governed by laws
> more uniform or certain than those which regulate the moral and
> political world.[26]

Just as important as his theoretical purpose was his political
purpose—his determination to refute criticisms by smug European
philosophes of American constitutions for conforming to what he
saw as the lessons of history. European views of America, Adams
thought, could threaten the success of American experiments in
government. If they believed that those experiments were based
on unsound principles, they would reject the United States as
an unworthy ally, an unsound trading partner, and a bad place to

settle. Adams also aimed his vast, disorderly treatise at his fellow Americans, to stiffen their resolve to stand by their own constitutional experiments. If the American people, lacking confidence in their constitutional handiwork, heeded the philosophes' mistaken counsel, the result would be disastrous for American liberty and for preserving the fruits of the Revolution.

Adams distilled wisdom from human history to justify his vision of sound constitutional government, but he also was doing something new. He was declaring American intellectual independence from Europe. He insisted not only that Americans should not listen to European thinkers but also that they had much to teach the Old World. Adams's *Defence* was an enormous sequel to his 1776 pamphlet on constitution-making, *Thoughts on Government*, but it also was a constitutional counterpart to Jefferson's *Notes on the State of Virginia*. In *Notes*, Jefferson refuted the arguments of European philosophes—led by the great naturalist the Comte de Buffon—that all life, including human life, degenerated in the New World.[27] Whereas Jefferson sought to defend the new nation's legitimacy and soundness from the perspective of natural history, Adams sought to uphold the legitimacy and soundness of American experiments in government from the perspective of constitutional history. Both men wrote in the spirit of the Enlightenment.

The two men swapped books, and each sent the other letters filled with compliments. From 1786 to 1788, the artist Mather Brown painted portraits of each man holding his new book, and both authors secured copies of the portraits for their homes. On May 22, 1785, Adams wrote to Jefferson: "I thank you kindly for your Book. it is our Meditation all the Day long.— I cannot now Say much about it. but I think it will do its Author and his Country great Honour. The Passages upon Slavery, are worth Diamonds. They will have more effect than Volumes written by mere Philosophers." This was the privately printed edition of *Notes*, which appeared two years before the public version. Jefferson addressed slavery in two different chapters: in chapter XVIII, he denounced the institution, but in chapter XIV, he proposed a scientific argument ("advanced as a suspicion only") for why people of African descent might be suited for slavery. We do not know whether Adams thought both chapters "worth Diamonds."[28]

In January 1787, the first volume of Adams's *Defence* appeared in London; an enterprising printer reprinted it in Philadelphia that spring in time for the convening of the Federal Convention, the body that was to frame the Constitution of the United States. Adams finished two more volumes within the year. At first, readers welcomed Adams's *Defence*, praising its author as a benevolent man seeking to put his profound knowledge at the service of his country. However, the praise faded, to be succeeded by puzzled, even bitter, criticism. Adams's critics charged him with adopting corrupt, decadent, European habits of thought. In particular, they attacked what they saw as his embrace of aristocratic government. These critics failed to grasp Adams's point. Adams never advocated aristocracy. Rather, in the *Defence*, he penned a clear-eyed, realistic assessment of aristocracy as an enduring political problem.[29] Adams insisted that every society would develop an aristocracy; that that aristocracy would seek to control the government to protect itself and to extend its power; and that the best way to meet this challenge was to give aristocracy a place in government, benefiting from its wisdom, while limiting its power with constitutional safeguards so that it could do as little harm as possible.

One reader sharing Adams's concerns about the American situation but rejecting Adams's arguments on substantive grounds was James Madison. The Virginian, who rivaled Adams as a leading American constitutional thinker, read Adams's first volume during the opening weeks of the Federal Convention. Writing to Jefferson on June 6, 1787, Madison began by making the usual critical claim—that Adams was defending aristocratic forms of government, particularly the British constitution: "Mr. Adams' Book which has been in your hands of course, has excited a good deal of attention. . . . It will probably be much read, particularly in the Eastern States, and contribute with other circumstances to revive the predilections of this Country for the British Constitution." But then he delivered one of the most devastating put-downs in the history of letters:

> Men of learning find nothing new in it. Men of taste many things to criticize. And men without either not a few things, which they will not understand. It will nevertheless be read, and praised, and become a powerful engine in forming the public opinion. The name & character of the Author, with the critical situation of our affairs, naturally account for such an effect. The book also has merit, and I wish many of the remarks in it, which are unfriendly to republicanism, may not receive fresh weight from the operations of our Governments.[30]

Madison's dismissal of Adams's book may have been in part the growl of a frustrated would-be author confronting a senior colleague's book on his chosen subject. Like Adams, Madison was a student of comparative constitutional government; in 1786, he had researched the history of ancient and modern confederacies, preparing an elaborate memorandum to guide his thinking.[31] By publishing first, Adams may have rubbed Madison's sensibilities raw.

More than authorial jealousy was at work in Madison, however. Exploring the contrast between their approaches to constitutional government illuminates the intellectual worlds of both men, and the ways that Adams was falling increasingly out of step with his countrymen as they pursued different lines of thought about what government should be and how it should work. It is no accident that Madison shared with Jefferson his disappointment with Adams's book on the same day that he delivered one of his most important speeches in the Federal Convention, setting forth his views on factionalism and the extended republic, issues on which Adams gave no guidance.[32]

Adams and Madison were thinking politicians of very different kinds.[33] Though they shared such traits as deep learning, bookishness, love of study, and fascination with the history of republican government, they approached these subjects in radically different ways. Adams was a student of comparative constitutional government and history. He worked to master the wisdom of Western civilization in general and that of comparative constitutional government in particular, seeking to teach the lessons that he derived from his study of that subject and seeking also to bring American constitution-making in line with those lessons. By contrast, Madison was a political technologist who sought not only to understand human experience with republican government and constitution-making but also to go beyond the conventional wisdom when it threatened to doom American efforts to create a new constitution. Instead of conforming constitution-making to the lessons of human nature and of history, Madison sought to manipulate human nature and history by devising new constitutional forms. He did not just reject history's conventional wisdom; sometimes he even stood it on its head.

Whereas problems flowing from aristocracy preoccupied Adams, Madison focused on problems flowing from federalism. In a sense, Adams was a vertical political thinker, starting from the conventional teaching that society was hierarchical, with top, middle, and bottom layers corresponding to the one, few, and many of humanity. For his part, Madison was a horizontal political thinker, stressing the effects of geography on constitution-making. For Madison, the problem was holding together an extensive republic under one constitutional system, including striking a proper balance between the general government and the states. Madison engaged with that problem throughout the 1780s, grappling with its theoretical and practical issues. Because Adams had never had to contend with issues of federalism, he never addressed those issues.[34]

The outcome of the convention's labors in Philadelphia was a new kind of government for the United States. This compound federal republic recognized the people as sovereign, making it possible for them to assign one share of that sovereignty to the general government and another share to the states. It then sought to regulate the balance of power between the federal government and state governments, and to regulate the balance of power among the federal government's branches.[35] Adams grasped only the Constitution's latter aspect; he never saw that the Constitution's federal framework was meant to solve problems different from those preoccupying him. Thus, Madison criticized Adams's book for failing to address the issues of constitutional design that he saw as truly central to the Constitution's creation.

Adams and Madison also diverged because they grounded their competing conceptions of constitutional government on differing visions of the United States. On the one hand, Adams crafted his vision of republican constitutional government for a nation that was like other nations in having to grapple with the perennial problem of aristocracy. On the other hand, Madison saw the United States as unique—a relatively equal people with a common national identity, yet with competing loyalties to the several states, while also forming factional groups, defined by loyalty to or hostility to a specific leader, by differing religious commitments, and above by all clashing economic interests.

Madison spurned what he saw as an outmoded model of society divided into aristocratic and democratic layers. For him, as he wrote in *The Federalist No. 10*, interests and factions posed the key problem: "The regulation of these various and interfering interests forms the principal task of modern legislation."[36] Because this calculus of interests and its interaction with federalism preoccupied Madison, he rejected Adams's *Defence* as missing the point. Adams's book focused on the wrong question, and its answer was irrelevant to what Madison saw as the real question. Further, though not all American politicians shared Madison's sophisticated understanding of interests and factions,[37] their sense of the American people as a relatively equal political mass was far removed from Adams's embrace of the old wisdom of the one, the few, and the many. Yet another difference between them was that Adams's political thinking was largely static, giving little attention to the American future, whereas Madison, like Jefferson, sought to extrapolate and provide for the United States' future political development.[38]

These intellectual differences between Adams and Madison—and, more generally, between Adams and his countrymen—about the nature of American politics and the challenges of constitution-making loom increasingly large in our effort to understand Adams.[39] Adams did not grasp the changes in the American intellectual and political climate wrought by the years since 1779 (his last extended time in the United States). In the closing pages of the third volume of his *Defence*, Adams sought to shoehorn the proposed US Constitution into his framework of political analysis, while missing its embrace of federalism and divided sovereignty. Adams saw the Constitution's inclusion of a Senate as part of a bicameral national legislature as vindicating his theories about aristocracy and the need for an upper house as its home in a balanced constitutional republic. By contrast, the Federal Convention created the Senate principally as a means of placating the small states, with its rule of equality of representation for all states and its assignment of the election of Senators to state legislatures. Its basis was not classical political thought but federalism.[40]

While writing volumes 2 and 3 of the *Defence*, Adams also began the slow process of concluding his diplomatic mission and preparing to return to the United States. The many letters between Adams and John Jay, the Confederation's secretary for foreign affairs, suggest how slow the process was. On January 24, 1787, Adams sent Jay an official request for permission to resign his post and return home by the beginning of 1788; he then wrote a private letter to Jay, asking Jay as a friend to do all he could to expedite permission from Congress.[41] On July 31, Jay sent an embarrassed apology for Congress's delay.[42] Nearly three months later, on October 16, Jay finally informed Adams that Congress had granted his request and had passed resolutions complimenting him on his service.[43] Still more logistical delays plagued the Adamses, so that they did not begin their voyage home until late April 1788.

On February 21, 1788, Adams reported to Jay on his last audience with George III. Peeping through the lines of his letter is Adams's satisfaction that, despite the frustration of dealing with the king's ministers, at least he was able to meet with the king on amiable terms:

> Yesterday I had my Audience of Leave of His Majesty. . . . The Substance of my address to His Majesty was no more than, a Renewal of assurances in Behalf of the United States, of their friendly Dispositions, and of their continued desire to cultivate a liberal Intercourse of Commerce and good offices which his Majestys Subjects and States; Thanks for the Protection and Civilities of His Court; and good Wishes of Prosperity to His Majesty, His Royal Family, His Subjects and Dominions.
>
> The Kings Answer to me, was in these Words "Mr Adams You may, with great Truth assure the United States that whenever they Shall fulfill the Treaty, on their Part, I, on my Part will fulfill it, in all its Particulars. As to yourself, I am sure I wish you a safe and pleasant Voyage, and much comfort with your Family and Friends."[44]

While he prepared to go home, Adams was eager to learn about the American struggle to adopt a new constitution. One great irony of American constitutional history is that the man who had a plausible claim to be the prophet of American constitutionalism had to watch from three thousand miles away as his countrymen struggled over ratifying the proposed US Constitution. When he received a copy of the Constitution, the only qualm that he expressed at first paralleled that of Jefferson and many other Americans on both sides of the ratification controversy: "What think you of a Declaration of Rights? Should not such a Thing have preceeded the Model?" Even so, he generally approved of what he read, as he told Jefferson:

> It seems to be admirably calculated to preserve the Union, to increase Affection, and to bring us all to the same mode of thinking.

They have adopted the Idea of the Congress at Albany in 1754 of a President to nominate officers and a Council to Consent: but thank heaven they have adopted a third Branch, which that Congress did not. I think that Senates and Assemblies should have nothing to do with executive Power. But still I hope the Constitution will be adopted, and Amendments be made at a more convenient opportunity.[45]

Jefferson thought that the House of Representatives would be inadequate to the burdens of business placed on it, and he strongly criticized the eligibility of the president for as many terms of office as he pleased.[46] Despite his insistence to Madison that the Constitution ought to have included a bill of rights and ought to be amended to include one, Jefferson never addressed that point with Adams. In a later letter to Jefferson, Adams spelled out his own criticisms. He pointed out that Jefferson feared monarchy whereas Adams feared aristocracy. Jefferson's apprehensions about a too-strong president who could serve for too long did not move Adams, for he saw such a strong president as a counter to the Senate. Both men worried about foreign efforts to corrupt the process of electing a president, but Adams drew from that fear the conclusion that, "as often as Elections happen, the danger of foreign Influence recurs. The less frequently they happen the less danger."[47] After sharing these reflections, they turned back to issues regarding American loans from bankers in Amsterdam and the news of potential constitutional upheavals in France.

The ratification controversy ground on from the fall of 1787 to midsummer 1788. On the other side of the Atlantic, Adams attempted only one indirect intervention.[48] On March 26, 1788, he wrote to Governor George Clinton of New York, introducing his daughter and son-in-law (who were traveling to New York) and offering his perspective from abroad on the desirability of adopting the Constitution. Adams apparently did not know that Clinton had emerged as a leading spirit among the Constitution's opponents and was the leader of the Constitution's adversaries in New York. Clinton seems not to have answered Adams's letter:

> It is expected in Europe that the new Constitution for the United States will be soon adopted by all. It is a general opinion that the old one, stood in great need of a Reform, and that the projected Change, will be much for our Prosperity. A federal Republick of independent Sovereign States was never known to exist, over a large Territory. inumerable Difficulties have been found in these which have been tried in small Countries. The question really seems to be, whether the Union shall be broken; or whether all shall come under one Soverignty. The Union is one object of such Magnitude: that every Thing but constitutional Liberty Should be Sacrificed to it.[49]

Adams did not know that his *Defence* was being quoted and attacked in the ratification debates. His critics cited his analysis of aristocracy, which they misread as a defense of aristocracy, to smear the Constitution as an aristocratic document. A notable pamphlet by John Stevens of New Jersey targeted the *Defence* as Adams's means of signaling his intentions to bring aristocracy to the new nation; we do not know if Adams ever saw Stevens's pamphlet.[50]

Adams's marginal role during the ratification controversy, and the rumblings at home of popular dissatisfaction with the *Defence*, indicated that an intellectual and political gap was opening between him and his countrymen. That gap raised ominous questions about Adams's political future—questions that he did not and perhaps could not see, let alone answer. As he and Abigail prepared to return to Massachusetts in the spring of 1788, Adams was teetering between his inclination to retire and his desire to take part in the Constitution's new political experiment, and to learn what the new American political world had in store for him.

Chapter Seven

"The most insignificant office"

Vice President (1788–1797)

In late April 1788, the ship *Lucretia* left Britain for Boston, carrying John and Abigail Adams. As the voyage's eight weeks dragged by, Adams pondered his future. Retirement attracted him, but his yearning for retirement clashed with his concern about his country. He pondered the new US Constitution, which he read as vindicating his arguments about a proper balanced government in his *Defence of the Constitutions*. He speculated whether enough states would ratify the US Constitution to make it the nation's new form of government. He also reflected on hints from friends and allies that he would be a leading candidate for office in that government, should it come into being. He little knew that the office he would be chosen to fill would be one of the most trying of his life, bringing him to some of the lowest points in his public career.

One powerful inducement for Adams to remain active in politics was his recognition that holding office under the Constitution might win him fame. He and his contemporaries understood fame as a reward for great achievements inspired by devotion to the public good; thus, winning fame was neither only nor mainly about personal gratification. For years, he had fretted that his service abroad might go unappreciated at home. He always was vigilant to assert his claims to what he thought due to him in terms of recognition (sometimes at his own cost). Thus, he welcomed the prospect that he might be chosen for high office in the new federal government.[1]

On June 17, 1788, the *Lucretia* reached Boston. Sailing into port, the ship was greeted by fusillades of cannon fire echoing across Boston Harbor. On landing, the Adamses received a hero's welcome far beyond what they had expected, featuring artillery salutes, cheering onlookers, and pealing church bells. Greeting the couple at the dock was an emissary from Governor John Hancock, Adams's ally from the Second Continental Congress, who threw open the governor's mansion to them.[2]

Though honored by Hancock's hospitality, John and Abigail were eager to settle into their new house. They would not return to the saltbox house in Braintree where they had spent the first twenty years of their married life and where their children had been born. The idea of buying a new house had taken form in 1787, when Abigail wrote from London to her older sister, Mary Cranch, asking her to measure the house in Braintree to guide purchases of new furnishings to be shipped home; Mary warned Abigail that the old house was too small for their family, which now included three grown sons.[3] She suggested that Abigail and John buy a larger house that had just come on the market, the Vassall-Borland House. After consulting with Mary, John and Abigail asked her uncle Cotton Tufts to negotiate the purchase.

The Vassall-Borland House sat on eighty-three acres a mile north of their old home. Built in 1731 by the West Indies sugar planter Major Leonard Vassall, it had passed through various hands; at one point, the Massachusetts government had confiscated it as a Loyalist property. Its last owner was Royall Tyler, the writer, lawyer, and rejected suitor of their daughter Abigail. When Tyler had defaulted on his attempt to buy the house, it returned to Vassall's grandson, Leonard Vassall Borland, who sold it to the Adamses.

After leaving Boston, John and Abigail traveled inland to stay with relatives while awaiting the arrival of their furniture in Braintree. At their new home, they found a scene of confusion. The renovations that Abigail had entrusted to Cotton Tufts's supervision were far from being finished. To her dismay, Abigail also saw that the house was less grand and elegant than she had remembered. It was smaller than the townhouse they had occupied in London; she plaintively called it a "wren's nest." Determined to set things right despite suffering from an arthritic hand, she set to work, intent on moving the renovations forward and planning an expansion of the house. John, captivated by the surrounding land and eager to return to farming, felt comfortable, even happy, in his new home. He named the house Peacefield, commemorating his role in negotiating the Treaty of Paris of 1783.[4]

Adams had to face another practical question—his finances. He and Abigail not only would have to maintain themselves but they also would have to support three sons. John Quincy, a fledgling lawyer, would have lean years as he launched his law practice. Charles and Thomas Boylston were undergraduates at Harvard who also were aiming at legal careers; they would need support while finishing their college studies and legal apprenticeships and then joining the bar. The costs of renovation were mounting, and Adams had to include in his financial calculations the mortgage that he had taken as part of the house's purchase. Sadly, he concluded that his expenses were nearly three times his income, ruling out retirement. New expenses would require a new salary. Not even the profits that Abigail had made from her financial enterprises, such as her skilled investments in government securities and her sales of goods that Adams had sent her from Europe—which persuaded him that she had greater fiscal sagacity than he did—could make up the shortfall.[5] Further, he realized that he had to collect moneys due him, specifically his back salary and funds owed to him by the federal government for expenses he had amassed during his diplomatic missions. During his first years as vice president, he kept up an insistent campaign to secure reimbursement for those expenses.[6]

Beyond financial worries and fame, other considerations brought Adams back into politics. His return to Massachusetts meant that others would seek to draw him into the political world unless he took active steps to prevent them—and he was not inclined to prevent them. Before he and Abigail had returned home, the Massachusetts legislature had chosen him as a delegate to the Confederation Congress—and Virginia delegate Tench Coxe saw Adams as a fine choice for president of Congress.[7]

Events moved more quickly than institutions did. In July 1788, Adams learned that the Constitution had been ratified, replacing the Articles of Confederation. He realized that that change would supersede his election to the Confederation Congress. Organizing government under the Constitution meant new offices and new possibilities. Which post should he seek? He knew that standing for the presidency was out of the question, because of the man whose name was on every tongue in discussions of that office—George Washington. Adams deferred to the national favorite.[8]

Adams decided that only one office under the Constitution would suit him—vice president of the United States. The second-highest office under the Constitution, the vice presidency seemed to Adams appropriate for a man with his extensive record of public service, suiting his status as a leading figure in the Revolution. Further, he knew that he could expect the backing of New England and perhaps most of the northern states. Most of his rivals withdrew from consideration as soon as they learned that he was interested—but one potential competitor remained. Governor George Clinton of New York expected support from the movement that had opposed the Constitution in 1787–88. Though the Constitution's foes had conceded defeat, they still wanted to battle over how to put the Constitution into effect. As part of that battle, they wanted to install an ally in a high office in the new government. They were committed to vigilance lest the Constitution's supporters expand the federal government's powers beyond the people's expectations. Some opponents of the Constitution were organizing to demand a second convention to revise or to replace the Constitution; Clinton's election would aid that movement.[9] Clinton also made a generous estimate of his own fitness for the nation's second-highest office.[10]

The possibility of Clinton's candidacy, the aftershocks of ratification, the agitation for a second convention, and the challenge
of launching the new government alarmed such supporters of the
Constitution as Alexander Hamilton. What worried him and his
allies most was the campaign by the Constitution's opponents to
use the first federal elections to influence how the new Constitution
would be put into effect. Interpreting its provisions could expand or
contract the new government's powers. Hamilton and his allies knew
that the electors had freedom to cast their votes for those vying to be
the first president and vice president. They therefore sought to guide
presidential electors to cast their votes for the right man and against
the wrong men. Two goals drove their efforts. First, they wanted to
ensure Washington's unanimous election; second, they wanted to
deny whoever came in second any chance to threaten Washington's
preeminence.[11]

Throughout the summer and fall of 1788, having allowed word
to circulate that he was available and interested, Adams fretted over
political gossip that one or another candidate was outpacing him for
vice president. The electoral process came to an end in January, when
electors in each state cast their votes and the nation's newspaper
published the results. Washington had won all sixty-nine first-place
electoral votes, which confirmed his election as the nation's first
president. To his dismay, however, Adams had eked out only thirty-
four of the sixty-nine second-place votes; it was enough to elect
him vice president with no other candidate coming close, but still
one vote less than a majority. He read into those numbers stinging
implications about what the people thought of him. Though he
suspected that some politicians had worked to reduce his electoral-
vote count, we do not know whether he learned of Hamilton's role.[12]

At first, Adams felt humiliation rather than joy at his election.
Certain that his countrymen did not value his merits, he grumbled
that perhaps he should turn down the vice presidency. This dour
line of thought lasted for only a short time, however, and he accepted election.[13] He received formal notification on April 12, in

a letter from Senator John Langdon, president pro tempore of the Senate, setting forth the official vote tally by a full, official open vote count before both houses of Congress.[14] Adams set out for New York City; Abigail was visiting their daughter and her husband in Jamaica, New York, waiting for the right time to join John in the new capital.

People in towns along Adams's route cheered him as he rode by, sometimes bestowing symbolic gifts. Militia units escorted him into and out of such towns as Hartford and New Haven. When he reached New York City, another militia unit conducted him to the home of his friend John Jay, who hosted him for his first days in the nation's temporary capital.

On April 21, 1789, Adams became the nation's first vice president in the renovated Federal Hall—formerly New York's City Hall, the first capitol building of the United States.[15] Because there was no set oath for federal officials to take, there was no ceremony. Langdon yielded his place to Adams at the front of the Senate chamber, a room forty by thirty feet and two stories high; a canopy of red damask shaded the president's chair. Adams then read the Senate a short speech, closing with a promise:

> It should be my constant endeavour to behave towards every member of this most honorable body with all that consideration, delicacy, and decorum, which becomes the dignity of his station and character. But if, from inexperience or inadvertency, any thing should ever escape me, inconsistent with propriety, I must entreat you, by imputing it to its true cause, and not by any want of respect, to pardon and excuse it.[16]

On April 23, President-Elect Washington arrived in New York City after his own journey from Mount Vernon. Washington dreaded assuming the presidency; he wrote that his journey to New York was like that "of a culprit who is going to the place of his execution."[17] Could he live up to his countrymen's hopes? He did not know what to think.

As New Yorkers welcomed Washington, the Senate met in its chamber on Federal Hall's second floor; the House of Representatives met in a similar chamber one floor below. As he gazed at the twenty senators who were present, Vice President Adams faced a body that was both a new institution and a recognizable descendant of the Confederation Congress.[18] The Senate was a council of representatives of the states, refashioned as the upper house of a bicameral Congress of the United States. Each state had two senators, who voted individually rather than by state delegation. Most states gave their legislature the task of choosing senators, though Connecticut guided its legislature's choices by popular vote. Only ten states were represented in the Senate. North Carolina and Rhode Island had not yet ratified the Constitution. Well into the summer of 1789, the two houses of New York's legislature were deadlocked over choosing the state's senators; for that reason, New York never chose presidential electors.[19]

The Senate had features drawn from institutions that Adams knew. As the upper house of Congress, it paralleled the British House of Lords, Parliament's upper house. It also resembled the executive council found in American colonial charters and state constitutions. The president could make treaties and appoint executive officials only with the Senate's advice and consent—features of the Senate that Adams found problematic because they varied from his strict version of separation of powers. As he had written to Jefferson in 1787, he would have given the president sole power to make treaties and to name and fire executive officials.[20] Such opinions risked making him look like an advocate of monarchy.

Adams noted a few former colleagues among the senators. Richard Henry Lee of Virginia, Robert Morris of Pennsylvania, George Read of Delaware, John Langdon of New Hampshire, and Ralph Izard of South Carolina all were veterans of the Second Continental Congress. A classmate from Harvard's class of 1755, Tristram Dalton of New Hampshire, also was there.[21] If the presence of these men gave Adams the sense that he was among friends, events proved him mistaken.

Adams's troubles as vice president began almost at once. In his first days in office, he voiced confusion about his role. He asked the senators for advice as to how he should act—expressing doubt, for example, on April 25, 1789, regarding his role when the president entered the Senate chamber. Senator William Maclay of Pennsylvania recorded Adams's words in his diary:

> Gentlemen I feel great difficulty how to act. I am possessed of two seperate powers, the one in esse, and the other in posse. I am Vice President. in this I am nothing, but I may be everything, But I am President also of the Senate. When the President comes into the Senate, what shall I be. I cannot be then, no Gentlemen, I cannot, I cannot—I wish Gentlemen to think what I shall be.[22]

Some senators, notably Connecticut's Oliver Ellsworth, shared Adams's discomfort with the question; Maclay recorded Ellsworth's response:

> Elseworth thumbed over the Sheet constitution, and turned it for some time: at length he rose, and addressed the Chair with profound Gravity. Mr. President I have looked over the Constitution (paused) and I find Sir, it is evident & Clear Sir, that wherever the Senate is to be, then Sir you must be at the head of them, but further Sir (here he looked agast, as if some tremendous Gulph had Ya[w]ned before him) I. shall. not. pretend. to. say.[23]

Maclay reacted with sardonic amusement to the dithering before him: "God forgive me, but it was involuntary, for the profane Muscles of my face, were in Tune for Laughter, in spite of my indisposition."[24] A newcomer to national politics, Maclay was a leading figure in Pennsylvania. His acidulous diary of his Senate service is a classic of American politics—resembling, in its self-revealing style, John Adams's diary. In some ways, the two men would have been very similar in outlook had Adams not gone to Europe. Adams's time in the Old World did more than shape his conduct as vice president; Maclay decided that Adams had been corrupted away from American republican values by his time in Europe, and therefore that he was not to be trusted.

Adams's self-consciousness during the inauguration was problematic enough, but he soon made matters worse. Alarmed by his belief that the Union risked losing the respect of European powers, he drew on his diplomatic experience and his study of European nations to educate the senators. Only one solution would work, he argued at great length—bestowing an august title on the president.[25] Only such a title, he insisted, would enable the new government to establish its dignity in the world's eyes. Reminding the senators that he was familiar with the Confederation Congress's failure to win respect, he identified the reason for that failure as Congress's inability to establish its dignity. Titles, he finished, would be a sure means to that end.[26]

The senatorial debate on titles took place behind closed doors. The Senate's creators at the Federal Convention of 1787 gave it legislative and quasi-executive functions. Making laws in partnership with the House of Representatives was its legislative function; advising and consenting on executive and judicial appointments and making treaties were its quasi-executive functions. Recognizing this mix of functions and powers and giving priority to their quasi-executive functions, the senators voted to meet in private. Choosing to follow a different path, the House of Representatives voted to meet in public, even admitting journalists. (Not until 1795 did the Senate open its sessions to the public and to journalists, belatedly joining the House in affirming the public's right to know the doings of their representatives.)[27]

Despite the Senate's decision to meet in private, word of its debates on titles, including Vice President Adams's strong advocacy of that proposal, soon became public knowledge. The leaks were inevitable, for a bill establishing titles would require action by both houses of Congress to become law, and the House of Representatives not only was meeting in public but also was holding its own debate on titles. Adams's suggestion of titles soon became the target of satire focusing not on the proposal but on its sponsor. It did not help that Adams's proposed title was an indigestible mouthful: "His High Mightiness the President of the United States, and Protector of Their Liberties." A mocking title forever attached itself to Adams: "Mr. [Ralph] Izard after describing [Adams's] air Manner deportment and personal Figure in the chair, concluded with applying the Title of *Rotundity* to him."[28] Others dubbed Maclay and Pennsylvania representative Henry Wynkoop, the tallest members of Congress, His Highness of the Upper House and His Highness of the Lower House.[29]

Adams soon ran into other difficulties. One resulted from his attempts to draw on his greatest strengths—his vast learning and his willingness to share that learning—in contributing to Senate debates. He not only was determined to expound the lessons that he had distilled from his study of governments but also believed that his diplomatic experience had taught him an immense amount about government and politics directly relevant to the American situation. He was determined to lay out that knowledge for the benefit of the senators in particular and Americans in general.

Adams did not realize how far he had fallen out of touch with his countrymen's political ideas, in the Senate or among the people. For one thing, Americans had come to think of themselves as different not just in geographical location but in kind from the peoples of Europe. Most Americans did not have Adams's experience of Europe, nor did he have direct experience, as they did, of the different course that American political thought had taken beginning in the 1780s. Most senators dismissed Adams's invocations of history and his discussions of European diplomatic customs; they found his disquisitions laughable at best and annoyingly irrelevant at worst. They, and many among the people, deduced from Adams's apparent obsession with the Old World that, having spent too much time in Europe, he had been corrupted away from his former attachment to American ideals and republican virtue. Every time he advocated titles, he seemed to speak for an obsolete and decadent political past.

Adams had another mistaken idea about his office that crippled his effectiveness as vice president; he thought that he would be the administration's prime minister in the Senate. He soon learned otherwise. The senators made clear that they did not want him to take part in debates, let alone guide them. They expected him to preside, not to speak, and certainly not to speak for them. After a few ill-considered attempts to lead the Senate, he acknowledged that the senators had no desire to be led. Thereafter, he restrained himself.[30]

President Washington further rebuffed Adams's attempts to become the Washington administration's leader in the Senate. Not only was the vice president to preside over the Senate rather than lead the senators; he also was to be barred from taking part in the executive branch's deliberations. Washington met with his cabinet—a group including only heads of executive departments—to secure their advice and discuss public policy. Because Adams was president of the Senate, Washington saw him as part of the legislative branch, not as part of the executive branch, and thus not as part of his cabinet.

Fallout from the controversy over titles also played a part in giving Washington a dim view of Adams, as did growing controversy over ceremony and pomp in the new government. Rumors spread through the country about the pomp with which the Washington administration was conducting itself—carriages drawn by too many horses, too-elegant dress for the leading members of the government, and so forth. Many Americans disapproved of how grandly the government seemed to be behaving. Word of the controversy reached John and Abigail Adams; they read into these rumors the clear implication that they were to blame. Yielding to the natural temptation to defend themselves, they complained in response that Washington was really at fault because of his love of pomp and ceremony. In turn, news of that criticism reached Washington via reports

from as far away as Virginia. Thereafter, he showed a decided cool-
ness toward Adams. Other contributing factors included occasional
clashes between them dating back to the Revolution, Adams's alignment with a Lee-Adams faction in the old Confederation Congress
that criticized and denigrated Washington, and Washington's dislike of Vice President Adams's joking tendency to call himself "the
heir apparent." Washington rarely consulted Adams, preferring to
confer with his advisers in the executive branch.[31] Thus, Adams was
sidelined during discussions of such pivotal issues as the location of
the permanent federal capital, the federal government's assumption
of state debts, and Congress's power to create the First Bank of the
United States.

Even Adams's attire attracted criticism. By dressing in finery
suited to a European court, his detractors charged, Adams was
giving himself airs as an aristocrat. Veering between sarcasm and anguish, he explained to his former law student William Tudor that,
having returned from Europe with only his diplomatic wardrobe, he
could not afford a new, simple republican wardrobe.[32] In Adams's
thinking, the attire question linked with his frustrating battle to get
Congress to arrange for his compensation for debts owed to him,
and his equally vexing battle to win a salary suitable to his needs in
office. Aghast that he was to be paid only $5,000 per year as vice
president when President Washington would get $25,000 per year,
he complained that both men had nearly equal burdens of providing
for guests and entertainment. Thus, Adams maintained, his salary
should be closer to that paid to the president—but he never got satisfaction on that point.

Adams's sole duties as vice president were to preside over the
Senate's debates; to break tie votes in the Senate; and to hold himself
in readiness should the president be unable to exercise his powers
and fulfill his duties, whether by death or illness. During President
Washington's first term, two health crises beset him.[33] In June 1789, a
large tumor on his left thigh required removal by a risky operation.[34]
In May 1790, Washington again fell ill, of influenza accompanied by

complications in his lungs. His illness left him near death for three days, affecting his sight, hearing, and strength. On both occasions, Martha Washington kept Abigail Adams informed of the president's health.[35] Aware that the men of his family tended to die before their fortieth year, Washington had assumed that he would not have a normal life span. After his bout with influenza, he resigned himself to the idea that another such illness "would put me to sleep with my fathers."[36] We have no record of Adams's feelings on these occasions, for by 1790 Adams was no longer keeping his diary regularly; thus, he never wrote about Washington's illnesses. Further, because he and Abigail were together, they exchanged few letters. Adams left no record, then or later, of his reactions to these potential crises over presidential succession and disability.

When he had to break tie votes as the Senate's presiding officer, Adams wielded power. He broke twenty-nine ties (thirty-one, according to some counts) in his eight years as vice president—a record still unmatched. Fifteen of these votes came during the First Federal Congress alone, five during the argument over the location of the nation's permanent capital.[37] He cast tie-breaking votes mostly to vindicate the federal government's authority. Sometimes, as in late summer 1789, when the Senate could not decide whether to rewrite one of the constitutional amendments proposed by the House, Adams broke a tie to preserve good relations between Congress's two chambers; the Senate gave up its attempt to rewrite the provision.

Adams had no other important official role in American public life. Unable to influence or intervene in Senate debates, barred from executive branch deliberations, he was officially silenced. It is no wonder that, on December 19, 1793, during the crisis provoked by the French envoy "Citizen" Edmond Genet, Adams mocked himself and his office in a letter to Abigail: "My Country has in its Wisdom contrived for me, the most insignificant Office that ever the Invention of Man contrived or his Imagination conceived: and as I can do neither good nor Evil, I must be born away by Others and meet the common Fate."[38]

In 1790, he decided to enter the political arena as an essayist—a role familiar to him from his days as a polemicist from the 1760s through the 1780s. He also hoped to salvage his most extensive work of constitutional argument, the *Defence of the Constitutions*, by extending that project in a new series of essays to be recast in book form.[39] Irritated that his countrymen had misread his *Defence* not as an anatomization and critique of aristocracy but as a vindication of it, he hoped to clarify matters with what would be a fourth volume of the *Defence*.[40]

Adams took up his pen in response to the French Revolution. Viewing the upheavals in France with suspicion, Adams thought that nothing good would come of them. He suspected that France would plunge into chaos, from which a tyrant would emerge, instead of becoming the constitutional republic that such pro-French Americans as Jefferson desired. Because Americans seemed to Adams to be too naive and enthusiastic about France, he was determined to set them straight.

As was his practice in planning his extended writings, he chose a text on which he could write commentary—the massive seventeenth-century *Historie of the Civil Warres of France* (1630) by the Italian historian and diplomat Enrico Caterino Davila.[41] Adams focused on Davila's reflections on how factional strife endangered liberty in France, drawing parallels with similar dangers facing the American republic.[42] He hoped that his *Discourses on Davila* would be a counterpart to Niccolò Machiavelli's greatest work, *Discourses on the First Ten Books of Titus Livius*. As Machiavelli had used the Roman historian Livy's account of the Roman Republic's origins to discuss problems affecting the republics of Renaissance Italy, Adams tried to use Davila's analysis of the sixteenth-century French civil wars to inspire his commentary on problems facing the United States. Adams also used another source for fourteen of the essays, which addressed moral and ethical themes—a passage in Adam Smith's influential book *The Theory of Moral Sentiments*, published in 1759 and reissued in a revised edition in 1790, just as Smith died.

Adams did not just track Smith's reasoning but borrowed his words without labeling his quotations, though he sometimes recast them in more vivid metaphors.[43]

Again, how Adams wrote his *Discourses* helped to undermine their effectiveness. Like the *Defence*, his new essays showed a lack of sustained argument and method; he later wrote mournfully that his essays made a "dull, heavy volume" that had "powerfully operated to destroy [his] popularity." He added, "It was urged as full proof that [Adams] was an advocate for monarchy, and laboring to introduce an hereditary President and Senate in America."[44] The *Discourses* also miscarried because Adams grounded his analysis on his faith in the continuing relevance of classical political thought to the modern world, despite its skepticism about democracy and about republican government.

Most Americans rejected his perspective, as he saw too late. The *Discourses* became a target for pamphleteers and controversialists, who not only disputed his arguments but also used those arguments as the basis for attacks on his character. They pulled from the essays passages that, taken out of context, would caricature Adams as an aristocrat and a would-be monarch. A man of such views, they argued, must be hostile to American political principles. Adams never found the respectful and attentive readership that he had hoped to have. Saddened, he broke off his *Discourses on Davila* after the thirty-first essay (though scholars have found a thirty-second published in a Federalist newspaper).[45]

Though he may not have understood the significance of his decision to end *Discourses on Davila*, Adams's laying down his pen also meant that he had given up his last sustained work of political thought and argument, ending his formal work as a thinking politician. That ending confirmed his failure to find his intellectual bearings in the American political world. The stormy reception provoked by his arguments forced him to recognize that his ideas of politics differed dramatically from those held by most Americans, citizens and politicians alike. Thereafter, although he expounded his understandings of politics and government brilliantly in private letters, he never again sought to undertake a formal work of constitutional and political analysis.[46]

Adams's immersion in the ideas and practices guiding Old World politics and diplomacy had wrenched his views out of alignment with conventional American wisdom. He had represented a fragile confederation in a world of great powers. He not only had studied how they interacted but also tried to master the assumptions shaping their interactions, viewed through the intellectual lenses formed by his observations of monarchy and aristocracy in action. As he insisted, he was neither a monarchist nor an aristocrat nor an advocate of monarchy or aristocracy. Rather, seeking to grasp the hows and whys of European politics, he had become so used to them that he could not perceive that in America he was now operating in a different political context from the one reigning in Europe. Nor did he see, for example, that Franklin, whose ideas about politics were more democratic than his, had not allowed his time in Europe to wrench him out of alignment with the ideas of his countrymen.

Adams was shocked that others saw differently the problems and challenges of politics, and the challenges of devising constitutional systems to solve those problems and meet those challenges. Other thinking politicians of his time experienced similar shocks. Rifts between such leading American politicians as Hamilton and Madison, Hamilton and Jefferson, and Washington and Madison all had in common each man's puzzled and horrified realization that someone else thought differently, with an accompanying sense of personal hurt and betrayal, as well as alarm because the stakes were so high.

American thinking politicians assumed, with the Scottish philosopher David Hume, that politics was an organized body of knowledge akin to "natural philosophy"—the era's term for science.[47] To them, politics was like physics or chemistry—it had clear postulates and assumptions, and equally clear principles and theories derived from them.[48] They assumed further that these assumptions, postulates, principles, and theories fit together naturally and neatly, with one right way to assemble and apply them. To someone who had arrived at a well-defined conception of the science of politics, anyone urging a different method of fitting these things together or a different way of applying them was wrong, evil, or both. Still, these differences not only emerged but multiplied, disrupting relations among American thinking politicians and the people in general. Dissension among thinking politicians was a drawback of American attempts to articulate the "divine science of politicks"—the failure to realize that different thinkers could assemble contrasting, even antithetical, visions of politics, government, and constitutionalism, with no generally accepted standard for deciding which was right and which was wrong.[49] All these competing visions of politics and methods of political reasoning ultimately fed the evolution of American constitutionalism and politics—but Adams and his contemporaries never grasped that development.

Adams and Jefferson both struggled to understand the political world that they found on their return home, but for different reasons. The experience of Europe affected the two friends in starkly different ways. Adams had accepted European ways as the ways of the world and saw the need to bring American politics into alignment with his perceptions of European politics and its lessons; he sought to use European politics to cast light on the likely evolution of American politics. Jefferson differed significantly from Adams. He had found European social and political corruption deeply traumatic; that traumatization sharpened Jefferson's understanding that American politics and governance stood in glaring opposition to those of Europe. Whenever Jefferson saw American public life seeming to echo European public life, he interpreted those echoes as symptoms of corruption and decadence.[50] Jefferson used European politics as a great array of warnings to Americans not to ape the ways of the Old World. Jefferson not only refused to see European politics as forecasting the development of American politics but also committed himself to preventing American political imitations of Europe.

When in 1778 Adams went to Europe, he left behind him an American political system starting to emerge from the British colonial mindset. On his return in 1788, he found a new American political world starkly different from its colonial past, insecure about but proud of its intellectual independence from the Old World in general and from Britain in particular. The Americans whom he found on his return would have liked a comment penned decades later by the Frenchman Alexis de Tocqueville, one that Adams would have rejected: "A new science of politics is needed for a world itself quite new."[51] Adams was dubious of that American world's new science of politics. Rejecting that world's political givens, he hoped to draw on his strengths—his knowledge of systems of government and politics and the evolution of Western political thought, past and present—to establish his place in that world. In the process, he hoped to educate his countrymen as he had educated himself, but it was not to be. Adams gave up the work of a thinking politician because he and his countrymen were talking past each other.

In the 1790s, personal and intellectual differences shaped differences over public policy at home and diplomacy abroad, helping to mold the evolution of politics under the Constitution. Such leading American thinking politicians as Madison and Hamilton were at odds, with ominous consequences. They agreed in seeing American politics as dynamic, evolving in line with currents of social and economic change and development. What they disagreed about was those currents' specific nature and their consequences for America's evolving constitutional and political systems. Leading spirits in Washington's administration, such as Hamilton and Jefferson, were at loggerheads over the proper ways to interpret the Constitution and to apply its commands and limitations to solving national problems.[52] In another kind of rupture, Vice President Adams, seeking to educate and guide his countrymen about the nature of politics, unintentionally created a widening rift between him and them, in the process dooming himself to political irrelevance.

Another factor helping to sideline Adams was the controversy in the United States over the French Revolution. In 1791, as he was about to discontinue his *Discourses on Davila*, a new controversy occasioned by the Revolution put him and his friend Jefferson at odds. The American printer J. B. Smith undertook the first American edition of Thomas Paine's *Rights of Man*, a powerful defense of the French Revolution against the strictures of such writers as the British Member of Parliament Edmund Burke. Smith went to Jefferson for support, and the secretary of state penned what he thought was a private letter praising Paine's book. To Jefferson's horror, Smith used that letter as the introduction to his edition of *Rights of Man*; Jefferson had to write apologetic letters to Washington and to Adams because his letter-preface attacked "the political heresies that have sprung up amongst us," and many readers understood that reference to point to Adams or Washington.[53] Jefferson's discomfort about explaining himself to Adams may explain the six-week delay between his letters to Washington and to Adams. In his gentle, friendly response, Adams reassured Jefferson that their friendship was not damaged by the printer's publishing of a private letter.[54]

What Adams himself could not do, John Quincy Adams, a young lawyer in his midtwenties, could do. Soon after the appearance in the United States of *Rights of Man*, John Quincy Adams began publishing a series of essays under the pen name "Publicola," which attacked Paine's support of the French Revolution, defended constitutionalism as understood in Britain and in America, and indirectly defended his father. So powerful were the "Publicola" essays that many Americans mistakenly identified them as John Adams's work. The essays—and two later series of essays defending the foreign policy of Washington's administration—brought John Quincy Adams to President Washington's attention. Washington helped to launch the younger Adams's diplomatic career by naming him American minister to the Netherlands (the same post his father had held in the early 1780s). Still, the elder Adams's opposition to the French Revolution remained a vulnerability for him.[55]

Adams's marginal status as vice president continued to vex him. His extensive learning and his questing mind seemed of no use to anyone. Only three avenues of expression remained open to him. He could vent his thoughts and feelings to his family. He could argue with European controversialists in the margins of their books, a pursuit that he continued during his presidency and into his retirement.[56] And he could immerse himself in private correspondence. Here, he found much to occupy him. Friends and allies, past and present, pelted him with letters asking him about his views. Had he abandoned republicanism? Was he a monarchist, an apologist for aristocracy, or both?

Adams answered that he had not changed, insisting that he was as much a republican as he had been during the Revolution. Still, in ways that he did not recognize, he had changed. As a man steeped in political history and political learning, he did not have the aversion to monarchy that so many Americans had. Rather, he thought that monarchy and aristocracy were natural political institutions, consequences of human nature, nor did he believe that Americans had banished such things from their future. Consider a letter that he wrote on June 9, 1789, to his friend and fellow signer of the Declaration, Dr. Benjamin Rush:

> I do not consider "hereditary Monarchy or Aristocracy as Rebellion against Nature." On the contrary I esteem them both Institutions of admirable wisdom and exemplary Virtue in a certain Stage of Society in a great Nation. The only Institutions that can possibly preserve the Laws and Liberties of the People, and I am clear that America must resort to them as an Asylum against Discord, Seditions and Civil War, and that at no very distant Period of Time. . . . I think it therefore impolitick to cherish prejudices against Institutions which must be kept in view as the hope of our Posterity. I am by no means for attempting any such thing at present. Our Country is not ripe for it in many respects, and it is not yet necessary, but our ship must ultimately land on that shore or be cast away.[57]

It was hard for Rush, Jefferson, or any other American getting such letters to discern the difference between Adams and an advocate of aristocracy or monarchy. But the difference is clear, though sometimes difficult to trace. It is the difference between a political advocate and a political diagnostician—between one who insisted that monarchy and aristocracy were desirable and one who, like Adams, recognized that these institutions were central to the evolution of government, politics, and society throughout history, and no more unnatural to humanity than was an oak tree. And yet the difficulty of understanding the difference between Adams's mindset and that of an advocate for these despised institutions—for most Americans did despise them—cost Adams dearly. Try as he would, he could not make himself understood; the result was that others abandoned him or wrote him off, and he seethed in frustration at his inability to acquit himself of charges that he felt he did not deserve to face and should not have to disprove.

Vexed at his enforced official silence, Adams found various ways to dissipate his exasperation. One was regularly returning to Braintree (absorbed in 1792 into the village of Quincy), sometimes for months at a time. His habit of leaving the scene of government paralleled that of President Washington. Both men, tired of their exalted offices, yearned for their homes, timing trips homeward to coincide with congressional recesses. In truth, their absences mattered little; the general government was part-time, and congressional recesses (with the executive branch in suspended animation) were the rule. After the Compromise of 1790, when Congress moved the nation's capital to Philadelphia, matters of public health combined with the lack of need for full-time government to give the nation an intermittent government.[58] Philadelphia was tormented by outbreaks of yellow fever; escaping the disease by fleeing the capital was common.[59] Adams growled to Abigail that he needed to go home regularly and would sooner resign than be forbidden to return to his home in Massachusetts:

> I will not sit here in Summer, in all Events. I would sooner resign my office. . . . Other Gentlemen of the Senate and House are frequently asking leave of absence: but my Attendance is perpetual and will if continued much longer disorder my Health, which hitherto has been very good. But I want my Horse, my farm, my long Walks, and, more than all, the Bosom of my friend.[60]

Retreating to his favorite part of the world, Adams devoted himself to his wife and his children. Four children born to Abigail and John had survived into adulthood. The marriage of his daughter Abigail to Colonel William Stephens Smith proved troubled, a source of pain not only to her but also to her parents. John Quincy was more a source of pride than of worry. By late 1794, he was at his new post in Amsterdam, an office that his father had held fourteen years earlier. In abandoning the law for diplomacy, John Quincy drew on his mastery of languages, his experience, and his pronounced gift for diplomacy. Thomas Boylston Adams served as his older brother's secretary, putting his own legal career on hold. Charles had launched his own law practice in New York City. John and Abigail, proud yet anxious parents, indulged themselves in pride, worry, and advice.

Adams was happy to turn to private concerns, for, though he was re-elected as vice president in 1792 with a majority of electoral votes, his second term in that office may have been the low point of his political career.[61] Political unhappiness, worsening health problems for him and his wife, and his vexation with his "insignificant Office" continued to annoy him. He seemed irrelevant to the great controversies roiling American politics and dividing the nation, his attempts to guide Americans to form a proper approach to the French Revolution had failed, and he saw little purpose in plunging into the controversy over President Washington's Neutrality Proclamation of 1793 or the tumult over the contentious

French envoy Edmond Charles Genet or 1794's crisis over the Whiskey Rebellion. On March 12, 1794, for example, he wrote to Abigail, "It is to be sure a Punishment to hear other Men talk five hours every day, and not be at Liberty to talk at all myself: especially as more than half I hear appears to me very young inconsiderate and inexperienced."[62]

Yet in the last year of his service as vice president, a new possibility opened. On January 5, 1796, he informed Abigail of the almost certain news—though then private—that President Washington had decided to retire at the end of his second term: "You know the Consequence of this, to me and to yourself. Either We must enter upon Ardours more trying than any ever yet experienced; or retire to Quincy Farmers for Life."[63] Conflicting feelings overwhelmed Adams. He desired peace and quiet and an escape from the public arena, but once again he felt the claims of ambition, relishing the idea that others saw him as a credible successor to Washington. For months, John and Abigail wrestled with the choice before them; political gossip named him and Jefferson (now in his third year of retirement from public life) as the leading contenders for the presidency.

On September 19, 1796, Washington announced his decision to retire, publishing a message (written with Hamilton's aid) in David Claypoole's *Pennsylvania Packet, and Daily Advertiser*. Adams first read Washington's Farewell Address in a Boston newspaper; Washington had neither consulted him nor informed him of his decision to publish his announcement. Washington's Farewell Address won fame as perhaps his most important statement on American politics. He warned the American people against "self-created societies" (his term for Democratic-Republican societies proliferating across the nation) and other forms of partisan strife, as well as against embrace of foreign adventures by the government or the people.[64] Washington's blend of sage counsel and embittered partisan rhetoric showed how the fevered political world of the 1790s had dragged even the central figure of American politics from his determination to stand above partisanship. Washington was no longer "the man who unites all hearts" but a staunch Federalist. The increasing polarization of the nation's public life intensified the challenge facing any man picked to succeed him.

Rumors of Washington's impending retirement prompted politicians throughout the nation to devise ways to name candidates to stand for the presidency in the nation's first contested presidential election. For example, in 1796 Massachusetts politicians used Washington's birthday celebrations to highlight their backing of Adams; in late 1795, supporters of Jefferson let one another know by letter that they would rally behind him. Within the Federalist partisan alliance, some, such as Hamilton, sought a palatable southern candidate to counter Jefferson and perhaps to supplant Adams.[65]

The four candidates emerging that fall were a heterogeneous group. Federalists rallied behind John Adams and Thomas Pinckney of South Carolina, a diplomat whose negotiation of a 1795 treaty with Spain made him an admired national figure (and an appealing alternative to Adams for Hamiltonian Federalists).[66] Republicans backed Thomas Jefferson, with New Yorker Aaron Burr emerging as the likely second candidate of that partisan alliance. Under the Constitution as it was in 1796, all four men stood for the presidency, making possible covert machinations by those looking to replace an "obvious" candidate with a more tractable alternative.

As was customary in that era, Adams, Jefferson, and Pinckney did not put themselves forth as candidates; only Burr campaigned for himself. By the time of Washington's announcement that he would not seek a third term, Federalists agreed on Adams and Pinckney, and Republicans backed Jefferson. In that fall's brief, hard-fought contest, the campaigning was in the hands of networks of Federalist and Republican politicians vying for states and votes, leading up to the choice by each state of presidential electors, who would vote in each state's capital on the same day throughout the United States.

Reports by newspapers around the nation made clear that Adams had narrowly defeated Jefferson to become president—but that, as the first runner-up in the electoral tally, Jefferson would become

Adams's vice president. The inventors of the Electoral College had not reckoned on partisan forces reaching across state lines to dominate presidential elections; thus, they had not foreseen the problems that could result from an election dominated by national partisan alliances. Again Hamilton had sought to manipulate the Electoral College, this time to edge Pinckney past Adams. Hamilton failed to undermine Adams in Pinckney's favor—and now Adams began to suspect and distrust Hamilton.

On February 8, 1797, before a joint session of Congress in Philadelphia's Congress Hall, Vice President Adams conducted the official count of electoral votes. He opened the sealed reports from each state and read the votes aloud, tallying them as he read. Once he had finished, he announced that he had been elected president, with 71 electoral votes; that Thomas Jefferson, with 68 electoral votes, would become vice president; that Thomas Pinckney and Aaron Burr had received 59 and 30 electoral votes, respectively; and that nine other candidates had received a total of 48 electoral votes. Adams had won 1 more vote than the 70 needed for election. He was the first vice president to announce his own election as president.

In a farewell speech to the Senate a week later, on February 15, 1797, Adams spoke with humility and affection; he concluded with a tribute to the Senate:

> Within these walls, for a course of years I have been an admiring witness of a succession of information, eloquence, patriotism, and independence which, as they would have done honor to any Senate in any age, afford a consolatory hope . . . that no council more permanent than this, as a branch of the legislature, will be necessary to defend the rights, liberties, and properties of the people, and to protect the Constitution of the United States.[67]

Adams was relinquishing the office that he had held for eight years—the longest duration of any in his career. In some ways, he was the office's first victim,[68] injured by his and his countrymen's confusion about what the vice presidency was or should be. His successor, Thomas Jefferson, would learn from Adams's experience and benefit by it.[69]

Vice President Adams had educated his countrymen—but in ways that he had not intended, shaping their perceptions of him in ways opposed to his ideas and hopes. What he did not realize was that he had failed to learn how politics in the new nation was really working. Though he never put it in those terms, he had failed to educate his countrymen, and he had failed to educate himself. Although relieved to give up the ordeal of the vice presidency, he knew that, in a few weeks, he would assume another, more demanding, role.

Chapter Eight

"May none but wise and honest Men ever rule under this roof"

President John Adams (1797–1801)

On March 4, 1797, wearing a suit of pearl-gray broadcloth and carrying a cockaded hat, John Adams entered the US House of Representatives chamber on the first floor of Congress Hall in Philadelphia. Taking the chair reserved for the Speaker of the House, Adams waited to be sworn in as the second president of the United States. Omitting the ceremony characteristic of President Washington's public appearances and hoping to counter his own reputation for pomposity, Adams had made sure that his inauguration would be simple. Chief Justice Oliver Ellsworth of the US Supreme Court was there to swear him in. Onlookers included the retiring president, George Washington; the new vice president, Thomas Jefferson; members of both houses of Congress; and a number of guests. Abigail Adams was back home in Quincy, tending to many domestic responsibilities, including caring for her dying mother-in-law.

Conscious of everyone's scrutiny, Adams worried that the audience was comparing him with his predecessor to his own disadvantage. Commanding in posture despite his sixty-five years, Washington attended the inauguration clad in black—the color that his era associated with political power. He looked relieved to be giving up the burdens of office. Because the day marked Washington's retirement as well as Adams's inauguration, Adams could not help feeling that Washington's last appearance on the national scene was eclipsing *his* inauguration.

Before taking the oath, Adams delivered his inaugural address. To allay fears that he wanted to create an American monarchy or aristocracy, he stressed his commitment to American independence, constitutional liberty, and republican government. His last sentence, more than seven hundred words long, presented a set of carefully framed "if" clauses sketching his life, career, and political values, as well as the challenges awaiting him. By his era's oratorical standards, it was an outstanding performance. He won approval for his speech's substance and for his skilled delivery, though he had not slept the night before and felt ill throughout the ceremony.[1]

After Adams finished, Chief Justice Ellsworth administered the constitutional oath of office. Adams then accepted congratulations from Washington and the other guests, and the inauguration was over. The next day, Adams wrote to Abigail, describing his self-consciousness about the contrast between him and Washington. He even imagined the other man's thoughts:

> My dearest Friend, your dearest Friend never had a more trying day than yesterday. A Solemn Scene it was indeed and it was made more affecting to me by the Presence of the General, whose Countenance was as serene and unclouded as the day. He Seemed to me to enjoy a Tryumph over me. Methought I heard him think Ay! I am fairly out and you fairly in! See which of Us will be happiest.[2]

An iconic figure for all Americans, Washington helped to define the presidency by his eight years in that office. To a greater extent than any later president, except perhaps Franklin Delano Roosevelt, Washington had fused his identity with the presidency; for decades, Americans used Washington as a measuring rod to assess his successors.[3] Adams was the first ordinary American (by comparison with Washington) to be president. He tried to emulate Washington's conduct—but fundamental differences between them in background and temperament doomed him to failure. Washington had been a veteran soldier and general. By contrast, Adams had no military experience; the short, stout lawyer from Braintree could not project authority, dignity, and gravity the way the tall, erect, powerfully built Washington could.

Washington had had nearly sixteen years' experience of wielding executive power—from his service as commander in chief of the Continental Army from 1775 to 1783 through his two terms as president from 1789 to 1797. In the process, he had come to embody the Revolution and the American nation.[4] Adams had never held an executive office. He was a veteran legislator and diplomat, he had chaired or served on countless committees in the Continental Congress, and he had spent eight years as vice president—but he had never been a state governor or the head of an executive department. And he was all too aware of that lack of experience. Moreover, Washington was a product of Virginia's colonial and revolutionary aristocracy, whereas Adams was a man formed by relatively democratic New England; Washington's Virginia background helped to groom him for national leadership in ways that Adams's New England origins did not.

As to temperament, Washington had a long and difficult history of restraining his formidable temper and cultivating his ability to project dignified calm, which sometimes came across as chilly formality. Adams knew that his own volcanic temper was set on hairtrigger; unlike Washington, he had not perfected the ability to keep himself in check. Adams also knew that his turbulent emotions raised doubts about whether he could muster the self-command that a president should have. His critics focused on his outbursts. At the height of the clashes between Adams and his cabinet, Secretary of War James McHenry wrote to Secretary of the Treasury Oliver Wolcott, mocking the president: "Whether he is sportful, playful, witty, kind, cold, drunk, sober, angry, easy, stiff, jealous, careless, cautious, confident, close or open, is almost always in the *wrong place* or to the *wrong persons*."[5]

Adams also brought with him inconvenient intellectual and political baggage that shaped Americans' perceptions of him. Recalling his writings and his service as American minister to England and as vice president, many Americans saw him as an advocate of high-toned government, believing that he yearned to bring aristocracy and monarchy to America. Not only did his *Defence of the Constitutions* and his *Discourses on Davila* contain passages that his foes used to indict him for those sins; his 1789 campaign for an ornate title for the president seemed to confirm these propensities.

Finally, unlike Washington, Adams had not been the Electoral College's unanimous first choice. Rather, he had won by a thin margin in the first contested presidential election, in which partisan alliances had backed candidates bearing partisan labels. Could a president who had won his office so narrowly in such a contest live up to the ideal of nonpartisan executive power?[6] Adams shared that ideal, but his version differed from the activist presidency embraced by Washington and Hamilton. Instead of energy and activism, Adams extolled balance. His view of constitutionalism in general and American constitutionalism in particular grew out of his allegiance to the principles of balanced government, shaping and reflecting a balanced society. He saw the presidency as the key institution in maintaining balance within the constitutional system.[7] Would he be able to remain true to those ideals?

Adams's first decision as president was to retain Washington's cabinet as his own. First, he wanted to avoid appearing to criticize his predecessor. Replacing Washington's appointees, he worried, might signal implied censure of Washington's judgment in making those appointments. As he explained to Benjamin Rush years later: "Till 1797 when I was chosen President of U.S. I had never had much intercourse with any of the secretaries of departments; but now it became my duty to look into them. Washington had appointed them, and I knew it would turn the world upside down if I removed any one of them."[8] Adams also preferred to keep incumbents in place because it was hard to persuade talented men to join the federal government. And he had no concerns that any of Washington's men would advance himself at the Adams administration's expense.

Retaining Washington's cabinet sowed the seeds of discord in Adams's administration, however, hampering its—and his—effectiveness. The heads of departments felt no loyalty to Adams. They were loyal to Washington (Secretary of War James McHenry) or to former Treasury secretary Alexander Hamilton (Secretary of State Timothy Pickering and Secretary of the Treasury Oliver Wolcott Jr.). The one cabinet member in neither camp—Attorney General Charles Lee—did not head a cabinet department (the Justice Department was not created until 1870); rather, he was a one-man law firm for the federal government, with his own private practice. As a cabinet member, he was largely ineffectual.[9]

Pickering, Wolcott, and McHenry had interlocking backgrounds, the nexus points being service in Washington's administration and intellectual kinship with Hamilton. Pickering, a fellow citizen of Massachusetts, succeeded Samuel Osgood as postmaster general in 1791 and Henry Knox as secretary of war in 1795; he replaced Edmund Randolph as secretary of state in 1795, following Randolph's resignation. Pickering and Hamilton, veterans of the Continental army, had served under Washington; they shared a skeptical view of human nature, a bias for England in foreign policy, and a commitment to a strong federal government. Wolcott, a citizen of Connecticut, assisted Hamilton from 1789 to 1791 as auditor of the Treasury; Hamilton helped to secure Wolcott's elevation to comptroller in 1791 and persuaded Washington to name Wolcott to succeed him as secretary in 1795. McHenry, a Marylander, had befriended Hamilton when they were aides to Washington during the Revolution. In 1787, with Washington, they were delegates to the Federal Convention; and McHenry succeeded Pickering as secretary of war in 1795. The web of relationships linking Pickering,

Wolcott, and McHenry gave Adams no entry, and it soon closed against him.

Adams's decision created another problem. A president's second-term cabinet often lacks the best and brightest. Once a president has gone through the best talent available in his first term, he finds his choices limited to the "second string," at best. In the 1790s, the burdens of service in the federal government eclipsed any attraction in becoming a department head; prospective appointees often declined to serve, making it harder for a president to find leading talents. Thus, Adams began his presidency with leftovers from Washington's presidency—not a guarantee of success.[10]

Not until Congress created the Navy Department in 1798 did Adams have a cabinet member loyal to him. Benjamin Stoddert of Maryland was an able administrator and a useful partner in building up the navy. Like the ancient Greek leader Themistocles, Adams and Stoddert believed in strengthening the nation's "wooden walls." The navy that they developed proved invaluable when the United States fought the Quasi-War with France; ships built under their supervision played distinguished roles in American naval history thereafter.[11]

Adams lacked support in Congress as well as in the executive branch. In the 1790s, Congress did not yet have the party structure that enabled later party leaders to discipline members and command support. Few congressional Federalists felt loyalty to Adams equal to their loyalty to Washington or to Hamilton. As Adams recognized, he had few or no tools or powers to enforce his will as president; he had only "speeches, written recommendations, and messages."[12] These limits, combined with the era's wariness of executive power, hampered the new president's ability to do his job.

Family difficulties plagued Adams. For much of his presidency, he felt keenly the absence of his wife. Abigail largely avoided the nation's capital, worrying about the climate's dangers to her health. She preferred to stay in Quincy, in the family home that she had labored to perfect since they acquired it in 1788. During their separations, John and Abigail regularly wrote to each other; as always, each derived comfort from their correspondence. The family was scattered, with some children doing well—or seeming to do well—and others dealing with personal problems. Abigail Adams Smith was mired in her unhappy marriage to Colonel William Stephens Smith, a rash financial speculator and an improvident provider. John Quincy Adams became American minister to Prussia during his father's presidency (with his younger brother Thomas Boylston Adams again serving as his secretary). Charles Adams had married a sister of Colonel Smith and appeared to be thriving as a lawyer in New York City.

The nation's domestic and foreign problems gave Adams reasons for disquiet. The United States was a fragile union seeking to hold itself together despite political strife. Most politicians viewed partisan competition as a danger to the republic, not a legitimate governing assumption of American political life.[13] The foremost problem facing the nation was the state of world politics—specifically the troubled relationship between the United States and France.[14] Since 1789, revolutionary unrest had consumed France; since 1792, the country had been at war with the rest of Europe.

Divisions over France pervaded domestic politics and interacted with domestic issues; when Federalist economic policies caused factional strife, it was because those policies resonated with foreign crises requiring the federal government to raise revenues. Republicans backed France as the nation's oldest ally, a fellow republic seeking to throw off monarchy and aristocracy. By contrast, Federalists distrusted France as a source of democratic chaos, an enemy of religion, law, and good order. Most Federalists embraced American neutrality; some urged that the nation join Britain and its European allies in opposing France. These political rifts dominated Washington's last years in office and persisted under Adams.

By comparison, American relations with Britain and with Native American nations were quiet under Adams. Two commissions established under the Jay Treaty of 1794 continued negotiations with

Britain, continuing their work into the nineteenth century. One commission was settling American claims for property destroyed by British forces during the Revolution; the other was adjusting claims by British subjects for debts owed by Americans from before the Revolution. Adams insisted that, in any joint action by Britain and the United States, the new nation had to maintain an independent stance so that the two countries would be on an equal footing[15] Careful work by Washington and his advisers, notably Pickering, placed US relations with Native American nations on a mutually respectful basis, quieting the clashes that had raged on American frontiers in the early 1790s. Adams continued these policies.[16]

Determined to ease tensions with France, Adams pondered a mission to resolve disputes between the two nations, modeled on John Jay's 1794 mission to Britain. At first, the French seemed uninterested; in 1796, the French foreign minister, the Comte de Talleyrand, had refused to receive Charles Cotesworth Pinckney when he sought to present his credentials as American minister. On receiving news of Talleyrand's rebuff, Adams called a special session of Congress, the first under the Constitution. On May 16, 1797, he read Congress an angry speech insisting that France owed the United States fair treatment: "We are not a degraded people, humiliated under a colonial spirit of fear and sense of inferiority, fitted to be the miserable instruments of foreign influence."[17] Yet he still wanted to find a route to peace.

Adams hoped to send a respected Republican to France, such as Vice President Jefferson or former representative Madison, but both men declined. Pickering, Wolcott, and McHenry opposed the idea, hinting that they would resign in protest if Adams named a Republican envoy. Hoping to mollify his cabinet, Adams adopted a different model for the mission. He chose three men, balanced geographically and ideologically: Charles C. Pinckney (Federalist from South Carolina), John Marshall (Federalist from Virginia), and Elbridge Gerry (Republican from Massachusetts). Adams's cabinet objected to Gerry; Adams had chosen him both because he wanted a balanced mission and because he trusted Gerry, an old friend from the Second Continental Congress and a fellow signer of the Declaration of Independence. Adams picked another old friend, Francis Dana, a Federalist, to replace Gerry—but Dana declined to serve, citing ill health. Adams restored Gerry to the mission.

When the Americans reached Paris, Talleyrand refused to receive them. As they debated what to do, three French agents met with them and demanded an apology for Adams's May 1797 message— and hinted at the payment of bribes to secure access to Talleyrand. The Americans spurned these terms; Pinckney replied, "No, no, not a sixpence!"—a flat phrase that gave rise to the slogan "Millions for defense, but not one cent for tribute!"[18] The American diplomats' report to Adams labeled the French agents as X, Y, and Z—hence, the "XYZ Affair." They agreed that Marshall would deliver the mission's documentation to Adams; Pinckney would follow, and Gerry would stay in France on the chance that the French might reconsider.

Even before Marshall's arrival in Philadelphia, news of the mission's failure reached American shores. Certain that France could not have refused negotiations, Republicans charged Adams with having sabotaged the mission. On his arrival, Marshall closeted himself with the president, who debriefed him and reviewed the documents he brought. At the right time, Adams made the mission's documents available to the public and to Congress. Proof of French responsibility for the mission's failure embarrassed Republicans; an enraged American public demanded war with France.[19] The United States abrogated its alliance with France; American and French warships clashed on the high seas in the Quasi-War, the first undeclared war under the Constitution. The people rallied around Adams; for the first time, he was popular.[20]

Adams ordered mobilization of the army to prepare for a French invasion. To lead the army, he named Washington commander in chief, stressing the general's military experience and his own lack of expertise. Second, Adams ordered that the navy be strengthened to meet the Quasi-War's demands, making the navy the primary safeguard against invasion. Bolstering his efforts, merchants in ten cities organized private subscription ventures to raise funds to build frigates for the navy.[21]

Seeking to defend the nation against subversion, Federalists in Congress drafted four bills, focusing on what they saw as the major domestic problems rooted in the threat of war. Targeting hostile resident aliens and journalists, Congress sought to strengthen American law on immigration and to tighten limits on press criticism of government or its officials.

Since the outbreak of the French Revolution in 1789, European refugees had poured into the United States, which had no immigration policy. Some were Irish refugees who had sided with the French; some were liberal French exiles fleeing France to save their lives; still others were backers of the French Revolution from other European nations, seeking refuge from persecution. Federalists worried that these new arrivals would subvert the US government, creating a regime like the revolutionary French Republic.[22]

Partisan criticism of the government and its leaders also alarmed the administration and its supporters, including Abigail Adams. The question Federalists asked was: What should the limits on freedom of speech and press be? English common law taught that criticizing the government or its officials was punishable as the crime of seditious libel. At common law, truth was no defense against a charge of seditious libel; the greater the truth, the greater the libel. True or false, seditious libel inflicted injury on the reputations of the government and its officials. Why did the government's reputation matter? Federalists saw the government under the Constitution as dangerously fragile. If its legitimacy was no stronger than its officials' reputations, an attack on one was an attack on the other—so both had to be protected.[23]

Congress framed three bills to prevent subversion by suspect aliens and a fourth limiting criticism of the government; Adams signed the bills into law.[24] The Naturalization Act imposed exacting requirements on foreign nationals seeking to become naturalized citizens. The Alien Enemies Act empowered the president to deport any alien resident who came from a country with which the United States was at war. The Alien Friends Act gave the president full discretion, without due process, to deport any alien national deemed a threat to domestic peace.[25]

The Sedition Act banned spoken or published criticism of the government or of specific officials—the president and Congress (leaving Federalists free to attack Vice President Jefferson)—though it made truth a defense to charges under the act. This act was to expire on March 3, 1801. Republicans charged that that expiration date proved the bill's political character; it could be used only against critics of the Adams administration. If Adams were re-elected in 1800, the Federalists could re-enact the bill; if not, the bill would be unavailable to any Republican successor to use against Federalist opponents.[26]

Federalists saw the Sedition Act as a weapon that the government could use to defend itself against a barrage of criticism. And yet such ardent Federalists as Hamilton and Marshall doubted the measure's wisdom, though they accepted its constitutionality.[27] By contrast, Abigail Adams was firmly convinced of the need to punish sedition. Like others backing the Sedition Act, she insisted that the statute was legally and politically warranted, a safeguard against those who would bring the Terror's bloodshed to American shores.[28]

Administration officials never used the alien statutes, but they did wield the Sedition Act against Republican printers—including Benjamin Franklin Bache of the *Philadelphia Aurora*, Matthew Lyon of Vermont, and James Thomson Callendar of Virginia.[29] The Sedition Act undergirds the most serious charge leveled by posterity against President Adams—that he had violated freedom of the press.[30] In the 1790s, the nation's press was a collection of newspapers and a few magazines; those writing for and editing them were not professional journalists but rather fiercely partisan writers and printers allied with or opposing a specific partisan alliance. Standards of journalistic objectivity did not exist.

Adams's views of the press were those of his era, not of ours.[31] Like his contemporaries, he viewed the press as a collection of partisan printers. Shaping his opinion was the viciousness with which opponents in the press assailed his character, views, and conduct as president. Their treatment of him left its mark—including his willingness to see the press as a hostile force whose power had to be checked to preserve the government. Even if he could remain unmoved under a hail of journalistic criticism, Abigail could not. She was outraged, both as a loyal wife and as a convinced Federalist. By the standards of his time, Adams's decision to sign the Sedition Act into law was not unreasonable or indefensible—though it was certainly open to severe criticism.[32]

Vice President Jefferson reassured Republicans that the "reign of witches" symbolized by the Alien and Sedition Acts was sure to pass away.[33] At the same time, he and Madison, who was in political retirement but working behind the scenes, sought to rouse Republican opposition to Adams's administration. Their tools were the Kentucky and Virginia Resolutions. The Kentucky Resolutions, drafted by Jefferson and adopted in 1798 by Kentucky's legislature, denounced the Alien and Sedition Acts as unconstitutional and claimed that a state had the authority to declare them null and void within its borders—*nullification*. The Virginia Resolutions, drafted by Madison and adopted in 1798 by Virginia's legislature, also attacked the statutes' constitutionality. They declared that a state could *interpose* its authority to protect its citizens from federal prosecutions under what it deemed to be an unconstitutional statute, while seeking help from other states.[34]

The Virginia and Kentucky Resolutions failed to unite popular opposition against the Alien and Sedition Acts; the other states rejected Virginia's and Kentucky's constitutional arguments—their visions of federal constitutional power and of press freedom; their readings of the statutes; and their proposed remedies, nullification and interposition.[35] Even so, federal prosecutions of editors for sedition began to shift public opinion in favor of those prosecuted and against the prosecutions. These cases persuaded many Americans that the government should not be able to prevent publication of criticism of the government or its officials, and the government should not prosecute printers for publishing criticism of the government if they published true criticism for good reasons and good motives.[36]

Adams was often an absentee president. Each year, he traveled to Quincy, staying there for months at a time, to be with Abigail. His absence from the capital troubled many of his supporters; Secretary of the Navy Benjamin Stoddert and General Uriah Forrest, among others, urged him to return to Philadelphia. Forrest wrote in 1799, "The public sentiment is very much against your being so much away from the seat of government, from a conviction that, when you are there, the public vessel will be properly steered; and that these critical times require an experienced pilot. The people elected you to administer the government. They did not elect your officers, nor do they (however much they respect them) think them equal to govern, without your presence and control."[37]

Adams had reasons for his absenteeism. He was following precedents set by Washington and by himself as vice president— but Adams was gone 385 days in four years whereas Washington was gone only 181 days in eight years.[38] During the early republic, the federal government was a part-time government, with long periods when Congress was adjourned and the rest of the government was on hiatus. Adams's times away coincided with these hiatuses. Delays in travel slowed the pace of events, reducing the need to respond to crises quickly. Moreover, outbreaks of yellow fever in Philadelphia forced government officials, including Adams, to relocate (with Trenton as a temporary capital) to avoid sickness.[39]

Adams insisted that being an absentee president was not the same as being an inactive president. He received and answered daily dispatches from his cabinet. He assured Forrest: "I do administer [the government] here at Quincy, as really as I could do at Philadelphia. . . . [N]othing is done without my advice & direction, when I am here. . . . The post goes very rapidly and I answer by the return of it, so that nothing suffers or is lost."[40] By these means, Adams sought to maintain control over his administration when he was away.

Unfortunately, Adams's long absences led not to coordinated government but to cabinet government. Pickering, Wolcott, and McHenry worked together in Adams's absence to strengthen the nation's armed forces on Hamiltonian terms. At their request, Hamilton guided their deliberations and their decision-making. Hamilton justified himself in running Adams's government behind the president's back, but his reasoning was tainted with the arrogance that his enemies often denounced in him: the nation had to be governed, he thought; if Adams would not oversee his own administration, and if the government needed overseeing, he would do it through Adams's advisers. Though in 1800 Adams at last took charge of his government, forcing McHenry and Wolcott to resign and firing Pickering, and though he denounced Hamilton as a potential Caesar, he never learned the full extent of Pickering's, Wolcott's, and McHenry's collaboration with Hamilton behind his back, nor did he grasp that his own quasi negligence was a contributory cause.

The division in Adams's administration between the president and most of his cabinet signaled another kind of trouble. No longer a unified partisan alliance, the Federalists were splitting into two factions, a process that began in the last years of Washington's presidency; "High" Federalists allied with Hamilton confronted a moderate group, Adams Federalists, loyal to the president. Any problem highlighting the differences between these groups might rupture the Federalist partisan alliance.[41]

Organizing the army gave rise to a host of administrative, political, and personal problems that highlighted divisions within Adams's administration and among Federalists. The first questions focused on Washington's staff officers: Who would choose them, and what seniority would they have? More allied with Washington and Hamilton than with Adams, Congress sought to write

Hamilton's and Washington's views into law, giving the general discretion to choose his aides and rank them in order of seniority as he saw fit. They hoped that Washington would choose Hamilton as second in command, inspector general, with Henry Knox and Charles C. Pinckney next in line. Adams, who distrusted Hamilton as too young and too ambitious, refused to give him so high a rank. Knox, indignant that anyone should be deemed to outrank him, withdrew from consideration. Pinckney offered to serve in any capacity. Washington insisted that Adams honor his preferences for seniority. The wrangling exacerbated Adams's distrust of Hamilton and provoked his annoyance with Washington for trying to dictate terms to him.

Exasperated, Adams reviewed the American-French crisis. In confidential letters sent through the second half of 1798, William Vans Murray, American minister to the Netherlands, reported to Adams that the French might welcome reopening negotiations. Delighted with the news, which reinforced his doubts about war with France, Adams instructed Vans Murray to open back-channel talks with the French. He was not yet ready to confide in his cabinet.[42]

At the same time that the French crisis provoked Adams, he and the cabinet also had to deal with a related crisis raging on the island of Saint-Domingue, then a French colony. In 1791, a slave revolt had brought civil war to Saint-Domingue. Defeating their masters, the rebels created Haiti, the only republic besides the United States in the Western Hemisphere. At first, the Washington administration sought to aid the French planters, but by 1794 relations between the United States and France were deteriorating. Federalists saw the Haitian Revolution as a chance to undercut French interests in the New World. One advocate for Haiti was Timothy Pickering; southern Federalists agreed with him on favoring independence for Haiti to strike a blow against French power. Through Pickering, the Adams administration continued to assist Haiti, to promote its interests, and to confirm its independence. The island became an American base during the Quasi-War with France, as American warships battled French privateers in the Caribbean. American pro-Haitian policy continued until 1801, when the Republicans succeeded the Federalists; the United States then reversed its stance on Haiti, continuing that hostility for decades. Adams was more interested in causing trouble for the French than in aiding the Haitian people.[43]

Private worries intruded into Adams's October 1799 travel from Quincy to the temporary capital at Trenton. Stopping to visit his son Charles in New York City, Adams discovered that Charles was alcoholic and penniless and had abandoned his wife and daughters. Adams disowned him. Reporting Charles's condition to Abigail, Adams wrote that he envied Washington's childless state.[44] Then, he continued his journey, heartbroken.

Based on hopeful reports from William Vans Murray and from John Quincy Adams about France's willingness to negotiate, Adams surprised and angered his cabinet with a set of abrupt decisions. He would send a peace mission to France. At first he wanted to send Vans Murray, in whom he already had confidence, but his cabinet insisted that he add members acceptable to High Federalists. Adams's first choices for a peace mission consistent with his cabinet's demands were William Vans Murray, Chief Justice Oliver Ellsworth, and former Virginia governor Patrick Henry, who had moved into Federalist ranks to oppose Virginia's Jeffersonian Republicans. When Henry declined, citing his age and bad health, Adams named Governor William Richardson Davie of North Carolina, a Jeffersonian Republican, instead. As with the XYZ mission, Adams balanced the trio geographically and politically. Like Gerry, Adams's choice of Davie angered and divided his cabinet; Pickering, McHenry, and Wolcott opposed Davie, while Stoddert and Lee stood by the president. Despite Federalist efforts to downplay the peace mission or to persuade its members not to serve, the three diplomats sailed for France in November 1799.

Another opponent of the peace mission made an unexpected intervention at this point. Inspector General Hamilton had come to

Trenton to meet with Secretary of War McHenry and General James Wilkinson to discuss troop deployments in the Old Northwest. Hamilton disputed Adams's decision to send negotiators to France and demanded that Adams suspend or cancel the mission. Adams refused, railing against Hamilton's opposition to his policies.[45] Each man left the meeting thinking the other mad. Adams pursued his peace efforts; Hamilton planned to manipulate Federalist politics against the president in 1800.

Washington's death on December 14, 1799, which prompted weeks of national mourning, exacerbated the rancor within the Adams administration. The passing of "the father of his country" freed Adams to be his own man in the presidency and to challenge his advisers. Washington's death also left the army without a commander; this vacancy gave Adams the chance to forestall a needless war with France.

At the beginning of May 1800, Adams abruptly ended his working vacation. Heeding the urgent appeals of Stoddert, Forrest, and other supporters, he traveled from Massachusetts to Trenton, having kept his travel plans to himself. On his arrival, Adams confronted his department heads. He declared his determination to end the Quasi-War, to support the peace mission, to reject Hamilton as Washington's replacement as head of the army, and to disband the army. His decisions left his cabinet shaken, appalled, and angry.

On May 5, in a vehement argument with McHenry, Adams rebuked him, denouncing Hamilton and mocking his ambitions while praising Jefferson. He concluded by demanding McHenry's resignation; McHenry resigned on May 12, making his letter effective at the end of June, to give Adams time to find a successor. Adams also wrote to Pickering, demanding his resignation; Pickering refused, citing his need for his government salary to support his family. Unmoved, Adams fired him a week later. This was the first time in American history that a president dismissed a cabinet member; Adams followed the "decision of 1789," by which the First Federal Congress recognized the president's constitutional power to fire heads of executive departments.[46] Though Adams kept Wolcott at the Treasury for the time being, he confined Wolcott to his Treasury responsibilities, barring him from discussions of war, peace, and foreign policy.[47]

Reorganizing his administration, Adams turned to John Marshall, who impressed him with his legal skill, his diplomatic record, and his loyalty.[48] At first, Adams wanted Marshall to become secretary of war, but, after dismissing Pickering, he nominated Marshall as secretary of state. Adams persuaded another ally, the Massachusetts politician Samuel Dexter, to lead the War Department. Wolcott resigned on December 31, 1800; Adams named Dexter secretary of the Treasury; Dexter also served as secretary of war through the end of Adams's term.

The Quasi-War raised domestic problems for Adams. In March 1799, federal taxes on dwelling houses, land, and slaves to raise revenue for the war sparked outrage in Pennsylvania; John Fries, a Continental Army veteran, organized a tax-resistance movement. After insurgents led by Fries clashed with local authorities, state militia, and US marshals, government officials arrested Fries and twenty-nine other men and tried them for treason and other crimes in federal court in Pennsylvania. Fries and two other defendants were convicted of treason and sentenced to hang. Reviewing their sentences, Adams decided that none of the convicted men had committed treason as defined by the Constitution. On May 21, 1800, in the face of his advisers' opposition, he pardoned all three men and granted amnesty to all participants in the rebellion. Notwithstanding Adams's generous measures, Pennsylvania's German voters, who had sided with Fries, voted against the Federalists in 1800.[49]

The 1800 election, which promised to be more stormy than that of 1796, was pivotal for the United States.[50] Federalists faced Republicans, but a dramatic split divided Federalist ranks, pitting Adams Federalists against High Federalists. The resulting fray seemed to nervous observers so bitter that it might tear the republic apart.

Republicans backed Thomas Jefferson and Aaron Burr; opposing them were Federalists John Adams and Charles C. Pinckney, a veteran of the XYZ mission. All four men were candidates for the presidency under the Constitution's definition of the process, but Federalists agreed that Adams was their choice for president and that Pinckney was their candidate for vice president; Republicans agreed that Jefferson was their candidate for president and that Burr was their choice for the vice presidency.

One Federalist who did not want Adams to have a second term was Alexander Hamilton. Angered by Adams's disbanding of the army and his canceling of Hamilton's plans for military preparedness, Hamilton launched a verbal war against Adams. He even sought to confront Adams again in person, demanding to know why the president had labeled him the head of a British faction and insisting on an apology for the slur. Hamilton echoed the preliminaries of an honor dispute—but Adams ignored Hamilton.

In October 1800, Hamilton published a furious, disdainful pamphlet eviscerating Adams's character and conduct. He hoped to circulate it privately among leading Federalists to persuade them to back Pinckney instead of Adams. Unfortunately for both men, the pamphlet leaked far beyond its intended audience. Republican operatives published a special edition "for the public" to spread Hamilton's intemperate attack far and wide. Instead of shifting the Federalists from Adams to Pinckney, Hamilton had proved that the Federalist partisan alliance was disintegrating, undermining both candidates and destroying his own stature as a Federalist leader. Even close friends of Hamilton bemoaned his imprudence and tactlessness.[51]

In this period, states held elections at different times of the year, rather than agreeing on one day in late fall (the modern practice). In the spring of 1800, the elections in New York City signaled the likelihood of a Republican victory nationwide; Burr devised and used new forms of electioneering and campaigning, overcoming the efforts of Hamilton and the Federalists. The Republicans carried

New York City and the state; further developments, state by state, confirmed the pattern foreshadowed by New York's results.

The 1800 election returns resembled those of 1796, with regional loyalties eclipsing party loyalties.[52] Adams (sixty-five votes) and Pinckney (sixty-four) finished one electoral vote apart, indicating Federalist planning to avoid a tie. But Adams finished eight votes behind Jefferson and Burr, who tied with seventy-three electoral votes each. This defeat was relatively close, rather than the national humiliation of historical myth.[53] The electoral results also indicated that the Republicans would capture both houses of Congress, ending Federalist majorities that had held Congress since 1789. Federalists complained after 1800 that the Constitution's three-fifths clause skewed the Electoral College results to favor Jefferson, a slave owner, arguing that the clause's augmentation of the representation of slave states in the House and thus in the Electoral College gave an unfair political edge to slave states. The three-fifths clause might have given states with large slave populations only a negligible advantage, in light of other factors at issue in 1800.[54]

With the omens of Republican success and Federalist failure arrived news of a family tragedy, making retirement increasingly welcome for John and Abigail Adams. On November 30, 1800, Charles Adams died, aged thirty, reportedly of cirrhosis of the liver.[55] (His widow, Sarah, known as Sally, had left him weeks before, taking their children with her; they visited with her mother. By the end of January 1800, Sally and her children went to live with Abigail.) With Charles's death, his father could mourn him; in later years, John even recognized that his insistence that Charles enter the law as a career might have contributed to his son's self-destruction.[56]

The Electoral College tie between Jefferson and Burr portended trouble for the nation. Competing interests tried to sway the lame-duck House of Representatives, which had the responsibility to break the tie. Although the Constitution specified how the House should decide a contested presidential election, political uncertainties put into play by the 1800 electoral-vote tie left the nation in a state of uncertainty.[57] Adams, whose third-place finish excluded him from consideration by the House, found bitter amusement in the election's results. He wrote to William Tudor, "Mr Hamilton has carried his Eggs to a fine Markett.... The ... very two Men, of all the World, that he was most jealous of, are now placed over him."[58]

Finding Jefferson dangerously radical and therefore unacceptable, some Federalists pondered making a deal with Burr. Burr was not tied to any particular set of principles; his supporters claimed, and Federalists agreed, that Burr was more open-minded and less ideologically rigid than Jefferson, and thus open to a deal by which he could win the presidency and Federalists could continue to shape policy. Alarmed at the threat of Burr allying himself with the Federalists, Jeffersonian Republicans demanded that Burr defer to Jefferson, which he was prepared to do, and that he declare himself unworthy to be president by comparison with Jefferson, which he was *not* prepared to do. Rejecting what he saw as a dishonorable slap at his fitness for leadership, Burr began to consider Federalist offers of support. Appalled, Hamilton wrote frantic letters to leading Federalists begging them not to back Burr—even at the price of accepting Jefferson. Hamilton pointed out that, though he disliked Jefferson's principles, Jefferson had principles, whereas, in Hamilton's eyes, Burr was committed only to forwarding his own career.[59]

Federalists alarmed by the tug of war between Jefferson and Burr in the House and unprepared to accept either suggested that Adams become a caretaker president—if need be, continuing beyond the end of his term of office. Stung by his defeat and increasingly looking forward to retirement, Adams rejected their proposal on principled and personal grounds. He was sick of the presidency and of politics, he declared; he wanted to rejoin Abigail in Quincy. Further, he insisted, he had to honor the people's decision to deny him a second term.

Adams and Jefferson had one last face-to-face meeting during the deadlock. According to Jefferson, Adams told him that he had the power to break the impasse: "You have only to say that you will do justice to the public creditors, maintain the navy, and not disturb those holding office, and the government will instantly be put into your hands." Jefferson declined to give such assurances, as they would violate his sense of integrity. He added, "It was the first time in our lives we had ever parted with anything like dissatisfaction."[60] Adams never wrote about this meeting, the only time that he played any direct role in the effort to resolve the electoral crisis.

Two weeks before the inauguration, the House broke the deadlock in Jefferson's favor on the thirty-sixth ballot. For the rest of his time in office, Adams worked to foster an orderly transfer of power. His actions during this crisis rendered a service to the nation and its constitutional system as great as Washington's in refusing to seek a third term. Adams's willingness to accept his defeat and to help smooth Jefferson's way to the presidency helped to ensure the first peaceful transfer of political authority from one partisan group to another under the Constitution. The 1800 presidential contest became a precedent governing later presidential elections.

The closing months of Adams's presidency gave rise to a myth that he sought political retribution against Republicans; the myth's focus was the federal judiciary, the Constitution's problem child. Since the federal courts began their work in 1790, federal judges had complained about their burdens—but their pleas for help went unanswered.[61] Though in 1799 Adams urged judicial reform, Congress ignored his suggestion. At the end of 1800, however, once the Federalists saw that the election had cost them the presidency and both houses of Congress, the need for judicial reform blended with partisanship to make the nation's courts a pressing subject.[62]

Article III, section 1, of the US Constitution authorizes "one supreme Court, and such other inferior Courts as the Congress may from time to time ordain and establish." This provision paralleled many states' approach to structuring their court systems—by enacting judiciary statutes. The Constitution's framers similarly left the federal judiciary's design to the first Congress under the

Constitution.[63] The Judiciary Act of 1789 created a three-tier court system, with the Supreme Court at its apex and federal district courts, with jurisdiction only over customs and revenue cases, at its base. Federal circuit courts, the middle layer, were the system's main trial courts, staffed by each state's US district judge and by two Supreme Court justices "riding circuit" from state to state. The statute divided the nation into three judicial circuits, Eastern, Middle, and Southern. Congress imposed circuit-riding on the justices to give them something to do while the Supreme Court's caseload developed, so that their idleness would not cause them to form dangerous ambitions.

Circuit-riding was onerous. Associate Justice James Iredell died in 1799 at forty-eight, after repeated complaints to his brethren about having to ride more than fifteen hundred miles, twice a year, on the Southern Circuit. Associate Justice Samuel Chase fell off his horse and nearly drowned while riding the Middle Circuit. For a decade, the justices petitioned Congress to reform the federal judiciary and lift their circuit-riding burden, but to no avail until early 1801.[64]

The Federalist effort at judicial reform produced the 1801 Judiciary Act, which freed the justices from the burden of circuit-riding and redesigned the federal judicial pyramid. District courts would henceforth be the main US trial courts. Each circuit court, with its own judges, would become an appellate court between that circuit's district courts and the Supreme Court. The justices would stick to the business of the Supreme Court. More important were two technical changes made by the 1801 statute that expanded the federal courts' caseload. First, the 1789 Judiciry Act had set the minimum "amount in controversy" (that is, the value of the legal dispute) for a case to be brought in federal court had to be $500. The 1801 statute lowered the amount in controversy to $100. Second, the 1801 statute for the first time empowered federal courts to hear cases posing federal questions under the Constitution and laws of the United States. These two new provisions dramatically expanded the number of cases that the federal courts could hear, enraging Jeffersonian Republicans, who already distrusted the federal judiciary.[65]

In his last two weeks in office, Adams nominated and the Senate confirmed loyal Federalists to the posts created by the 1801 Judiciary Act. These actions gave rise to the myth of the "midnight judges"—supposedly, Adams stayed up until well after midnight on his last day as president naming federal judges to the posts created by the 1801 act. Nominating and confirming federal judges are indeed complicated processes, too much so to make this tale possible, but the tale of the "midnight judges" seized the Republicans' imagination; they were ready to believe that Adams would treat them treacherously.[66]

As Congress struggled to redesign the judiciary, Adams faced a new vacancy on the Supreme Court. On December 5, he received a letter from Chief Justice Ellsworth. He sent Adams the Convention of 1800 (the Treaty of Mortefontaine), which ended the Quasi-War between France and the United States and resolved other disputes between the two nations. Having led the negotiations of that treaty, he also resigned from the Court, citing ill health.[67] Ellsworth's letter dumped a large problem into Adams's lap: Who should be Ellsworth's successor? Could Adams keep the Supreme Court's leadership in Federalist hands? Must he yield to pressure from High Federalist senators to name a chief justice acceptable to them though not to him? If he did not find a candidate acceptable to the Senate, would he have to leave the choice of a chief justice to his Republican successor? Should he listen to the entreaties of some Federalist senators and name himself chief justice?

Adams rejected the most often named candidates—Associate Justices William Cushing (too old and frail) and William Paterson (preferred by High Federalists). Instead, he nominated Governor John Jay of New York. He reasoned that Jay's familiarity with the Court (he had been its first chief justice) and the esteem he had from both High Federalists and Adams Federalists might make him an ideal candidate. The Senate swiftly confirmed him. Nobody had asked Jay whether he wanted the office, however. Writing Jay to inform him of his appointment, Adams conceded that he had not sought Jay's consent but assured him of the Senate's and his own high regard for him, as well as his confidence that Jay would do his duty to the nation and its courts.[68]

Adams rightly worried that Jay might decline reappointment. On January 2, 1801, Jay wrote a respectful but coldly blunt letter of refusal. He made his reasons clear—the burdens of the chief justiceship and the record of congressional indifference to the justices' pleas for help through the 1790s. Thanking Adams for the honor, Jay was firm in saying no.[69]

In mid-January, according to Marshall's account, Adams opened Jay's letter and informed Marshall, "Mr. Jay has declined his appointment." After a colloquy with Marshall, Adams declared, "I do not know whom I shall appoint. . . . I believe that I must appoint you."[70] Marshall suited Adams. He was young enough, at forty-five, to serve a long time as chief justice. Also, he was loyal to Adams, which pleased Adams and discomfited High Federalist senators. He was popular after his role in the XYZ Affair. He had diplomatic experience, fitting the era's view that the Court should be a source of expertise in national security and diplomacy.[71] Finally, he was a Virginian and a protégé of Washington. Thus, Adams solved the problems posed by Ellsworth's resignation. Reluctantly, the Senate confirmed Marshall; he served both as chief justice and as secretary of state for the remaining weeks of Adams's term.

Exhausted and knowing that Abigail needed him at home, Adams left the capital very early on March 4, 1801. There is no evidence for the myth that he refused to attend Jefferson's inauguration because he was deeply hurt by his defeat in 1800. The conditions of travel facing Adams were so inconvenient that a carriage leaving the nation's capital at 4:00 a.m. on inauguration day was his only chance for a swift exit. It appears that neither Adams nor Jefferson contemplated Adams's attendance at Jefferson's inauguration.[72]

Adams and Jefferson had a brief correspondence suggesting anything but bitterness or resentment on Adams's part. Writing just after the House made Jefferson president, Adams informed him that the seven horses and two carriages housed in the Executive Mansion's stables with harness and other property belonged to the United States; he added that "they will certainly save you a considerable Expence as they belong to the stud of the President's Household."[73] Adams wrote again to thank Jefferson for forwarding a letter addressed to "the President" that he had inadvertently opened, only to reseal it when he recognized that it was for Adams. Adams sadly informed Jefferson of the death of his son Charles, the subject of the forwarded letter. He added, "This part of the Union is in a state of perfect Tranquility and I See nothing to obscure your prospect of a quiet and prosperous Administration, which I heartily wish you."[74]

On November 2, 1800, his first night in the Executive Mansion, he had written to Abigail, "Before I end my Letter I pray Heaven to bestow the best of Blessings on this House and all that shall hereafter inhabit it. May none but honest and wise Men ever rule under this roof."[75] Did Adams deserve being numbered among those "honest and Wise men"?

When Adams became president, the "age of experiments in government" had come to an end. The thinking politicians focused on supervising experiments already established. Their greatest challenge was making sure that the government would continue as a workable system. In this new political world, politicians were tense and prone to overreaction. For anyone, it would have been a difficult time to become president. Fearful of appearing inadequate by contrast with his predecessor or his vanquished rival, unsure of the loyalty and competence of those serving under him, and wondering whether he could meet the obligations that he had sworn to undertake, Adams found being president "a splendid misery," as Jefferson called it.[76]

One of Adams's greatest achievements as president is that he proved that someone *not* George Washington could be president, showing that the office was not uniquely crafted to fit "the Father of His Country." Taking charge of the presidency and becoming his own man after Washington's death, Adams helped to shape the office in his own image. Only then could he show what a presidency tailored for him, suited to his intellect, personality, and political virtues, would look like. By then, however, it was too late to alter the public's views of him.

Adams was deeply proud that he had averted a disastrous war with France. Throughout that crisis, he drew on his expert awareness of diplomacy's pitfalls and possibilities. His patience steadied the nation's response to the crisis with France, enabling him to resolve that crisis and to stabilize French-American relations. He showed prudent firmness in resisting demands for war from the people and from his advisers.

Many scholars consider Adams's greatest presidential legacy his appointment of John Marshall to the Supreme Court. On August 17, 1825, Adams proudly wrote to Marshall: "There is no part of my Life that I look back on with more pleasure, than the short time I spent with you. And it is the pride of my life that I have given to this nation a Chief Justice equal to Coke or Hale, Holt or Mansfield."[77] Marshall was the most creative, politically adept chief justice in US history; his nationalist vision and legal skill raised the Court to an eminence rarely questioned.[78]

Adams not only accepted his defeat in 1800 but cooperated in making a smooth transition of power to Jefferson. He also spurned efforts by Federalists to persuade him to continue as a caretaker president after the end of his term. Adams thus helped to establish the tradition of orderly transitions of power from one party to another in presidential elections.

Given these achievements, Adams's presidency was not the failure that many have deemed it. Against these successes, we must revisit the greatest blots on his record—his signing the Sedition Act into law and his concurrence in enforcing it against critics of himself and his administration. To be sure, the statute was not unique. In England and in the states, the common-law crime of seditious libel was well known, and states also had sedition statutes. The difference between harsh laws on the books and freer, less stringent law as applied meant that most American printers felt free to publish, and in fact did publish, material that some viewed as seditious. Even so, we cannot dismiss the sedition prosecutions of 1798 to 1800. Further, the Sedition Act had an unintended consequence. It created a libertarian counterblast enshrining a new understanding of freedom of speech and press, recognizing the people's right to criticize their elected officials and their government, free of threat of prosecution. That libertarian counterblast helps explain why the Sedition Act is the indelible taint on Adams's presidency.[79]

On March 4, 1801, John Adams began his long trip home to Quincy and to Abigail. He was content to end his public career quietly and privately. He knew that he was entering the closing stage of his life—retirement and reflection.

Chapter Nine

"In dogmatizing, laughing, and scolding
I find delight"

Retirement and Reflection (1801–1812)

On March 17, 1801, two weeks after leaving Washington, DC, John Adams reached Peacefield, his home in Quincy. Until his death in 1826, this house was his home. In keeping the name Peacefield, he was commemorating one of his presidency's greatest triumphs—his avoidance of war with France in 1800. (Later in his life, he jokingly named the house Montezillo—Italian for "little hill," half in emulation and half in mockery of Jefferson's Monticello.)[1] Living with him were Abigail and the widow and children of their son Charles. He and Abigail enjoyed frequent visits by their son Thomas Boylston Adams and less frequent visits by their other surviving children, Abigail Adams Smith and John Quincy Adams.

Adams was the second former president of the United States, but in 1801 the modern role of ex-president did not yet exist; its invention awaited Jefferson's retirement in 1809.[2] In 1797, when George Washington left the presidency, he was still the acclaimed "first citizen" of the United States—but the national veneration he received owed more to his service during the Revolution than to his presidency. At his death, his countrymen identified him with the Revolution and the creation of the American nation, mourning him as "the first of men" and (in a phrase borrowed from the Roman

Republic) the "father of his country."[3] In 1812, Adams speculated sourly that, if Washington had not died in 1799, the Virginian would have allowed himself to be persuaded to stand for a third term as president in 1800, and probably would have won.[4]

As the first president defeated for re-election, Adams played a unique role in the history of the presidency; his defeat thrust him into obscurity rather than into eminence. Few recognized what posterity has come to admire—Adams's sense of fair play in relinquishing the presidency after his defeat in 1800 and in ensuring a peaceful transition from the Federalists to the Republicans. Despite his willingness to leave office as a defeated former president, his bitterness at having been rejected by the people hung like a storm cloud over his first years in retirement. Adams felt that rejection especially keenly because he contrasted it with his lifetime of public service and the high points of his administration.

Soon after his return, the members of the Massachusetts state legislature journeyed from Boston to Quincy to pay Adams honor and to thank him for his decades of public service. Though the occasion moved him to tears, as the first time that a public body had done him honor,[5] it was the only such visit. For the rest of his life, Adams had visits only from family members and a few friends; his retirement was quiet. His electoral defeat led too many of his fellow citizens to forget him; few sought his opinions on issues of the day, and, reluctant to expose himself to further political brickbats, he decided to keep his opinions to himself or to share them only with family members and trusted friends.

Convinced that the people had spurned and forgotten him, Adams veered between accepting his situation and complaining about it. When he complained, the usual suspects were at hand—his principal foe, Hamilton; his adversaries among the Federalists, notably Pickering; his erstwhile friend and victorious rival, Jefferson; the august Washington; the venerated Franklin; and lesser players, the journalist-printers who had used him as a convenient target.

Adams was struggling to decide what to do with his remaining years. The question of his future was pressing; the United States had no system of presidential pensions, and he was at a loss to know how to support himself and his family. He briefly considered resuming the practice of law, but he gave up that idea because of his age (he was sixty-five in 1801), his years away from the bar, and the loss of his teeth, which would have garbled any attempt he made to address a judge or a jury.

Adams's financial situation worsened soon after his return home. While in Europe, John Quincy Adams had transferred his parents' and his own funds overseas to a London bank, Bird, Savage, and Bird. But, in the spring of 1803, the younger Adams discovered to his horror that the bank had failed, taking with it $18,000 of his parents' funds as well as $13,000 of his own money. Blaming himself for not having monitored the bank's fortunes, John Quincy Adams reorganized the family's finances. As part of his plan, he made a series of gradual purchases from his father of the family mansion and its adjoining lands; he used the payments of the purchase price to create an annuity supporting his parents, while granting them a life estate in Peacefield. John Quincy Adams's financial acumen and his ability to recover swiftly from a disaster helped ease his parents' financial worries. Nonetheless, John Adams reproached himself for his preference for investments in land, instead of heeding advice (particularly from Abigail) to liquidate some of his holdings and make use of the cash.[6]

His financial future put on a secure footing by his son's management, Adams lived quietly, receiving the occasional visitor and sitting in his study and looking out the window as he smoked. As long as his health permitted it, he worked side by side with the hired workers who cultivated his farm. He also made repairs to the house and to stone fences on the property. For the most part, he lived the life of the mind, reading widely and deeply on a host of subjects, including comparative religion and government, and revisiting the political battles of his life.

John Adams's retirement is a story of intellectual adventures— of exploring new ideas, bodies of knowledge, and the world of the past. Like other Founding Fathers, he faced an increasing flow of letters seeking his recollections of the Revolution, in particular the year 1776. These inquiries stimulated his memories and spurred his desire to represent himself to the inquirers, and to posterity, as a leading figure of the Revolution. With each such letter, Adams felt a more urgent need to explain himself and the history that he had helped to make.

Though he had abandoned thoughts of resuming his law practice, Adams's focus on the past committed him to a different kind of law-yering, with himself as his client—pleading his own case for his life and career, with posterity as the court. Having left office repudiated and disgraced (as he saw it), Adams wanted to turn his back on politics and government, to lose himself in family concerns and running his home and his farm—and yet he wanted to justify himself to his countrymen and to the future.

Adams's efforts to defend his legacy and to shape his historical reputation resembled the actions of such other leading Founding Fathers as Thomas Jefferson and James Madison. Their last great battle was to demonstrate that they deserved to be remembered. In particular, Adams hoped that what his contemporaries seemed to have denied him—gratitude and remembrance—future generations would grant him. But he would receive that gratitude and remembrance from them only if they understood why he deserved them. He hoped that posterity would form a just estimate of his efforts—one, he hoped, that would not be tainted by ignorance, malice, or prejudice.[7]

Aided by his sons, Adams launched a valiant effort to organize his massive collection of papers—the raw material from which he planned to make his case for himself at the bar of history. These papers spanned his busy and eventful life and also generations of Adams family history stretching back to the early seventeenth century. Exploring his family's past, he thought, was essential to understanding and explaining his own story. The process took months, but at last, his papers in order, Adams was ready to take up his pen.

Adams then began to write his autobiography, which he launched with great energy in 1802. He worked on it intermittently for the next five years, breaking off in 1807, when he had reached the middle of the year 1780. The manuscript comprises 440 pages, divided into three parts—"John Adams," "Travels and Negotiations," and "Peace." The first part, completed in 1802, addressed both his own life and, as prologue, his family's history from the first Henry Adams's arrival in America. He completed the second part in 1806 and left the third part unfinished. At first, Adams wrote from memory, but he made extensive use of his papers, incorporating and reworking extracts from his diaries and letters into his autobiography.[8]

A prolific and assiduous correspondent, Adams drew on his past in writing letters, many of which read like draft material awaiting amalgamation into his autobiography. Adams wrote letters for many reasons beyond communication with his correspondents. He wanted to clarify his thinking, to test ideas, to retell stories of his life, and to revive friendship with former political friends and allies. The most notable early example of this last use is his rich and intimate correspondence with the Pennsylvania physician, revolutionary, and public servant Benjamin Rush, spanning the years from 1805 until Rush's death in 1813.[9] Adams explained to Rush his use of letter writing: "[Samuel] Johnson said when he sat upon his throne in a tavern, there he dogmatized and was contradicted, and in this he found delight. My throne is not in a tavern, but at my fireside. There I dogmatize, there I laugh, and there the newspapers sometimes make me scold, and in dogmatizing, laughing, and scolding I find delight, and why should I not enjoy it, since no one is the worse for it, and I am the better."[10]

Though Rush was more than ten years younger than Adams, the two men had much in common. Both had served as delegates to the Second Continental Congress, both had signed the Declaration of Independence, and both had played prominent and controversial roles in winning independence. Rush counted Adams and Jefferson among his valued friends, though he charted an independent political course, allowing him to maintain cordial relations with both even as politics divided them. Rush also shared with Adams a simmering resentment of George Washington. During the Revolutionary War, when he was inspector general of the Continental Army's medical facilities, Rush clashed bitterly with Washington, who engineered his dismissal. For the rest of his life, Rush insisted that Washington had showed criminal indifference to the health of the men under his command. Adams sympathized with Rush's wounded feelings, for they paralleled his own resentment, which sometimes broke through the surface of his letters, of Washington's eclipse of Adams despite what Adams deemed to be Washington's meager talents. In one letter, Adams presented for Rush's edification a list of ten reasons that Washington was deemed a great man and then pointed out: "Here you see that I have made out a list of ten talents without saying a word about reading, thinking, or writing."[11]

Opening their hearts to each other through their frank and candid letters, Adams and Rush recognized that they were kindred spirits. For example, both not only loved their country and were proud of their respective parts in the Revolution that gave it birth but also were thin-skinned when contemplating the injuries that they had suffered from those whom posterity had anointed as the Revolution's leading figures. In writing to Rush, Adams could not resist sniping at Franklin and Jefferson. In particular, he enjoyed drawing contrasts between his and Jefferson's administrations— always to Jefferson's discredit.[12] Further, as Adams pointed out, Washington, Franklin, and Jefferson shared a valuable trait, the gift of silence, that neither he nor Rush had.[13] Adams's correspondence with Rush evoked from him a broad, generous sense of humor about himself, Rush, the claims of history, and the vicissitudes of politics.

On January 8, 1810, Adams wrote to another friend, Judge Joseph Ward, a newsy and chatty letter that took up the subject of Jefferson. In the course of his criticisms, Adams not only cited the Virginian's funding of journalists and printers to attack Adams but addressed a charge made by one particular printer formerly in Jefferson's employ. Adams addressed the publication in 1802 by James Thomson Callendar of charges that Jefferson had had a sexual relationship with one of his slaves, Sally Hemings. Though Adams noted that Callendar was so untrustworthy that "I believe nothing that Callendar Said, any more than if it had been said by an Infernal Spirit," he also discussed Callendar's accusation, its source, and its consequences. Adams made clear that he saw the Hemings-Jefferson liaison as directly attributable to the existence of "Negro Slavery"; for him, such reports, true or not, exemplified "infamy . . . [and] black Licentiousness." This letter illustrates the feelings on race intermingled with slavery that occasionally emerged in Adams's reflections and letters:

> Callender and Sally will be remembered as long as Jefferson as Blotts in his Character. The story of the latter, is a natural and almost unavoidable Consequence of that foul contagion in the human Character Negro Slavery. In the West Indies and the Southern States it has the Same Effect. A great Lady has Said She did not believe there was a Planter in Virginia who could not reckon among his Slaves a Number of his Children. But is it Sound Policy will it promote Morality, to keep up the Cry of such disgracefull Stories, now the Man is voluntarily retired from the World. The more the Subject is canvassed will not the horror of the Infamy be diminished? and this black Licentiousness be encouraged?[14]

Another friend with whom Adams corresponded eagerly was Dr. Benjamin Waterhouse. Nearly twenty years younger than Adams, Waterhouse had been a student at the University of Leyden in the Netherlands in the early 1780s; he and Adams had roomed in the same boardinghouse during Adams's mission to the Netherlands, and the doctor had befriended the diplomat and his son John Quincy. Waterhouse became a leading American physician, distinguishing himself by his research and experiments in combating smallpox; after his work spurred controversy, he reached out to the senior Adams as a kindred spirit and an old friend. Their correspondence continued, by fits and starts, until nearly the end of Adams's life.[15]

Just as Adams told Waterhouse that the young physician had much in common with Rush, Adams's letters to Waterhouse resemble his letters to Rush—wide-ranging, philosophical, and playful. For example, in 1805, thanking Waterhouse for a pamphlet on tobacco, Adams held forth in two letters about his own uses of tobacco and his matured skepticism about it.[16] Adams also wrote revealingly to Dr. Waterhouse about his evolving feelings about his political career. For example, on March 13, 1811, after President Madison had dismissed Secretary of State Robert Smith, who took his case to the people by publishing a pamphlet, Adams expostulated to Waterhouse on the plight of a president dealing with an incompetent and recalcitrant secretary of state. The Smith crisis reminded him of his own struggles with Timothy Pickering:

> Must a President publish a justificatory Proclamation containing all his Reasons, for dismissing a Secretary of State? And when every one of his Reasons is contradicted, misrepresented, abused, insulted, must he answer all these Libels? How many Clerks and Secretaries must he employ? or must he write all this himself? Twenty Scribes would not be sufficient. What would become of the Business of the State? . . .
>
> Suppose a President has a Secretary, fastened upon him by a Predecessor, whom he finds incompetent to the high Duties of his office, and thinks it necessary to dismiss him for his Incapacity; or suppose he knows another, infinitely better qualified; must he reveal the whole History of his Administration, and detail every Fact upon which he grounded his Opinion? Every Fact will be denied, every Inference disputed. How long must the Controversy continue[?] It will be a Subject of dispute with Posterity as well as the present Age.[17]

Similarly, in 1805 Adams treated Dr. Waterhouse to a memorable blast against the fame of another favorite target, Thomas Paine, as a symbol of the Age of Reason:

> I am willing you should call this the Age of Frivolity as you do; and would not object if you had named it the Age of Folly, Vice, Frenzy, Fury, Brutality, Daemons, Buonaparte, Tom Paine, or the Age of the bottomless Pitt: or anything but the Age of Reason. I know not whether any Man in the World has had more influence on its inhabitants or affairs for the last thirty years than Tom Paine. There can be no severer Satyr on the Age. For such a mongrel between Pigg and Puppy, begotten by a wild Boar on a Bitch Wolf, never before in any Age of the World was suffered by the Poltroonery of mankind, to run through such a career of mischief. Call it then the Age of Paine.[18]

Another of Adams's correspondents was Francis Adrian Van der Kemp, a Dutch Mennonite clergyman and writer whom Adams had met in Holland during his service as American minister in the 1780s. In 1788, Van der Kemp fled Holland to escape persecution and settled in upstate New York. The two men maintained an episodic, wide-ranging correspondence on matters as diverse as religion, natural history, government, religious freedom, and their memories. Both John and John Quincy Adams exchanged letters with Van der Kemp, and John Quincy Adams maintained contact with Van der Kemp until his death.[19]

In 1807, Adams launched another correspondence under less happy circumstances, and with far more painful emotions. He and Abigail had long been friends with James Warren and his wife, the essayist, poet, and historian Mercy Otis Warren, the sister of Adams's old hero James Otis. In 1805, Mercy Otis Warren published her *History of the Rise, Progress, and Termination of the American Revolution*. This book, the first history of the United States written by a woman, presented its author's strong-minded version of the recent past, critically viewing the development of the United States since independence.[20] Mrs. Warren told a tale of decline from patriotic virtue and selflessness to greed, luxury, and decadence, in which the promise of the Revolution had been lost. A vigorous opponent of the Constitution during the ratification controversy of 1787–88, Mrs. Warren showed no inclination to temper her opinions, even when they might be critical of old friends; Adams was both an old friend and a target. Critics and readers alike welcomed Mrs. Warren's history as one of the most valuable accounts of the Revolution. President Jefferson predicted that her book "will furnish a more instructive lesson to mankind than any equal period known in history."[21] Adams did not know of Jefferson's praise for Mrs. Warren's volumes, but he did not share Jefferson's high opinion of them.

In 1807, Adams began to read Mrs. Warren's *History*—and was aghast at what he found there, particularly her treatment of him and his diplomatic and political service. Adams discovered that he was a key figure in her denunciation of the corruption and degradation eroding the Revolution's democratic promise. She charged him with ambition for seeking appointment after appointment and office after office. Worse yet, she accused him of having been corrupted by his years in Europe, returning to the United States as a monarchist:

> Mr. Adams was undoubtedly a statesman of penetration and ability; but his prejudices and his passions were sometimes too strong for his sagacity and judgment.
>
> ... Mr. Adams ... resided [in England] four or five years; and unfortunately for himself and his country, he became so enamoured with the British constitution, and the government, manners, and laws of the nation, that a partiality for monarchy appeared, which was inconsistent with his former professions of republicanism. Time and circumstances often lead so imperfect a creature as man to view the same thing in a very different point of light.
>
> After Mr. Adams's return from England, he was implicated by a large portion of his countrymen, as having relinquished the republican system, and forgotten the principles of the American revolution, which he had advocated for near twenty years.[22]

Though these and other accusations in Mrs. Warren's pages echoed charges against him that he had had to endure as vice president and as president, it was different for Adams to see them set forth in a book, in a historical work addressed to posterity, written by someone whom he had thought of as a friend. Beginning on July 11, 1807, and continuing for nearly a month, Adams wrote ten long, hurt, angry letters to Mrs. Warren, defending himself and disputing what he insisted was her unfair treatment of him.[23] Though at first he tried to preserve a tone compatible with the long friendship between the Adamses and the Warrens, he could not restrain himself. Soon an anguished, hectoring tone crept into his letters:

> Corruption! Madam, I shall not very easily or very soon quit this topic; and I have a right to demand of you, and of General Warren, too, a more explicit acknowledgment of my uncorrupted integrity than any you have made in your History.... I would not hesitate to appeal to all Europe, and am confident you would not find one man or woman who would question my integrity in any transaction of mine abroad, public or private.[24]

Adams followed his usual writing practice of tracking his source, chapter by chapter and paragraph by paragraph, amassing qualifications, refutations, and disputations. Infuriated and astonished by his tirades, Mrs. Warren wrote back six equally long, angry, and pointed letters, defending her book and herself. The correspondence makes painful reading. Adams became increasingly distraught as he sought to refute what he deemed libels on his character and his reputation. Mrs. Warren fought equally hard for her work's integrity and her right to present her opinions, even at the risk of wounding an old friend. Each became more offended with the other, more angry and defensive. Mrs. Warren closed the correspondence with a pointed reproof:

> I now forbear further remarks. The lines with which you concluded your late correspondence cap the climax of rancor, indecency, and

vulgarism. Yet, as an old friend, I pity you; as a Christian, I forgive you; but there must be some acknowledgment of your injurious treatment or some advances to conciliation, to which my mind is ever open, before I can again feel that respect and affection towards Mr. Adams which once existed in the bosom of—Mercy Warren.[25]

Despite Mrs. Warren's efforts to maintain friendly relations with Abigail Adams, and despite an attempt in 1814 by John Adams to offer an olive branch to Mrs. Warren, the damage between them was done; they never resumed their former friendship.[26]

Concern for his reputation combined with smoldering anger against another foe (this one deceased) led Adams back into the political arena in 1809. Breaking his public silence for the first time since his return to Massachusetts, Adams launched what became a series of newspaper articles in the *Boston Patriot* lasting three years.[27] He began by responding to a public letter in the *Patriot* from two Massachusetts members of the US House, Erastus Lyman and Daniel Wright, seeking his counsel in a time when the United States confronted Europe at war. Seeing parallels between 1809 and the Quasi-War of 1798–1800, when the nation also had faced a war between Britain and France, Adams published his answer in the *Patriot* on March 24, 1809. As he continued writing letters, he was drawn into composing and publishing a lengthy defense, in essay installments, of his presidency and his public career.

Adams shifted his focus from a general defense to a particular attack—refuting the charges made against him by Alexander Hamilton in his 1800 pamphlet assailing Adams's character and conduct. The tone and substance of Adams's essays shifted from refuting Hamilton's charges to attacking Hamilton, voicing the anger that he had nursed against Hamilton for more than a decade. Yet again, Adams followed his preferred method in his longer theoretical and polemical writings, presenting an almost line-by-line response to Hamilton's pamphlet. With each correction and contradiction, Adams struck a blow at an antagonist who for him was very much alive, given that Hamilton's pamphlet lay open on his desk. It is not clear why the printer of the Boston *Patriot* bore with Adams's torrent of essays explaining, defending, justifying, and attacking—in particular attacking Hamilton, a man five years in his grave.

That Hamilton was dead did not matter to Adams, for his own feelings of anger and injury were as vivid as ever. The hurts inflicted on Adams by Hamilton's intemperate attack were fresh in his mind; his need to defend himself and repair his standing in the eyes of posterity drove him onward. Another possible reason for the timing of Adams's newspaper defense of himself was that he began only after Jefferson had left the presidency and returned to private life at Monticello. His restraint was a matter of propriety that, in various forms, has guided subsequent ex-presidents. Adams chose to remain in the private realm while his old adversary was the nation's chief executive; only after Jefferson had relinquished the presidency and returned to private life did Adams feel able to re-enter the public sphere.

Adams's re-emergence in the political arena perplexed and dismayed one of his other correspondents, a distant relative and Federalist political operative named William Cunningham, who had begun corresponding with him in 1803.[28] In their letters, Cunningham repeatedly sought to elicit from Adams quotable attacks on Jefferson or the Republicans for use against Jefferson in the 1804 election. Still smarting from his defeat in 1800, Adams obliged, though he set a condition for his candor: none of his letters could be published until after his death. Though frustrating Cunningham's purpose, that restriction did not affect the correspondence, which continued intermittently for several years.

Beginning in 1809, however, after Adams began his Boston *Patriot* essays and asked Cunningham what he thought of them, Cunningham responded with a mix of agitation and criticism. He questioned Adams's loyalty to the Federalists and attacked Adams for having abandoned them. Cunningham charged Adams with attacking Hamilton and the Federalists, of whom Hamilton had been a martyred leader, under the pretense of defending himself. As Adams ignored his reproofs, Cunningham raised the stakes. He hinted that he would violate the rule of secrecy that Adams had set for their correspondence and publish their letters while Adams was alive. Aware of the danger posed by his agitated relative, Adams reminded Cunningham of his pledge of secrecy. He then backed off, at first writing guardedly and then declining to answer Cunningham's increasingly troubled letters. In 1812, after a series of bitter, hectoring letters that Adams left unanswered, Cunningham stopped writing. Hoping that Cunningham's silence meant that the business was closed, Adams put the correspondence out of his mind.

Jefferson, by contrast, remained on Adams's mind for reasons beyond their former political rivalry, or others' attempts to elicit criticism of the Virginian from him—and both men were on Benjamin Rush's mind. As Adams and Rush exchanged warm, friendly, and ruminative letters, Rush repeatedly suggested to Adams and to Jefferson that they resume writing to each other. Whenever either man referred to the other in favorable terms, or whenever either man mentioned anything else that provided Rush an opening, the warmhearted doctor seized the opportunity to urge each man to make overtures to the other.[29]

There already had been a brief exchange of letters between Quincy and Monticello that Rush did not know about—one between Abigail Adams and Thomas Jefferson, which did not end as Rush would have wished. In 1804, Jefferson's younger daughter, Maria Jefferson Eppes, died after a difficult childbirth, as her mother had; she was less than four months shy of turning twenty-seven. Abigail had been close to Maria in the 1780s when the little girl had been sent to Europe to live with her father, so Maria's death moved Abigail to write Jefferson a condolence letter. Even on such an occasion, she felt deeply the partisan wounds from the election of 1800. Not just the storm of abuse and criticism that had buffeted her husband rankled with Abigail. One casualty of Jefferson's purging opponents from government jobs to make way for supporters was

John Quincy Adams, who lost his post as magistrate in the US district court for Massachusetts; no loyal mother could forgive such a crass political move. She therefore signed her letter as "one who once took pleasure in subscribing herself your friend."[30]

Choosing to ignore her ominous closing, Jefferson wrote a warm and friendly response.[31] To his astonishment, Abigail rejected his friendliness, taking him to task for actions by himself and his allies that were unfriendly to her husband and her family.[32] Abigail was a firm, vigorous, and determined antagonist, giving and asking no quarter. Though Jefferson defended himself as best he could, Abigail remained unmoved, closing the correspondence with a curt observation: "I will not Sir any further intrude upon your time."[33] She distilled this short, sharp exchange of letters in the phrase, "Faithfull are the wounds of a friend."[34] Soon after she broke off their correspondence, she showed the exchange of letters to John, who penned a terse note of his own declaring that he had no comment to make.[35]

In 1811, answering one of Rush's hopeful letters proposing reconciliation, Jefferson forwarded to Rush copies of his exchange of letters with Abigail Adams, implying that Rush's hopes were doomed. Jefferson added a sad reflection: "Judge for yourself whether they admit a revival of that friendly intercourse for which you are so kindly solicitous."[36] Nonetheless, Rush took each hopeful sign from the two estranged comrades as reason to hope that their friendship could be restored. By contrast, Adams treated Rush's entreaties with self-mocking wit. Writing on Christmas Day 1811, Adams challenged Rush directly, though jokingly: "I see plainly that you have been teasing Jefferson to write to me, or me to write to him." What reason, he asked, could justify resuming their correspondence? Why, he asked Rush, should he write to Jefferson or should Jefferson write to him, unless each were to wish the other an easy journey to the grave? Adams continued in this vein, and then he dropped a sly hint: "Time or chance, however, or possibly design, may produce ere long a letter between us."[37]

Though he did not tell Rush, he had made his decision. The "time" that he mentioned was one week. On New Year's Day 1812, he wrote Jefferson a gentle, friendly letter hinting at the delivery of a gift—two pieces of "homespun" from a person in whose education Jefferson had taken an interest. What Adams referred to as "two pieces of homespun" actually was a book, a two-volume set of lectures on rhetoric and oratory by John Quincy Adams, then Boylston Professor of Rhetoric at Harvard.[38]

The letter signed and the package and letter mailed, Adams awaited developments. The letter and the package separated in the mail, the letter arriving before the books. But Adams did not know that yet. As 1811 faded into 1812, he had taken a remarkable step that signaled his emergence from the cloud of despondency and resentment that had enveloped him after his electoral defeat in 1800. Relishing his restored sense of humor and his renewed spirits, Adams was about to enter on one of the intellectually richest and most satisfying periods of his life. He was ready to become the Sage of Quincy.

Chapter Ten

"What do We mean by the Revolution?"

The Sage of Quincy (1812–1826)

John Adams's decision to resume contact with Thomas Jefferson launched a new chapter of his retirement and a new conception of himself. He not only was free to rebuild his friendship with the Sage of Monticello but also was free to become a sage himself, based in Quincy. In this last period of his life, Adams read, wrote letters, conversed with visitors, enjoyed his family, and faced the growing burdens and lessons of old age. Just as, generations later, Henry David Thoreau wrote in *Walden*, "I have traveled a good deal in Concord,"[1] Adams traveled a good deal in Quincy.

Adams and Jefferson never saw each other in the years left to them, but their correspondence revived and deepened their friendship. Rich with reflection, argument, humor, and wisdom, their letters became a literary monument to the strength of friendship and to the power of words.[2] Their correspondence helped to define the central theme of the last fourteen years of John Adams's life, which echoed through his other letters and his conversations: exploration of the American Revolution and its meaning for the present and for posterity.

Adams and Jefferson offered each other a remarkable mix of reminiscence, history, prophecy, philosophy, religion, speculation, literature, and language. They exchanged congratulations on the fall of Napoleon in 1815 and shared their alarm about Pope Pius VIII's

1814 revival of the Jesuits. They shared their opinions on Plato and on Native Americans. They compared reading lists and swapped news of contemporaries. Only in the few years before their deaths in 1826 did old age diminish the river of letters passing between the two men. This correspondence was the core of the last phase of John Adams's life.

Receiving Adams's New Year's Day 1812 letter before the package, Jefferson eagerly wrote back on January 21, 1812.[3] Whatever hurt feelings he had described to Rush seemed to dissolve as he read Adams's letter. If anything, Jefferson's response was even more sincere in friendship and in affectionate memory of their labors together in the cause of independence. Jefferson assumed that Adams was serious about the pieces of homespun that were supposed to accompany his letter. Thus, he treated Adams to a thoughtful, informative disquisition on homespun and how desirable it would be for Americans to promote its making. In closing, he shifted back to a warm meditation on their former friendship and the happy prospect of resuming it. A few days after the arrival of Adams's letter, the package containing the "homespun" surfaced in the Charlottesville post office and made its way to Monticello, where Jefferson welcomed it with approving comments about John Quincy Adams's scholarship and writing.[4]

Adams wrote nearly four letters to Jefferson for every one that Jefferson wrote to him, at one point noting the difference in output but reassuring Jefferson: "Never mind it, my dear Sir, if I write four Letters to your one: your one is worth more than my four."[5] Seeking to put their disagreement from 1804 aside, Abigail added a postscript to one of Adams's letters, and twice wrote to Jefferson independently, prompting him to write back.

Sadly for both men, the friend who had worked unceasingly to reunite them died on April 19, 1813, of typhus fever, little more than a year after his campaign to reconcile Adams and Jefferson had triumphed. Jefferson lamented, "Another of our friends of 76. is gone, my dear Sir, another of the Co-signers of the independance of our country. and a better man, than Rush, could not have left us, more benevolent, more learned, of finer genius, or more honest."[6] Adams agreed: "I lament with you the loss of Rush. I know of no Character living or dead, who has done more real good in America."[7]

Hungry for an intellectual sparring partner, each man jumped from subject to subject, from the antiquarian to the philosophical to the literary to the political, often in the same letter. Each recognized that he needed the other as friend and intellectual counterpart. As Jefferson wrote to Adams, "Why am I dosing you with these Antediluvian topics? because I am glad to have some one to whom they are familiar, and who will not recieve them as if dropped from the moon."[8] They sought to entertain each other with unexpected reflections on great themes, as when Adams listed what he had learned from Plato, a philosopher whom both men detested:

> Two things only did I learn from him. 1. that Franklins Ideas of exempting Husbandmen and Mariners &c, from the depredations of War, were borrowed from him. 2. that Sneezing is a cure for the Hickups. Accordingly I have cured myself and all my Friends of that provoking disorder, for thirty years with a Pinch of Snuff.[9]

Sometimes, Adams could not resist baiting Jefferson on politics past and present, but he forsook combative anguish (as in his letters to Mercy Otis Warren about her *History*) for playful mockery. One fine example is the letter that he sent Jefferson on July 13, 1813, exploring a central and long-standing political difference between them:

> The first time, that you and I differed in Opinion on any material Question; was after your arrival from Europe; and that point was the french Revolution.
>
> You was well persuaded in your own mind that the Nation would succeed in establishing a free Republican Government: I was as well persuaded, in mine, that a project of such a Government, over five and twenty millions of people, when four and twenty

millions and five hundred thousands of them could neither write nor read: was as unnatural irrational and impracticable; as it would be over the Elephants Lions Tigers Panthers Wolves and Bears in the Royal Menagerie, at Versailles.[10]

At the same time, delighting in his bibliophilia, he reported the happiness and frustration that he felt as his friends "Overwhelm me with Books from all Quarters"—rhetorically asking himself and Jefferson: "What Should I do, with all this lumber? I make my 'Woman kind' as the Antiquary expresses it, read to me, All the English: but as they will not read the French, I am obliged to excruciate my Eyes to read it myself. And all to what purpose? I verily believe I was as wise and good, Seventy Years ago, as I am now."[11] Still, he kept reading. Jefferson marveled at his friend's energy:

> Forty three volumes read in one year, and 12. of them quartos! dear Sir, how I envy you! half a dozen [octavos] in that space of time are as much as I am allowed. I can read by candlelight only, and stealing long hours from my rest; nor would that time be indulged to me, could I, by that light, see to write. from sun-rise to one or two aclock, and often from dinner to dark, I am drudging at the writing table. and all this to answer letters into which neither interest nor inclination on my part enters; and often for persons whose names I have never before heard. yet, writing civilly, it is hard to refuse them civil answers. this is the burthen of my life, a very grievous one indeed, and one which I must get rid of.[12]

In particular, Adams shared his extensive reading on comparative religion—he was particularly fond of a twelve-volume study by Charles Francois Dupuis, *Origin de tous les cultes* (*Origin of All Religious Worship*), to which he devoted letter after letter. An envious Jefferson answered, "Your undertaking the 12. vols of Dupuis is a degree of heroism to which I could not have aspired even in my younger days."[13] Both men also exchanged musings on the classics, philosophy, and aristocracy.

Aristocracy became a regular theme for Adams and Jefferson, who disagreed about the nature of aristocracy, having differing conceptions of the term. Adams disputed Jefferson's insistence that there is a natural aristocracy among men, grounded in virtue and talent; he insisted that a wide range of personal qualities can make someone an aristocrat. Thus, Adams concluded, we could not define a solely natural aristocracy but had to provide for possible threats to balanced constitutional government from various kinds of aristocracy. Adams complained that, though he had written on aristocracy for much of his life, "I have been So unfortunate as never to be able to make myself understood." He added, "Your [aristocrats] are the most difficult Animals to manage, of any thing in the whole Theory and practice of Government. They will not Suffer themselves to be governed."[14]

In an extensive exchange of letters between Adams and the Virginia agrarian writer John Taylor of Caroline, Taylor rejected the idea of aristocracy altogether, insisting that the United States had perfected popular sovereignty and eliminated the different orders of mankind that classical political thought recognized. In his letters to Taylor, Adams gave no ground, maintaining the position that he had taken in the *Defence of the Constitutions*, but he admitted to Jefferson his amusement ("I gravely composed my risible muscles") that Taylor took his *Defence* so seriously when nobody else did: "Is it Oberon? Is it queen Mab, that reigns and Sports with Us little Beings? I thought my Books as well as myself were forgotten. But behold! I am to become a great Man in my expiring moments."[15]

Occasionally Adams and Jefferson plunged into such metaphysical questions as whether they would be willing to live their lives over again. Adams called the letter in which he launched that discussion "the most frivolous letter, you ever read."[16] Undaunted, Jefferson jumped into the subject as well, and both men gravely delivered their judgments on whether they would relive their lives or accept annihilation.

They treated one constellation of subjects with deadly seriousness—the history of the Revolution, their own places in that history, and the conflict between posterity's need to understand that history and the forces threatening to deprive later generations of reliable historical knowledge. For example, writing to Jefferson on July 30, 1815, Adams demanded, "Who shall write the History of the American Revolution? Who can write it? Who will ever be able to write it?"[17] Adams noted that extemporaneous speeches had not been preserved, and that texts of preserved speeches veered from hearers' recollections of what those speakers actually said. Some weeks later, he again asked Jefferson about the Revolution, but this time his focus was different—exploring "ideas [that] may be peculiar, perhaps singular":

> What do We mean by the Revolution? The War? That was no part of the Revolution. It was only an Effect and Consequence of it. The Revolution was in the Minds of the People, and this was effected, from 1760 to 1775, in the course of fifteen years before a drop of blood was drawn at Lexington. The Records of thirteen Legislatures, the Pamplets, Newspapers in all the Colonies ought be consulted, during that Period, to ascertain the Steps by which the public opinion was enlightened and informed concerning the Authority of Parliament over the Colonies.[18]

Preserving his preoccupation with the Revolution, Adams often took it upon himself to defend the place in history of friends and relatives—particularly his cousin Samuel Adams. In 1814, Adams noted sadly, "I am sometimes afraid that my 'Machine' will not 'Surcease motion' Soon enough; for I dread nothing So much as 'dying at top' and expiring like Dean [Jonathan] Swift 'a driveller and a Show' or like Sam. Adams, a Grief and distress to his Family, a weeping helpless Object of Compassion for years."[19] Five years later, he upbraided his former law student William Tudor for seeming to want to downgrade a man whom Adams revered as a key leader of the Revolution in Massachusetts: "You seem to wish me to write something to diminish the fame of Samuel Adams to show that he was not a man of profound learning, a great lawyer, a man of vast reading, a comprehensive statesman. In all this I shall not gratify you."[20]

All the letters that Adams wrote in retirement display a remarkable mix of wisdom, humor, learning, combativeness, and occasional cynicism about his own historical reputation and his likely fate at posterity's hands. Adams had recovered much of his youthful optimism about America, though he still disputed Jefferson's views on American exceptionalism, insisting that Americans were not exempt from the forces that had shaped human nature and human experiments in government throughout history. Adams's retirement letters display the playful, intellectually venturesome, and self-mocking facets of his personality that have endeared him to later generations.

Jefferson, on the other hand, was more formal, more disciplined, and more poised in tone. His letters resemble distilled essays; they are more considered performances on paper, lacking the spontaneity that Adams delighted to indulge—though they often show an intellectual energy and verbal nimbleness matching Adams's. Both men modeled their letters on Cicero's letters to his friend Atticus, a body of Roman literature that they both treasured.

Painful events intruded, and at such times each man sought solace from or offered comfort to the other. After Rush's death, the first such tragic event was the death of John and Abigail's oldest child, Abigail Adams Smith, who succumbed to breast cancer on August 15, 1813, after a long and difficult illness (including a mastectomy in 1811). Having begun a playful letter on Greek literature, Adams changed course, adding a postscript:

> Your Friend, my only Daughter, expired, yesterday morning in the Arms of Her Husband her Son, her Daughter, her Father and Mother, her Husbands two Sisters and two of her Nieces, in the 49th year of her Age, 46 of which She was the healthiest and firmest

of Us all: Since which, She has been a monument to Suffering and to Patience.[21]

Abigail wrote to Jefferson, as an inconsolable mother seeking to share her sorrow with a father who had also lost a daughter.[22] Both parents felt the loss deeply, and not only because of the ordeal of their daughters' last illnesses. Both remembered the younger Abigail's difficult marriage, her frequent unhappiness with her irresponsible and spendthrift husband, and the suffering that their daughters' unhappiness brought them. Jefferson addressed the younger Abigail's death in a sympathetic postscript; he knew all too well what it was to lose a daughter before her time:

> On the subject . . . , I am silent. I know the depth of the affliction it has caused, and can sympathise with it the more sensibly, inasmuch as there is no degree of affliction, produced by the loss of those dear to us which experience has not taught me to estimate. I have ever found time & silence the only medecine, and these but assuage, they never can suppress, the deep-drawn sigh which recollection for ever brings up, until recollection and life are extinguished together.[23]

Adams's most painful loss came in 1818. Jefferson had explained to Adams that the long gap in their correspondence was caused by various ailments that had forced him to visit the local warm springs. On October 20, Adams began his response as an encouraging and humorous letter to raise Jefferson's spirits—but abruptly he changed tone, reporting that his beloved Abigail had fallen gravely ill: "Now Sir, for my Griefs.! The dear Partner of my Life for fifty four Years as a Wife and for many Years more as a Lover now lyes, in extremis, forbidden to Speak or be Spoken to." Adams then mused on the nature of human existence: "If human Life is a Bubble, no matter how Soon it breaks. If it is as I firmly believe an immortal Existence We ought patiently to wait the Instructions of the great Teacher." He signed himself, "your deeply affected Friend[,] John Adams."[24]

On October 28, 1818, before Jefferson received Adams's letter reporting his wife's illness, Abigail Adams died, three days after their fifty-fourth wedding anniversary and three weeks short of her seventy-fourth birthday. Jefferson wrote an eloquent condolence letter, referring obliquely to his own losses of his wife and children and to the hope of a future existence:

> Tried myself, in the school of affliction, by the loss of every form of connection which can rive the human heart, I know well, and feel what you have lost, what you have suffered, are suffering, and have yet to endure. the same trials have taught me that, for ills so immeasurable, time and silence are the only medecines. I will not therefore, by useless condolances, open afresh the sluices of your grief nor, altho' mingling sincerely my tears with yours, will I say a word more, where words are vain, but that it is of some comfort to us both that the term is not very distant at which we are to deposit, in the same cerement, our sorrows and suffering bodies, and to ascend in essence to an ecstatic meeting with the friends we have loved & lost and whom we shall still love and never lose again. God bless you and support you under your heavy affliction.[25]

Adams responded with humble gratitude, moved deeply by Jefferson's words: "While you live, I Seem to have a Bank at Monticello on which I can draw for a Letter of Friendship and entertainment when I please." He then reaffirmed his hopes for life after death, and his belief that the Almighty would not be so cruel as to make human beings and then consign them to life on earth only. There must be something after death, he insisted. To try to restore a sense of daily life, Adams noted that the artist John Trumbull had brought him to Boston's Faneuil Hall (though he did not mention that it was to view the original of Trumbull's iconic painting *The Presenting of the Declaration*, featuring Jefferson and himself), but he did mention that the trip gave him a cold: "Sick or Well the Friendship is the Same of your old Acquaintance, John Adams."[26]

Both men's reflections on a future life after death highlighted two other issues on which their ideas had begun to converge: religion and the relationship between church and state. Having left behind as a young man the Congregationalism of his ancestors, the elderly Adams embraced Unitarianism, as Jefferson had, but they followed differing versions of Unitarianism. Jefferson was a deist Unitarian, believing only in God as creator who had left humans on their own after creation, and in Jesus as a human being who had all human virtues and never claimed or had anything more. Adams believed in a personal deity, in Jesus as the redeemer of humanity, and in the miracles of the New Testament. Still, they agreed that the state should not be entwined with the church.[27]

In his last act of public service, Adams gave voice to these beliefs. He accepted election as a Quincy delegate to the Massachusetts constitutional convention of 1820 (which met from November 15, 1820, to January 9, 1821), forty-one years after serving at the first Massachusetts constitutional convention in 1779.[28] When the eighty-five-year-old Adams entered the hall, the other delegates stood, their heads uncovered, as a mark of respect.[29] They then elected him their president, an honor that he declined on account of his age.[30]

Adams's only action in the convention was to propose the rewriting of the religious-liberty provision of the Declaration of Rights, which read: "All men of all religions, demeaning themselves peaceably, and as good subjects of the Commonwealth, shall be equally under the protection of the law."[31] Adams so phrased his amendment to achieve the broadest measure of religious liberty possible under the Massachusetts form of multiple religious establishments. To seek to disestablish religion would clash with the prevailing religious values of the people of the state and therefore would fail. Adams thus sought to keep his proposal within the structure of church-state relations established by Articles II and III of the 1780 Declaration of Rights, while expanding the category of citizens whose religious liberty would be protected. His motion failed. Adams confided to Jefferson his estimation of his own performance:

> My appearance in the late convention was too ludicrous to be talked of. I was a member in the Convention of 1779 and there I was loquacious enough I have harrangued and scribbled more than my share but from that time to the convention in 1820 I never opened my lips in a publick debate after a total desuetude for 40 years I boggled and blundered more than a young fellow just rising to speak at the bar, what I said I know not, I believe the Printers have made better speeches than I made for myself. Feeling my weakness I attempted little and that seldom. What would I give for nerves as good as yours but as Westley said of himself at my age, "old time has shaken me by the hand, and parallized it."[32]

In the same letter, Adams addressed an issue that both he and Jefferson found troubling and dangerous to the Union—slavery, then dominating the nation's politics in the Missouri crisis:

> Slavery in this Country I have seen hanging over it like a black cloud for half a Century, if I were as drunk with enthusiasm as Swedenborg or Westley I might probably say I had seen Armies of Negroes marching and countermarching in the air shining in Armour. I have been so terrified with this Phenomenon that I constantly said in former times to the Southern Gentleman, I cannot comprehend this object I must leave it to you, I will vote for forceing no measure against your judgements, what we are to see *God* knows and I leave it to him, and his agents in posterity.[33]

Adams never more clearly stated his hesitant approach to slavery than in this letter. He first identified white southerners as having expertise and thus authority in dealing with slavery and with slaves; second, he deferred to their supposed expertise and authority. This was but the latest example of Adams's gingerly approach to slavery and to race and to the constellation of issues that they symbolized. In 1810, for example, Adams had cited James Thomson Callender's charges against Jefferson concerning Sally Hemings as epitomizing the bad effects of slavery on slaveowners.[34] In 1813, writing to Richard Rush, the noted attorney who was the son of Benjamin Rush, Adams expressed similar views: "I have all my life been so sensible of the dangers and difficulties attending this thing that no Southern Gentleman can reproach me with a word or action tending to give discontent to their domesticks or to embarrass them in their intercourse with them, or government of them." As to his own family history concerning slavery, Adams boasted:

> I have the sweet consolation to reflect, that I never owned a Slave. Not one of my ancestors by my Father, for five generations in this Village of Mount Wollasten, now Quincy, ever owned a Negro. My Mothers Father in Brookline had an old African, named Sharper whom I remember, more than 70 years ago, who was treated by my Grand Father and Grand Mother as kindly as their Son and daughters. And this old creature treated me with so much kindness that I loved him almost as well as any of the family.[35]

With such reflections, Adams closed an intermittent and confused lifelong struggle with his ideas about slavery and race. Throughout his life, though finding slavery distasteful, he believed that it was a historical constant in human civilization. He never developed the antislavery stance associated with Benjamin Franklin, John Jay, or Alexander Hamilton. Not only did he never come out publicly against slavery; he also was mute on issues of race, confiding his discomfort with people of African descent only to a few friends and correspondents. Adams may fit within a category proposed by modern legal scholars, "unconscious racism"; though not a deliberate, self-conscious advocate of racism and white supremacy, he held unexamined assumptions that specified whiteness as the default position for Americans and citizens. His posthumous reputation as a foe of slavery and an advocate of equal rights regardless of race is open to serious question.[36]

Though in his old age Adams shied away from such loaded political issues, he found that politics would not leave him alone. In 1823, his unresolved dispute with William Cunningham revived after Cunningham's suicide. After discovering his father's correspondence with Adams, Cunningham's son decided that he was not bound by his father's commitment not to publish Adams's letters while Adams was alive, and so informed Adams. Ephraim May Cunningham was as partisan as his father, but whereas William Cunningham had been a High Federalist, his son was a supporter of Andrew Jackson and thus was hostile to Secretary of State John Quincy Adams, his leading opponent in the impending 1824 presidential election. Hoping that publication of the Adams-Cunningham correspondence would be political dynamite to the younger Adams, Ephraim May Cunningham published in 1823 *Correspondence between the Hon. John Adams, Late President of the United States, and the Late Hon. Wm. Cunningham, Esq., Beginning in 1803, and Continuing until 1823.*[37] Cunningham directed his enmity at both Adamses.

Jefferson got wind of the impending publication. Determined not to sacrifice to politics a friendship that meant so much to both men, Jefferson wrote to Adams with sympathy and understanding about the younger Cunningham's betrayal of Adams's trust. Pointing out that those with invidious motives might wish to poison relations between them "by filling our ears with malignant falsehoods, by dressing up hideous phantoms of their own creation, presenting them to you under my name, to me under your's," Jefferson refused to be fooled:

> Be assured, my dear Sir, that I am incapable of recieving the slightest impression from the effort now made to plant thorns on the pillow of age, worth, and wisdom, and to sow tares between friends who have been such for near half a century. beseeching you then not to suffer your mind to be disquieted by this wicked attempt to poison it's peace, and praying you to throw it by, among the things which have never happened, I add sincere assurances of my unabated, and constant attachment, friendship and respect.[38]

Deeply touched, Adams wrote back, indulging his gift for dramatic scene-setting in describing the arrival of Jefferson's letter:

> Your last letter was brought to me from the Post office when at breakfast with my family. I bade one of the misses open the budget, she reported a letter from Mr. Jefferson and two or three newspapers. A letter from Mr. Jefferson says I, I know what the substance is before I open it; There is no secrets between Mr. Jefferson and me, And I cannot read it, therefore you may open and read it—When it was done, it was followed by an universal exclamation, The best letter that ever was written, and round it went through the whole table—How generous! how noble! how magnanimous! I said that it was just such a letter as I expected only it was infinitely better expressed—A universal cry that the letter ought to be printed, No, hold—certainly not without Mr. Jefferson's express leave.

Adams explained to Jefferson his correspondence with Cunningham: "The peevish and fretful effusions of politicians in difficult and dangerous conjectures from the agony of their hearts are not worth remembering, much less of laying to heart." He closed with a self-mocking quip: "In the 89. year of his age still too fat to last much longer. John Adams."[39]

For Adams, the 1824 presidential campaign was about more than the threats and publications of the Cunninghams. He was so anxious about John Quincy Adams's chances to win the presidency in that election that he made a great sacrifice—he said nothing in public about John Quincy's candidacy or fitness for the presidency, lest his words be taken as an effort to impose monarchy on America in the form of his son. When the news arrived of John Quincy's election after a prolonged tussle in the House of Representatives, John Adams was nearly overcome by emotion.

Though Jefferson had supported Treasury secretary William Crawford, disdaining Andrew Jackson and regarding John Quincy Adams as too committed to a vigorous national government, on

February 15, 1825, he sent his congratulations to the proud father: "It must excite ineffable feelings in the breast of a father to have lived to see a son to whose educn & happiness his life has been devoted so eminently distinguished by the voice of his country."[40] Meanwhile, on February 18, Adams wrote a loving and proud letter to his son: "Never did I feel so much solemnity as upon this occasion— the multitude of my thoughts and the intensity of my feelings are too much for a mind like mine in its ninetieth year—May the blessing of God Almighty continue to protect you to the end of your life as it has heretofore protected you in so remarkable a manner from your cradle. I offer the same prayer for your Lady and your family."[41]

By 1826, Adams was ninety and Jefferson was about to turn eighty-three. Musing on whether they would like to live their lives over or to advance to what comes next, Adams assured Jefferson on December 1, 1825, that he would rather move forward: "I had rather go forward and meet whatever is to come—I have met in this life, with great trials—I have had a Father, and lost him—I have had a Mother and lost her—I have had a Wife and lost her—I have had Children and lost them—I have had honorable and worthy Friends and lost them—and instead of suffering these griefs again I had rather go forward and meet my destiny."[42]

Recognizing that their increasing frailty meant that they would not live much longer, Adams and Jefferson reluctantly declined invitations to attend ceremonies marking the fiftieth anniversary of the declaration of American independence, to be held on July 4, 1826.[43] They disagreed about the significance of the anniversary— Adams saw it as an event restricted to the American people, whereas Jefferson hailed it as a landmark of the age of the democratic revolution, with meaning for people all over the world. Nonetheless, both men were equally determined to live to see the day. They just barely realized their shared wish. Jefferson died early on the afternoon of July 4; Adams died several hours later that day, murmuring, "Thomas Jefferson survives." Americans regarded this unusual occurrence as a sign from Providence not only that the torch of responsibility for

American freedom was passing from the revolutionary generation to its successors but that heaven itself was conferring a sign of divine favor on Adams, Jefferson, and the American nation.[44]

In Massachusetts and particularly in Quincy, John Adams's death and funeral were events of state. He was interred beside his wife in the family crypt maintained by the Adamses in Hancock Cemetery. In 1828, he and Abigail were transferred to their current resting place, joined there in 1852 by John Quincy Adams and his wife, Louisa Catherine. They lie in cenotaphs in the crypt of the "Church of the Presidents," the United First Parish Church in the heart of Quincy, Massachusetts.[45]

Unlike Thomas Jefferson, John Adams composed no epitaph. Rather than distilling his life's meaning, he recorded it at daunting length in letters, diary entries, autobiographical writings, and manuscripts of books, articles, pamphlets, and legal pleadings. He emerges from his writings as a thinking politician driven by commitment to public service. He focused his commitment on the rule of law, seeing himself as a man of law, in many ways the leading man of law among the nation's founders. He insisted on preserving the rule of law, in particular its subset constitutionalism. That insistence helped to ensure that the Revolution was devoted to upholding and preserving law and constitutional government.

Adams stood for what later scholars have called law-mindedness, and he helped to make that value central to American history and culture. His greatest contributions to the Revolution—his mastery of constitutional advocacy, constitutional analysis, and constitution-making—had deep roots in his law-mindedness. By contrast, when he could not draw on his law-mindedness, he failed. At such times, he could not perceive law-mindedness's boundaries as well as its strengths. Today's flowering of our knowledge of the Revolution's legal and constitutional histories has helped us to see anew the significance of John Adams and his life's work—as well as his limits. As he would have been the first to admit, a great lawyer cannot necessarily do everything well.[46]

Epilogue

"Whether you or I were right Posterity must judge": The Legacies of John Adams

John Adams worried about his historical legacy, doubting that posterity would venerate him or even remember him. On March 23, 1809, he complained to Benjamin Rush:

> I am weary, my Friend of that unceasing Insolence of which I have been the object for twenty years. I have opposed Nothing to it but stoical Patience, unlimited submission, passive obedience and Non Resistance. Mausauleums, Statues, Monuments will never be erected to me. I wish them not. Panegyrical Romances will never be written, nor flattering orations spoken to transmit me to Posterity in brilliant Colours. No nor in true Colours. All but the last I loath. Yet I will not die wholly unlamented.[1]

After Rush had persuaded Adams and Jefferson to resume their friendship, Adams wrote with candor to Jefferson about their political differences: "Whether you or I were right Posterity must judge."[2] He thus identified the purpose of their correspondence.

Adams was right to submit himself to posterity's judgment—although posterity has taken a long time to do him justice. Following decades of neglect, he has rejoined the leading ranks of the Founding Fathers. Statues of him and of Abigail and the young John Quincy stand in the town of Quincy, and there are monuments to him of various kinds across the nation.[3] Adams has been portrayed on stage and screen by actors as various and talented as William Daniels, George Grizzard, Paul Giamatti, Vic Morrow, and Henry Thomas.[4]

How do we remember John Adams? How should we remember him? Popular culture presents him as a character—crusty, tactless, "obnoxious and disliked," yet also honest, brave, patriotic, lovable, and lucky enough to be married to Abigail Adams.[5] Disgruntled critics reject that version of Adams as sanitized for popular consumption and thus historically suspect. Refusing to venerate him, they invoke reasons valid and invalid. They attack him for favoring or hoping to found an American monarchy and titled aristocracy. They denounce Adams for signing the Alien and Sedition Acts into law, for presiding over his administration's prosecutions of Republican newspaper editors under the Sedition Act, and for the Alien Act's threats (never put into practice) to deport aliens. Some take part with the victims of these measures; others regard these actions and statutes as foreshadowing the USA PATRIOT Act, Guantanamo Bay, Abu Ghraib, and "extraordinary rendition."[6]

Understanding Adams rather than forgiving or demonizing him requires us to see him in context.[7] Because Adams's life and career are documented more thoroughly and accessibly than ever before, such an approach is both possible and necessary, as the availability of more evidence in more accessible forms drives scholarship. In response, a profusion of scholarship has illuminated many dimensions of his life. We may know John Adams better than he knew himself.

The central theme of Adams's life is his immersion in politics and law, focusing on the American Revolution. Repeatedly, he sacrificed family happiness and domestic bliss to his public duty to the Revolution. Though it imposed painful costs on his family and on himself, he saw the cause as worth those costs. His commitment to the Revolution was so strong because he identified with and cherished the constellation of ideas about human nature, society, politics, law, and government that he advocated then. Even in old age, he marshaled those ideas in service of the nation that the Revolution created and the history that it made. Reinforcing his intellectual, political, and legal fealty to the Revolution was his personal stake in his ideas and in his record of public service.

Recognizing how integral his Revolution-centered career was to his life, posterity has cast Adams as a leading Founding Father—a twentieth-century phrase with cultural and political weight.[8] That label's modern significance and the veneration given those who qualify for it resonate with Adams's ultimate goal—enduring fame. Adams wanted to make sure that posterity would remember him for his disinterested labors in the service of the public good. For Adams, achieving fame was an irrefutable sign that he *deserved* to be remembered, for he knew that one had to merit fame to achieve it.

Did Adams achieve that goal? The record is uneven. In his lifetime and since his death, Adams's critics have neglected his achievements while highlighting ways that he went too far, said too much, claimed too much, and otherwise got himself in trouble. Even those making a case for him have tended to stress the personal rather than the political.

Unwittingly, Adams gave his critics help. He clashed with the icons of the American founding in ways tailor-made to affront contemporaries and to disgust later generations seeking a usable past.[9] Long before his death, he dug his reputation's grave with his mouth and his pen. Theodore Parker rightly noted of Adams: "He was terribly open, earnest, and direct, and could not keep his mouth shut."[10] Adams quarreled with Benjamin Franklin in Paris and upbraided him in heated letters to Congress, only to be skewered forever by the sage's angry wit. He mocked the icon of icons, George Washington, only to have his mockery rebound against himself, cited as proving his own petty jealousy. Most people remember his vice presidency for his failed campaign to confer an elaborate, unwanted title on the president. And though he twice stood for the presidency against his friend and rival Thomas Jefferson, winning once and losing once, his victory in 1796 turned to ashes in his mouth, and his defeat in 1800 embittered him. He spent the rest of his life trying to overcome what he saw as an epic repudiation. In retirement, he vented indignation at posterity's preference for Jefferson over himself, disputing what he saw as Jefferson's devious claims to an outsized place in American memory. Jefferson's admirers paid Adams back in full measure, denouncing him for jealousy, vanity, and arrogance.

Unlike Jefferson, Adams did not write the words or the music to the American democratic epic; he missed the chance to define his own vision of American national identity and values. The Declaration—often called "Jefferson's Declaration"—is the American political testament, inspiring people around the world with its affirmation of "unalienable rights." Adams focused on systems of constitutional government and problems of constitutional design, but these matters rarely capture the popular imagination.

Thus, for example, the resolution that Adams drafted for the Second Continental Congress in May 1776 calling on the colonies to frame new state constitutions seems technical, lawyerly, and dry by contrast with the Declaration. Similarly, his 1774–75 *Novanglus* essays and his other formal writings on politics and constitutionalism remain embedded in their argumentative context. Adams would not be surprised by their neglect, for, by his own admission, his books were too heavy and dull to win an enthusiastic readership.

Neglect would be sad enough, but hostile critics past and present have used Adams's writings to torpedo his reputation. Misusing what he wrote about monarchy and aristocracy, they have tried to prove him a perfidious foe of the Revolution from within or a revolutionary fallen from grace. They have assumed that anyone who wrote so much about monarchy and aristocracy must favor them. So often have they convicted Adams of these antidemocratic sins by using his own words against him that condemnation of Adams echoes to this day.[11] (Never mind that most Americans before 1776, and most European philosophes before 1789, would have seen monarchy and aristocracy as Adams did, as default positions of human government.)[12]

Other factors helped to consign John Adams to the margins of history.

Adams had no political heirs to keep his memory green. He had broken with the Federalists; too many of them had been allies of Hamilton, and thus had no inclination to honor Adams or to promote his legacy. Even had they been sympathetic to him, by 1820 the Federalists were politically extinct, in no position to advocate for anyone. Adams's one plausible heir, Chief Justice John Marshall, spent his judicial career shifting his focus from politics to law, to protect the federal judiciary from Republican attack and to advocate his own jurisprudential nationalism. He showed no interest in advocating for Adams's political legacy.

Adams found himself sidelined in the new republic's partisan battles, both because the vice presidency was a hopeless office for one who wanted to remain active in public life and because Jefferson and Hamilton emerged as the leading contenders in the battles over public policy and politics. Their political heirs continued their passionate rivalry, refighting their original brawls or staging sequels to them. This ongoing contest has preoccupied politicians, polemicists, and historians up to our own day. That obsession with partisan fireworks eclipsed Adams, the man who despised party.

The controversial acts of Adams's presidency—signing the Alien and Sedition Acts into law and enforcing the Sedition Act—made him look like an enemy of freedom of speech and press. Further, the myth of the "midnight judges"—the bumper-sticker term for the Federalists' reshaping of the federal judiciary in 1801—has fastened itself to Adams, without justification.

Adams's failure to win re-election in 1800 eroded his significance in American history. Particularly in the twentieth century, scholars of American government defined as a test of a president's success or failure his ability to win a second term. On this theory, most one-term presidents fall into historical irrelevance. As the first one-term president, Adams became the prototypical presidential failure.

The lack of interplay between the issues dominating Adams's writings and those preoccupying later generations also undercuts Adams's claim to fame. Adams never grappled with the nature of federalism. Yet that issue pervading American constitutional controversy between the 1820s and the 1860s ultimately was crucial, in its interaction with slavery, to defining what kind of nation the United States would be. The terrible war that the crisis over slavery and federalism spawned was pivotal to that process of national definition. Adams's silence on federalism excluded him from those controversies. Moreover, his views on slavery and race put him on what might be called the wrong side of those political, moral, and intellectual battles, the side dismissed by later generations as the doughfaces—northerners fearful of challenging slavery or even sympathetic with it.[13] Adams also missed the court cases in 1783 that ended slavery in his native state, and most New Englanders found it easy to forget that they once had had both slavery and the racial ideology that undergirded it.[14] In any event, John Adams played no role in the constitutional, political, moral, and cultural controversies that we associate with the Civil War.

Following that war, the nation's constitutional agenda diverged more sharply from the issues to which Adams had given priority. Adams was irrelevant to the task of reconstructing the Union from 1865 to 1877. After Reconstruction's end, American constitutional argument shifted from issues of federalism, union, slavery, and rebuilding the Union to contests regarding competition between the federal government and the states to exercise regulatory power over the economy. Those contests unfolded in a nation shaped by new and powerful forces that Adams had barely perceived—urbanization, immigration, and industrialization.[15] Seeking support from the past for their positions in these arguments, scholars, jurists, politicians, and polemicists ransacked writings by Jefferson, Hamilton, Marshall, and Madison, but they never deemed John

Adams relevant. Adams's political thought describes a world of static constitutional and political principles. By contrast, arguments about politics, government, and constitutional change offered by those whom later controversialists invoked presuppose development over time, a concept overlooked in Adams's thought.[16]

Finally, historical neglect of Adams may also have roots in his descendants' overzealous guardianship of his papers. Charles Francis Adams published only selections from his grandparents' letters and other writings; the capstone of his efforts was a ten-volume selected edition of John Adams's writings (1850–56). For a century thereafter, the family refused scholars access to Adams's unpublished papers. Writing history and biography depends on the availability of sources; as Arnold Rampersad commented on writing his intellectual life of W. E. B. Du Bois, "I've since joked that an intellectual biography is what you write when you don't have access to the papers."[17] By guarding his papers from view, the Adams family gagged John Adams, leaving him represented only by his grandson's somber and stuffy edition. Although Charles Francis Adams was his era's best historical editor, he purged his grandfather's writings of his erratic spelling and punctuation, his earthiness, his humor, and his candor.[18] As one scholarly admirer wrote with regret in 1952, "He has been silenced after all."[19]

Even the first book-length treatment of Adams's political thought showed less interest in Adams than in the concerns of the author's time. In 1915, the political scientist Correa M. Walsh juxtaposed Adams's faith in separation of powers and checks and balances unfavorably with the Progressive movement's rejection of such concepts in favor of an agenda promoting efficient governance.[20] A reader of Walsh's study can only wonder why he bothered.

By contrast, after World War II, Adams's ideas attracted growing, respectful interest. The first to reinvent Adams as a sage for modern times were such conservative thinkers as Russell Kirk, who saw in the Cold War a return of the controversy swirling around the French Revolution, and such defenders of a moderate conservative tradition as Clinton Rossiter.[21] The Cold War revived arguments about revolution's origins, history, and development, contrasting the American and French Revolutions—and bracketing the French and Russian Revolutions. As part of that revival, conservatives and liberals embraced Adams's critique of the French Revolution, yoking Adams with Edmund Burke and enlisting both men in their battle against the twentieth century's Communist revolutions.[22] This antirevolutionary canon began with Adams and Burke, finding new targets in Lenin, Stalin, Mao, and the Gulag archipelago. So, too, in 1952, the literary scholar Zoltan Haraszti published a monograph examining the marginalia that Adams wrote in his books, rearranging them in dialogue form to show Adams arguing with the authors he was reading. In the process, he not only created a remarkably fresh, intimate portrait of Adams as thinker—his Adams was also an honorary Cold Warrior, combating the French Revolution and its supposed twentieth-century heirs.[23]

In the 1950s and 1960s, a surge in popular attention, sparked by the opening of the Adams papers, evolved in parallel with scholarly investigations of John Adams. In 1954, perhaps to take advantage of tax benefits conferred by the 1954 Internal Revenue Code, and also to follow the lead of *The Papers of Thomas Jefferson*, the flagship of the documentary-editing revolution, the Adams family unsealed the Adams papers.[24] Working with the Massachusetts Historical Society and Harvard University Press, the family created the Adams Manuscript Trust; the Adams project produced a 608-reel microfilm edition and an ongoing letterpress edition of the Adams papers.

The first product of opening the Adams papers was Lester J. Cappon's 1959 edition of the full correspondence between John and Abigail Adams and Thomas Jefferson. Reviewers hailed the two volumes as an American literary classic, heaping praise in particular on Adams's literary and philosophical talents. In 1961 appeared the first installment of the *Adams Papers*, L. H. Butterfield's edition of *The Diary and Autobiography of John Adams*. *Life* magazine serialized extracts from those volumes. Reviews, including one commissioned by the *American Historical Review* from President John F. Kennedy, were many and glowing. The *Adams Papers* revealed Adams as an unexpectedly vivid, funny, and human writer. The acclaim continued with the publication of the first volumes of Adams family correspondence, which brought renewed admiration for Abigail Adams as a writer, and an edition of John Adams's legal papers.

These publications separated Adams's two identities by focusing on differing bodies of his writings. One identity—Adams as character and literary figure, drawn from his diary, autobiography, and letters—captured the public's attention. The other identity—Adams as political and constitutional thinker, drawing on his more formal political and constitutional writings—remained the province of scholars. Thus, monographs published in the 1960s by Edward Handler and John R. Howe Jr. illuminated Adams anew as a political thinker, though neither book made an impression beyond academic circles. This evolving split has dominated the history of Adams's reputation ever since, as evidenced, for example, by David McCullough's *John Adams*. McCullough's approach to Adams, emphasizing character and personality and downplaying ideas, has overshadowed work by such biographers as John Ferling and James Grant, and monographic examinations of his thought by such scholars as C. Bradley Thompson, Luke Mayville, and Richard Alan Ryerson.

Nonetheless, Adams's overarching perspective as a thinking politician is an essential component of his intellectual legacy. Adams offered a realistic understanding of American politics; he focused on the American constitutional experiment's interactions with such social forces as aristocratic power and ambition, and the need for vigilance against abuses of power from any source. He imagined himself hectoring posterity about the Revolution's nature and American constitutionalism's future. The new scholarship would have captivated him.

Resigned to having no intellectual legacy at all, to his books and other writing being ignored by posterity, Adams chose instead to hope that he would be remembered for his part in the Revolution. Perhaps, however, there is a way to salvage John Adams's thought—reviewing how it worked might help us ponder how it might be of use again today.

We know that Adams was skeptical of the idea of popular sovereignty that came to be central to American political thought. Those advocating popular sovereignty argue that, if the people are the governors, then we can set aside the old idea of government as hostile to the people. Adams rejected that belief, insisting that the people had violated their own liberties often and that a government based on popular sovereignty could easily do the same thing. If we remain willing to reconsider skeptically the claims of popular sovereignty in general, or those of a government grounded on popular sovereignty in particular, then we can heed the potential threats to liberty and democracy masked by a government endangering those great goods under the mask of popular sovereignty.

At the same time, we should reconsider the idea that the theory about factionalism, constitutionalism, and the extended republic devised by James Madison is a stark alternative to Adams's arguments about aristocracy, like matter and antimatter—or that Madison's work rendered Adams's ideas and conceptions of government and politics obsolete. Maybe the two bodies of thought are not antithetical, nor one obsolete and the other dominant; maybe they are complementary.

Imagine Adams's analysis grounded in classical political thought—in the theory of the one, the few, and the many—as hierarchical or vertical, and then imagine Madison's political thought as emphasizing the horizontal: a politics of relative equality among political actors in an extended geographical realm. If we intersect those two bodies of thought, as if they were the x-axis and y-axis of analytical geometry, that synthesis produces a more complex and nuanced vision of American politics and of American constitutionalism; it enables us to draw on the wisdom of both models without sacrificing either. Such an approach to American political thought might well establish that Adams's political thought has renewed relevance for our time.

In that light, the story of Adams's legacies has one final, ironic twist. In 1809, he mocked the idea that anyone would erect monuments to him, mixing self-conscious wistfulness, self-denying nobility, and self-satirizing humor. In our time, contradicting his expectations, there is a campaign to create such a monument in the nation's capital.[25] And yet the premise of that campaign—that Adams deserves a national monument because he has none—is erroneous. The capital does have a monument to John Adams—one peculiarly suited to him.

In 1800, President John Adams signed into law the bill creating the Library of Congress. In 1871, Congress launched a plan to build a separate home for the library, which until then had been housed in the US Capitol. Congress had many reasons to move the library to a separate location. For one thing, in 1851 a fire had nearly consumed the collection and endangered the Capitol; for another thing, the spectacular growth of the library's holdings required the institution to grow.[26] More than a generation in the making, the library's magnificent building opened in 1897.

In 1928, more than thirty years later, Librarian of Congress Herbert Putnam argued that the library needed an annex to accommodate its collection's continued growth. Creation of that building took another decade. The large, boxy structure, known as the Annex, opened at the end of 1938.

On April 13, 1976, the Library of Congress renamed the Annex the Thomas Jefferson Building, marking Jefferson's birthday in the bicentennial year of the Declaration of Independence. A little more than four years later, on June 13, 1980, the library renamed its original building the Thomas Jefferson Building and opened the James Madison Memorial Building. At that time, the library again renamed the building first known as the Annex (and then as the Thomas Jefferson Building) as the John Adams Building, honoring its namesake for his role in creating the Library of Congress.[27]

Thus, John Adams has his monument—a building lacking architectural distinction or grace, but stuffed with books. It is an appropriate monument for a man who cared little about architecture but who expressed his revolutionary zeal and wrought his greatest intellectual and political achievements by daring to read, think, speak, and write.

CHRONOLOGY

1735

October 30 N.S. (October 19 O.S.): John Adams born in Braintree, Massachusetts, the first son of (Deacon) John Adams and Susanna Boylston.

1738

Birth of John Adams's first brother, Elihu Adams (dies 1775).

1741

Begins school at Dame Belcher's house, where he studies arithmetic, reading, and religion.

Birth of John Adams's second brother, Peter Adams (dies 1823).

1743

Begins attending Braintree's Latin School, headed by Joseph Cleverly.

1744

November 25: Birth of Abigail Smith (later Abigail Adams).

1749

John persuades his father to send him for schooling to Joseph Marsh, who prepares him for his admission exams to Harvard.

1751

John Adams is admitted to Harvard College.

1753

June 8: John Adams begins his diary.

1755

July: John is graduated from Harvard College. The Worcester clergyman Rev. Thaddeus McCarty hires him as a schoolmaster.

1756

August 21: John reaches apprenticeship agreement with James Putnam, who is to supervise his study of law.

1758

November 6: John is admitted to the bar of Suffolk County.

1759

Summer: John Adams and Abigail Smith meet for the first time.

1761

January: John Adams and Samuel Quincy observe the writs of assistance case (*Petition of Lechmere*) in Massachusetts Superior Court held in Town House in Boston.
May 25: Deacon John Adams dies of influenza.

1763

Treaty of Paris ends French and Indian War (Seven Years' War).

1764

John undergoes inoculation for smallpox and endures quarantine for two months.
Parliament enacts Sugar Act.
October 25: John marries Abigail Smith after two years of courtship.

1765

March: Parliament enacts the Stamp Act.
July 14: Birth of John and Abigail's first child, Abigail Amelia ("Nabby").
August: Stamp Act Crisis.
August: John Adams publishes anonymously "A Dissertation on Canon and Feudal Law."
October: Forty Massachusetts towns adopt the "Braintree Instructions" written by Adams.

1766

March 18: Parliament repeals the Stamp Act and adopts the Declaratory Act.

1767

June: Parliament enacts Townshend Acts.
July 11: Birth of John and Abigail's first son, John Quincy.

1768

January: The Adams family moves to Boston, settling in a white house on Brattle Street.

October: British authorities send four thousand soldiers to Boston to keep civil order.

December 28: Birth of John and Abigail's second daughter, Susanna.

1770

February 4: Daughter Susanna dies, thirteen months old.

March 5: Boston Massacre—five Bostonians slain by British soldiers after skirmish.

May 29: Birth of John and Abigail's second son, Charles.

June: Adams is elected to the Massachusetts General Court.

October: Boston Massacre trials. Adams defends Thomas Preston and the soldiers; jury acquits Preston and six of the eight soldiers but convicts two soldiers of manslaughter.

1771

John moves his family back to Braintree.

1772

September 15: Birth of John and Abigail's third son, Thomas Boylston.

1773

As newly elected member of the Massachusetts General Court, Adams wages polemical duel with Massachusetts governor Thomas Hutchinson, writing responses to the governor's addresses.

December 16: Boston Tea Party.

1774

May: Parliament enacts Coercive Acts (Intolerable Acts) to punish Boston for the Tea Party.

September–October: Adams is a Massachusetts delegate to First Continental Congress in Philadelphia.

1775

Adams writes *Novanglus* essays to answer *Massachusettensis*.

April 19: Battle of Lexington and Concord.

May: Adams is a Massachusetts delegate to the Second Continental Congress.

June: Adams nominates George Washington as commander of the Continental army.

June: Battle of Bunker Hill, witnessed from Braintree by Abigail and John Quincy Adams.

July 5: John Adams signs Second Continental Congress's Olive Branch Petition to George III.

October: Deaths from dysentery of Abigail's mother and John's brother Elihu.

1776

January: Thomas Paine publishes *Common Sense*.

April: Adams publishes *Thoughts on Government*.

May 10–15: Second Continental Congress adopts Adams's resolution authorizing colonies to frame new state constitutions.

June: Adams frames Plan of Treaties for alliances with European nations.

June 8: Richard Henry Lee of Virginia introduces package of resolutions for independence in Congress.

June: Adams named to committee to prepare declaration of American independence.

July 2: Second Continental Congress adopts Virginia resolutions on independence, on articles of confederation, and on United States seeking alliances with foreign nations.

July 4: Congress adopts Declaration of Independence.

September: British troops occupy New York.

1777

January: Adams returns to Continental Congress.

July: Abigail gives birth to stillborn daughter, Elizabeth.

November 15: Congress proposes Articles of Confederation to states.

Congress chooses Adams as American commissioner to go to France.

1778

February 8: Benjamin Franklin signs treaty of alliance and commerce, including French recognition of US independence.

February–April: Adams sails to France, with John Quincy.

1779

March–August: John Adams and John Quincy Adams sail home to Massachusetts.

October: Adams drafts Massachusetts Constitution for the state's constitutional convention.

November: Adams, with John Quincy and Charles, returns to Europe as peace commissioner.

1780

February 8: The Adams party reaches Paris after overland trek across Spain and France.

June–July: Congress authorizes Adams to negotiate a loan with the Netherlands; Adams travels to Amsterdam to undertake the mission.

October 25: Massachusetts constitutional convention declares the state constitution sent to town meetings in 1779 ratified and in effect.

1781

March 1: Articles of Confederation ratified by Maryland (the thirteenth state). Adams falls ill, suffering from strain of talks with Netherlands.

Adams gets word from home of political steps in Congress against him.

October 19: US victory at Yorktown, Virginia. British surrender and agree to negotiate peace. Dutch authorities welcome American victory, and American-Dutch negotiations progress.

1782

April 19: The Netherlands recognizes American independence.

June: Adams secures a $2 million loan from Dutch bankers.

June 23: John Jay arrives in Paris.

October: Jay and Adams form common cause in preparing for peace negotiations with Britain.

November: American and British diplomats agree on Preliminary Treaty of Peace.

1783

July 22: Benjamin Franklin writes letter to Congress declaring John Adams "always an honest Man and often a Wise One, but sometimes and in some things absolutely out of his senses."

September 3: Adams, Franklin, and Jay sign the Treaty of Paris, ending war with Britain and securing British recognition of US independence.

September: Benjamin West paints unfinished group portrait of American diplomats, *The Peacemakers*.

1784

August: Thomas Jefferson arrives in Paris.

Adams, Franklin, Jay, and Jefferson serve as commissioners to secure commercial treaties.

Adams negotiates a second loan with the Netherlands.

June–July: Abigail and Nabby sail from Boston to Paris.

August 7: Abigail and Nabby reunite with John.

1785

February 24: Congress names Adams first US minister to Great Britain.

May 2: Adams gets news of his appointment as US minister to Great Britain.

June 1: Adams has first audience with George III.

Adams secures treaty of alliance and commerce with Prussia.

Adams lays groundwork for treaty of alliance and commerce with Portugal (completed 1791).

1786

June: Nabby Adams marries Colonel William Stephen Smith, John Adams's secretary in London.

The Adamses and Jefferson hear of Shays's Rebellion in Massachusetts.

1787

January: Adams publishes volume 1 of *Defence of the Constitutions of the United States* in London (two more volumes follow within the year).

September 17: Federal Convention signs proposed US Constitution.

September: Ratification contest over US Constitution begins.

1788

February 21: John Adams has his final audience with King George III.

April: John and Abigail leave Britain, arriving in Boston on June 17.

June: John and Abigail settle into Vassall-Borland House, which John names Peacefield.

July 26: US Constitution wins eleventh state ratification, replacing Articles of Confederation.

September: Confederation Congress launches process to put Constitution into operation.

1789

April 1: Government under Constitution is launched in New York City, temporary capital of the United States.

April 6: George Washington and John Adams elected first president and vice president.

April 12: Adams receives official word of his election and leaves for New York City.

April 21: Adams takes office as vice president.

April 30: Washington inaugurated as president.

May: Titles dispute.

June: Washington falls ill but recovers.

July 14: Storming of Bastille in Paris launches French Revolution.

1790

April 17: Benjamin Franklin dies.

May: Washington again falls ill but recovers.

Adams begins publishing *Discourses on Davila* in *Gazette of United States*.

1791

April: Adams breaks off *Discourses on Davila*, ending his work as a thinking politician.

December 15: Virginia is eleventh of fourteen states to ratify the ten constitutional amendments later known as the US Bill of Rights, adding them to the US Constitution.

1792

September: France abolishes monarchy and becomes a republic.

Washington and Adams are re-elected as president and vice president.

1793

January 21: French government tries and executes Louis XVI.

February: Great Britain, Prussia, and Austria declare war on France.

April: Washington issues Proclamation of Neutrality keeping United States out of European war.

Citizen Genet Affair (ends in January 1794 when France recalls Genet as minister to United States and President Washington grants Genet's petition for asylum).

1794

John Quincy Adams becomes American minister to the Netherlands.

Whiskey Rebellion.

1795

August 29: Charles Adams marries Sarah (Sally) Smith in New York.

1796

September 19: Washington publishes Farewell Address in newspapers. Announcing that he will step down from the presidency at the end of his term, he establishes two-term tradition.

Adams is elected second president; his opponent, Thomas Jefferson, is elected vice president.

1797

February 8: Vice President Adams conducts official count of electoral votes, announces his election as president.

February 12: Adams delivers farewell speech to the Senate.

March 4: Adams is sworn in as president.

May 16: Adams delivers speech to Congress attacking French rebuffs to United States.

June: Adams appoints John Quincy Adams US minister to Prussia.

July: John Quincy Adams marries Louisa Catherine Johnson in London.

Negotiators Charles C. Pinckney, John Marshall, and Elbridge Gerry sent to Paris.

1798

Department of the Navy created.

March–April: XYZ Affair.

John Marshall returns home bearing documents of XYZ Affair and failed American mission.

Adams times XYZ documents' release for maximum political effect.

Quasi-War: naval clashes between French and US warships.

Adams names Washington as commander of US Army.

Enactment of Alien and Sedition Acts.

William Vans Murray, US minister to Netherlands, reports to President Adams that France is willing to engage in peace talks. Adams encourages Vans Murray to pursue the matter.

United States providing covert aid to rebel government in Haiti.

1799

March: Fries' Rebellion in Pennsylvania against taxes levied to support the Quasi-War.

Adams discovers his son Charles's alcoholism and pennilessness and disowns him.

Adams begins organizing peace mission to France, rebuffs dissent from his cabinet.

November: On Adams's orders, negotiators Chief Justice Oliver Ellsworth, William Vans Murray, and William Richardson Davie sail for France.

Bitter argument between Adams and Hamilton.

December: George Washington dies at age sixty-seven.

1800

Capital relocates from Philadelphia to Washington, DC.

Adams demands McHenry's resignation, fires Pickering, and confines Wolcott to Treasury duties.

May: Adams named Federalist candidate for president, with Charles C. Pinckney as running mate. Vice President Jefferson is Republican candidate, with Aaron Burr as running mate.

May 21: Adams pardons Fries and other defendants convicted of treason.

October: Alexander Hamilton publishes *A Letter on the Character and Conduct of the Hon. John Adams, Esq., President of the United States*. Pamphlet divides Federalists, damages both Adams and Hamilton.

November 2: Adams moves to President's House in Washington, DC.

November 30: Charles Adams dies at age thirty.

December: Republicans win 1800 national election, carrying presidency, House, and Senate.

Treaty of Morfontaine negotiated by Ellsworth, Vans Murray, and Davie settles hostilities between United States and France, ending the Quasi-War.

Adams receives Ellsworth's resignation as chief justice and nominates Jay to succeed him. Senate confirms Jay's nomination.

1801

January 2: Jay declines reappointment to the Supreme Court.

February: Adams nominates and Senate confirms John Marshall as fourth chief justice.

Judiciary Act of 1801 reshapes federal judiciary; Adams nominates and Senate confirms circuit court judges and other officials, including justices of the peace in the District of Columbia.

On thirty-sixth ballot, House of Representatives declares Jefferson elected president, with Aaron Burr as vice president.

March 4: Adams leaves Washington, DC, for Quincy; Jefferson inaugurated as president.

March 17: Adams arrives in Quincy.

Massachusetts state legislature journeys from Boston to Quincy to welcome Adams home.

1802

October: Adams begins autobiography.

1803

Failure of London bank threatens John's and Abigail's finances, but John Quincy Adams resolves the crisis.

William Cunningham launches correspondence with Adams.

1804

Correspondence between Abigail Adams and Thomas Jefferson.

November: Jefferson elected for a second term.

1805

Discourses on Davila is published in book form in Boston, reproducing thirty-one of thirty-two essays.

May 16: Thomas Boylston Adams marries Ann Harrod.

John Adams and Benjamin Rush resume their correspondence.

Rush repeatedly urges Adams and Jefferson to resume their friendship.

1807

Bitter quarrel between Adams and Mercy Otis Warren over her depiction of him in her *History*.

Adams breaks off writing autobiography.

1808

James Madison is elected fourth president.

1809

Adams begins writing *Boston Patriot* essays, continuing until 1811.

William Cunningham begins series of increasingly agitated letters attacking Adams's political views.

1812

Adams writes to Jefferson, resuming their correspondence, which continues until 1826.

War of 1812.

Adams breaks off correspondence with William Cunningham.

1813

April 19: Death of Benjamin Rush.

August 15: Nabby Adams dies of breast cancer at age forty-eight.

1815

John Quincy Adams leads peace negotiations culminating in the Treaty of Ghent, which ends the War of 1812.

1817

John Quincy Adams becomes James Monroe's secretary of state.

1818

October 28: Abigail Adams dies of typhoid fever at age seventy-three.

1819

Volume collecting *Novanglus* and *Massachusettensis* essays published in Boston.

1820

November 15: Adams serves as delegate to 1820 Massachusetts constitutional convention (ending on January 9, 1821).

1823

Ephraim May Cunningham publishes William Cunningham's correspondence with John Adams, hoping to damage John Quincy Adams's presidential hopes in 1824.

Jefferson reassures Adams that the Cunningham letters make no difference to their friendship.

1825

February: John Quincy Adams is elected president of the United States.

1826

July 4: John Adams dies at age ninety. He is buried alongside his wife in the Adams family crypt at Hancock Cemetery in the heart of Quincy, Massachusetts.

Thomas Jefferson dies at age eighty-three.

1828

John and Abigail transferred to their final resting place in the crypt in the "Church of the Presidents." John Quincy Adams and Louisa Catherine Adams also transferred to the crypt in 1852.

A NOTE ON SOURCES

This book uses various types of sources to cite and quote John Adams's writings. In choosing between print sources and online databases, I have preferred the databases, for they are accessible to all readers. I list reliable sources, both online and print, here.

For the diary and autobiography of John Adams and for the correspondence between John and Abigail Adams, I use Adams Family Papers: An Electronic Archive, online at http://www.masshist.org/digitaladams/archive/.

For sources from the Massachusetts Historical Society digital archive, I have given letter writers and recipients, dates, and the abbreviation AFPEA/MHS. (These documents are also available online at the Founders Online website maintained by the National Archives [NA], http://founders.archives.gov—with annotation from the published volumes of the *Adams Papers* series)

The Massachusetts Historical Society website offers a profusion of other Adams papers. The MHS also has digital editions of published volumes of the *Adams Papers* series, including *The Legal Papers of John Adams*, the first fifteen volumes of the *Adams Family Correspondence*, and the first seventeen volumes of *The Papers of John Adams*. Readers may browse the contents of these volumes or pursue specific documents at http://www.masshist.org/publications/adams-papers/index.php/browse.

I also use Founders Online (URL given two paragraphs earlier), a comprehensive database and search engine allowing access to the published volumes of the Adams Papers; this database also includes the scholarly editions of the papers of George Washington, Benjamin Franklin, Thomas Jefferson, James Madison, and Alexander Hamilton.

In citing Founders Online, I have used the abbreviated citations FO/NA and I have omitted the citation to the original print edition.

The only previous edition of Adams's papers, Charles Francis Adams, ed., *The Life and Works of John Adams*, 10 vols. (Boston: Charles C. Little and James Brown, 1850–56), is accessible online through the Liberty Fund's Online Library of Liberty. It is also accessible online, though with occasional difficulties, through Google Books. It is available in print through various publishers' print-on-demand editions.

As to print editions, Gordon S. Wood's three-volume edition for the Library of America of selected papers of John Adams, *Revolutionary Writings 1755–1775, Revolutionary Writings 1775–1783*, and *Writings from the New Nation, 1784–1826* (New York: Library of America, 2011, 2016), and Edith Gelles's selected edition, *Abigail Adams: Letters* (New York: Library of America, 2016), are indispensable guidebooks to the high points of these rich manuscript sources; they are based on the published volumes of the *Adams Papers* project. The classic edition of John Adams's *Diary* and *Autobiography* is L. H. Butterfield, ed., *The Diary and Autobiography of John Adams*, 4 vols. (Cambridge, MA: Belknap Press of Harvard University Press, 1961), supplemented by L. H. Butterfield, ed., *The Earliest Diary of John Adams: June 1753–April 1754, September 1758–January 1759* (Cambridge, MA: Belknap Press of Harvard University Press, 1966). For the correspondence between John and Abigail Adams and Thomas Jefferson, the classic edition is Lester J. Cappon, *The Adams-Jefferson Letters* (Chapel Hill: University of North Carolina Press for the Institute of Early American History and Culture, 1959). See also Margaret A. Hogan and C. James Taylor, eds., *My Dearest Friend: Letters of Abigail and John Adams* (Cambridge, MA: Belknap Press of Harvard University Press, 2007), supplanting L. H. Butterfield, ed., *The Book of Abigail and John: Selected Letters of the Adams Family, 1762–1784* (Cambridge, MA: Belknap Press of Harvard University Press, 1975); Charles Warren, ed., *Correspondence between John Adams and Mercy Otis Warren* (New York: Arno Press, 1972; reprinting material from *Collections of the Massachusetts Historical Society*, vol. 4, 5th series, 1878); Massachusetts Historical Society, *The Warren-Adams Letters, Being chiefly a correspondence among John Adams, Samuel Adams, and James Warren*, 2 vols. (New York: AMS Press, 1972, reprinting *Collections of the Massachusetts Historical Society*, vols. 72–73 [Boston: Massachusetts Historical Society, 1917–25]); Worthington Chauncey Ford, *Statesman and Friend: The Correspondence of John Adams with Benjamin Waterhouse, 1784–1822* (Boston: Little, Brown, 1927); and John A. Schutz and Douglass G. Adair, *The Spur of Fame: Dialogues of John Adams and Benjamin Rush,*

1805–1813 (San Marino, CA: Huntington Library, 1966; reprint with different pagination, Indianapolis, IN: Liberty Fund, 2001), based on *Old Family Letters, Copied from the Originals for Alexander Biddle, Series A* (Philadelphia: J. B. Lippincott, 1892).

I preserve original spelling and punctuation. For letters, I give the writer and the recipient and the date. For other primary sources, I give the writer, the title, and the date.

I use the following abbreviations:

Cappon	Lester J. Cappon, ed., *The Adams-Jefferson Letters: The Complete Correspondence between Thomas Jefferson and John and Abigail Adams.* 2 vols. Chapel Hill: University of North Carolina Press for the Institute of Early American History and Culture, 1959.
Howe	John R. Howe Jr., *The Changing Political Thought of John Adams* (Princeton, NJ: Princeton University Press, 1966).
Ryerson, *Republic*	Richard Alan Ryerson: *John Adams's Republic: The One, the Few, and the Many* (Baltimore: Johns Hopkins University Press, 2016).
WJA	Charles Francis Adams, ed., *The Works of John Adams, Second President of the United States,* 10 vols. (Boston: Little and Brown, 1850–56).
Wood *JA 1755–1775*	Gordon S. Wood, *John Adams: Revolutionary Writings, 1755–1775* (New York: Library of America, 2011).
Wood *JA 1775–1783*	Gordon S. Wood, *John Adams: Revolutionary Writings, 1775–1783* (New York: Library of America, 2011).
Wood *JA 1784–1826*	Gordon S. Wood, *John Adams: Writings from the New Nation 1784–1826* (New York: Library of America, 2016.).

NOTES

Preface: "Let us dare to read, think, speak and write"

1. John Adams, "VI. 'A Dissertation on the Canon and the Feudal Law,' No. 4, 21 October 1765," FO/NA. The quotations in this and the next paragraph are from this source.

2. The memoir by Adams's great-grandson Henry Brooks Adams inspired this book's title. Henry Adams, *The Education of Henry Adams* (Boston: Houghton Mifflin, 1918). This book is a free-standing companion volume to a similar life in context, R. B. Bernstein, *Thomas Jefferson* (New York: Oxford University Press, 2003).

3. See the otherwise illuminating studies by Peter Shaw, *The Character of John Adams* (Chapel Hill: University of North Carolina Press for the Institute of Early American History and Culture, 1975), and by John E. Ferling, *John Adams: A Life* (Knoxville: University of Tennessee Press, 1992). A best-selling popular life stressing his character to the exclusion of nearly all else is David McCullough, *John Adams* (New York: Simon and Schuster, 2001).

4. See, e.g., Correa Moylan Walsh, *The Political Science of John Adams: A Study in the Theory of Mixed Government and the Bicameral System* (New York: G. P. Putnam's Sons, 1915); and, to a lesser extent, C. Bradley Thompson, *John Adams and the Spirit of Liberty* (Lawrence: University Press of Kansas, 1998).

5. Precursors of this book's approach include James Grant, *John Adams: Party of One* (New York: Farrar, Straus and Giroux, 2005), and Joseph J. Ellis, *Passionate Sage: The Character and Legacy of John Adams* (New York: W. W. Norton, 1992). See also Luke Mayville, *John Adams and the Fear of American Oligarchy* (Princeton, NJ: Princeton University Press, 2016); Richard Alan Ryerson, *John*

Adams's Republic: The One, the Few, and the Many (Baltimore: Johns Hopkins University Press, 2016). Page Smith's Bancroft Prize–winning biography, *John Adams*, 2 vols. (Garden City, NY: Doubleday, 1962), is more a collection of information than a sustained biographical treatment. By contrast, the brilliant, concise essay in Edmund S. Morgan, *The Meaning of Independence: John Adams, George Washington, and Thomas Jefferson* (Charlottesville: University of Virginia Press, 2004 [1976]), 3–27, has been of great aid to me.

6. Douglass Adair, "Fame and the Founding Fathers," in *Fame and the Founding Fathers: Essays of Douglass Adair*, ed. Trevor Colbourn (New York: W. W. Norton for the Institute of Early American History and Culture, 1974; repr., Indianapolis: Liberty Fund, 1998), chap. 1. For helpful discussion of a similar problem affecting Marcus Tullius Cicero, whom Adams saw as a hero and role model, see Kathryn Tempest, *Cicero: Politics and Persuasion in Ancient Rome* (London: Continuum, 2011), esp. 2–7.

7. Edith B. Gelles, *Abigail and John: Portrait of a Marriage* (New York: William Morrow, 2009). Other treatments include Joseph J. Ellis, *First Family: Abigail and John Adams* (New York: Alfred A. Knopf, 2010), and G. J. Barker-Benfield, *Abigail and John Adams: The Americanization of Sensibility* (Chicago: University of Chicago Press, 2010). On Abigail, see generally Edith B. Gelles, *Portia: The World of Abigail Adams* (Bloomington: Indiana University Press, 1992); Edith B. Gelles, *First Thoughts: Life and Letters of Abigail Adams* (Boston: Twayne, 1998), reprinted in paperback as *Abigail Adams: A Writing Life*, London: Routledge, 2002); and Woody Holton, *Abigail Adams* (New York: Free Press, 2009).

8. The works of Merrill Jensen, Jack P. Greene, and David Hackett Fischer have been of immense aid. Merrill M. Jensen, ed., *Regionalism in America* (Madison: University of Wisconsin Press, 1951); Jack P. Greene, *Pursuits of Happiness: The Social Development of Early Modern British Colonies and the Formation of American Culture* (Chapel Hill: University of North Carolina Press for the Institute for Early American History and Culture, 1988); David Hackett Fischer, *Albion's Seed: Four British Folkways in America* (New York: Oxford University Press, 1989). I am deeply indebted for this point to conversations with Professor William E. Nelson of New York University School of Law.

9. L. Kinvin Wroth and Hiller Zobel, eds., *The Adams Papers, Series III: The Legal Papers of John Adams*, 3 vols. (Cambridge, MA: Belknap Press of Harvard University Press, 1965). Draft legal pleadings and essays are scattered through Adams's diary, showing how central Adams's legal work was to his understanding of himself. For excellent treatments of that legal world, see William

E. Nelson, *Americanization of the Common Law: The Impact of Legal Change on Massachusetts Society, 1760–1830* (Cambridge, MA: Harvard University Press, 1975; reprint, with a new introduction, Athens: University of Georgia Press, 1994), and Daniel R. Coquillette, ed., *Law in Colonial Massachusetts, 1630–1800* (Charlottesville: University Press of Virginia for the Colonial Society of Massachusetts, 1984). See also William E. Nelson, *The Common Law in Colonial America*, 4 vols. (New York: Oxford University Press, 2008–17). Finally, I am deeply indebted to Professor Charles L. Zelden of Nova Southeastern University, particularly for his biography of Thurgood Marshall, another great man of law. We eagerly await Richard Samuelson's forthcoming study, "John Adams and the Republic of Laws."

10. Gordon S. Wood, *The Americanization of Benjamin Franklin* (New York: Penguin, 2004), 154–57.

11. Gerald Stourzh, *Benjamin Franklin and American Foreign Policy*, rev. ed. (Chicago: University of Chicago Press, 1969 [1954]); see also Wood, *Americanization of Benjamin Franklin*, 153–200; James H. Hutson, *John Adams and the Diplomacy of the American Revolution* (Lexington: University Press of Kentucky, 1980).

12. James T. Patterson, *Grand Expectations: The United States, 1944–1974* (New York: Oxford University Press, 1997), 283 (Winston S. Churchill on US secretary of state John Foster Dulles).

13. Kathleen Bartolini-Tuazon, *For Fear of an Elective King: George Washington and the Presidential Titles Controversy of 1789* (Ithaca, NY: Cornell University Press, 2014).

14. Roy Porter and Mikulas Teich, eds., *The Enlightenment in National Context* (Cambridge: Cambridge University Press, 1981). On the radical Enlightenment, see Jonathan I. Israel, *A Revolution of the Mind: Radical Enlightenment and the Intellectual Origins of Modern Democracy* (Princeton, NJ: Princeton University Press, 2010). For the contrast between the European and American Enlightenments, see Henry Steele Commager, *Empire of Reason: How the Europeans Imagined and the Americans Realized the Enlightenment* (New York: Anchor Books/Doubleday, 1977).

15. On the English Enlightenment, see Roy Porter, *The Creation of the Modern World: The British Enlightenment* (New York: W. W. Norton, 2000).

16. JA to AA, after May 12, 1780, AFPEA/MHS.

17. This phrase, a favorite with Adams, appears most famously in "Thoughts on Government": "III. Thoughts on Government, April 1776," FO/NA.

18. Niccolò Machiavelli to Francesco Vettori, December 10, 1513, in *Machiavelli and His Friends: Their Personal Correspondence,* ed. and trans. J. B. Atkinson and David Sices (DeKalb: Northern Illinois University Press, 1996), 262–65 (quotation at 264).

19. "From John Adams to Alexander Jardine, 1 June 1790," FO/NA [Early Access document].

20. C. Bradley Thompson, "John Adams's Machiavellian Moment," *Review of Politics* 57, no. 3 (Summer 1995): 389–417.

21. Stephen G. Kurtz, "The Political Science of John Adams: A Guide to His Statecraft," *William and Mary Quarterly,* 3rd ser., 25, no. 4 (October 1968): 605–13.

22. Joanne Pope Melish, *Disowning Slavery: Gradual Emancipation and "Race" in New England, 1780–1860* (Ithaca, NY: Cornell University Press, 1998); Jared Ross Hardesty, *Unfreedom: Slavery and Dependence in Eighteenth-Century Boston* (New York: NYU Press, 2017); Lorenzo Johnston Greene, *The Negro in Colonial New England, 1620–1776* (New York: Atheneum, 1963 [1942]).

23. John R. Howe Jr., "John Adams's Views on Slavery," *Journal of Negro History* 49, no. 3 (July 1964): 101–6. And see Arthur Scherr, *John Adams, Slavery, and Race: Ideas, Politics, and Diplomacy in an Age of Crisis* (Santa Barbara, CA: Praeger, 2018).

24. "*The Federalist No. 1* [October 27, 1787]," FO/NA; Henry Steele Commager, "Leadership in Eighteenth-Century America and Today," *Daedalus* 90, no. 4 (Fall 1961): 652–73, reprinted in Henry Steele Commager, *Freedom and Order: A Commentary on the American Political Scene* (Cleveland: World Publishing Company, 1966), 149–70 (notes at 318–20).

25. Thompson, *John Adams and the Spirit of Liberty*; John R. Howe, *The Changing Political Thought of John Adams* (Princeton, NJ: Princeton University Press, 1966); Zoltan Haraszti, *John Adams and the Prophets of Progress* (Cambridge, MA: Harvard University Press, 1952); Timothy H. Breen, "John Adams' Fight against Innovation in the New England Constitution: 1776," *New England Quarterly* 40, no. 4 (December 1967): 501–20; C. Bradley Thompson, ed., *The Revolutionary Writings of John Adams* (Indianapolis: Liberty Fund, 2000); John Patrick Diggins, ed., *The Portable John Adams* (New York: Penguin, 2004); George A. Peek, ed., *Political Writings of John Adams* (Indianapolis: Bobbs-Merrill/Library of Liberal Arts, 1954); and George W. Carey, ed., *The Political Writings of John Adams* (Washington, DC: Regnery, 2000). The two newest and best examinations of John Adams's political thought are Mayville, *John*

Adams and the Fear of American Oligarchy, and Ryerson, *John Adams's Republic*. See also Scherr, *John Adams, Slavery, and Race*. Nancy Isenberg and Andrew Burstein, *The Problem of Democracy: The Presidents Adams Confront the Cult of Personality* (New York: Viking, 2019), came out just as I was doing the final edit of this book; I have tried to take account of its arguments.

26. Jane E. Calvert, *Quaker Constitutionalism and the Political Thought of John Dickinson* (Cambridge: Cambridge University Press, 2009). I am grateful to Jane Calvert for her emendation of this sentence.

27. Gregory Claeys, *Thomas Paine: Social and Political Thought* (Boston: Unwin Hyman, 1989); Eric Foner, *Tom Paine and Revolutionary America*, updated edition (New York: Oxford University Press, 2004 [1976]); Eric Foner, ed., *Thomas Paine: Collected Writings* (New York: Library of America, 1994); Jack Fruchtman, *The Political Philosophy of Thomas Paine* (Baltimore: Johns Hopkins University Press, 2009); and R. B. Bernstein, "Review Essay: Rediscovering Thomas Paine," *New York Law School Law Review* 39, no. 4 (1994): 873–929. On Franklin, see Wood, *Americanization of Benjamin Franklin*; Stourzh, *Benjamin Franklin and American Foreign Policy*; Carla J. Mulford, *Benjamin Franklin and the Ends of Empire* (New York: Oxford University Press, 2015); Paul W. Conner, *Poor Richard's Politicks: Benjamin Franklin and His New American Order* (New York: Oxford University Press, 1965); Lorraine Smith Pangle, *The Political Philosophy of Benjamin Franklin* (Baltimore: Johns Hopkins University Press, 2007); J. A. Leo Lemay, ed., *Benjamin Franklin: Writings* (New York: Library of America, 1987); Ralph Ketcham, ed., *The Political Thought of Benjamin Franklin* (Indianapolis: Hackett, 2003 [1965]); and Alan Houston, ed., *Franklin: The Autobiography and Other Writings on Politics, Economics, and Virtue* (Cambridge: Cambridge University Press, 2004).

28. On Madison, see Lance Banning, *The Sacred Fire of Liberty: James Madison and the Origins of the Federal Republic* (Ithaca, NY: Cornell University Press, 1995); Drew R. McCoy, *The Last of the Fathers: James Madison and the Republican Legacy* (Cambridge: Cambridge University Press, 1989); Jack N. Rakove, *James Madison and the Creation of the American Republic*, 3rd ed. (New York: Pearson/Longman, 2007); Rakove, *A Politician Thinking: The Creative Mind of James Madison* (Norman: University of Oklahoma Press, 2017); Ralph Ketcham, *James Madison* (New York: Macmillan, 1971; repr., Charlottesville: University Press of Virginia, 1990); Colleen Sheehan, *James Madison and the Spirit of Republican Self-Government* (Cambridge: Cambridge University Press, 2009); Jack N. Rakove, ed., *James Madison: Writings* (New York: Library of America, 1999); Marvin Meyers, ed., *The Mind of the*

Founder: Selected Writings of James Madison, rev. ed. (Hanover, NH: University Press of New England, 1981); Irving N. Brant, *James Madison,* 6 vols. (Indianapolis: Bobbs-Merrill, 1941–61); and Colbourn, *Fame and the Founding Fathers.*

29. On Jefferson, see, e.g., Bernstein, *Thomas Jefferson;* Peter S. Onuf, ed., *Jeffersonian Legacies* (Charlottesville: University Press of Virginia, 1993); Onuf, *Jefferson's Empire: The Language of American Nationhood* (Charlottesville: University Press of Virginia, 2000); Onuf, *The Mind of Thomas Jefferson* (Charlottesville: University of Virginia Press, 2007); Onuf, *Jefferson and the Virginians: Democracy, Constitutions, and Empire* (Charlottesville: University of Virginia Press, 2018); David N. Mayer, *The Constitutional Thought of Thomas Jefferson* (Charlottesville: University Press of Virginia, 1994); Dumas Malone, *Jefferson and His Time,* 6 vols. (Boston: Little, Brown, 1948–81); Merrill D. Peterson, *Thomas Jefferson and the New Nation: A Biography* (New York: Oxford University Press, 1971); and Peterson, ed., *Thomas Jefferson: Writings* (New York: Library of America, 1984). On the "age of the Democratic Revolution," see R. R. Palmer, *The Age of the Democratic Revolution: A Political History of Europe and America, 1760–1800,* 2 vols. (Princeton, NJ: Princeton University Press, 1959–64; one vol. ed., Princeton, NJ: Princeton University Press, 2014), supplemented by Janet Polasky, *Revolution without Borders: The Call to Liberty in the Atlantic World* (New Haven, CT: Yale University Press, 2015).

30. On Hamilton, see Joanne B. Freeman, ed., *Alexander Hamilton: Writings* (New York: Library of America, 2001); Gerald Stourzh, *Alexander Hamilton and the Idea of Republican Government* (Stanford, CA: Stanford University Press, 1970); Karl-Friedrich Walling, *Republican Empire: Alexander Hamilton on War and Free Government* (Lawrence: University Press of Kansas, 1999); John Lamberton Harper, *American Machiavelli: Alexander Hamilton and the Origins of U.S. Foreign Policy* (Cambridge: Cambridge University Press, 2004); Clinton L. Rossiter, *Alexander Hamilton and the Constitution* (New York: Harcourt, Brace and World, 1964); Harvey Flaumenhaft, *The Effective Republic: Administration and Constitution in the Thought of Alexander Hamilton* (Durham, NC: Duke University Press, 1994); John C. Miller, *Alexander Hamilton: Portrait in Paradox* (New York: Harper, 1959); Forrest McDonald, *Alexander Hamilton: A Biography* (New York: W. W. Norton, 1979); Michael P. Federici, *The Political Philosophy of Alexander Hamilton* (Baltimore: Johns Hopkins University Press, 2012); and Ron Chernow,

Alexander Hamilton (New York: Penguin, 2004). On John Jay, see Richard B. Morris, *John Jay, the Nation, and the Court* (Boston: Boston University Press, 1967), and Walter Stahr, *John Jay: Founding Father* (New York: Hambledon and London, 2005).

31. On Washington, see Jeffry H. Morrison, *The Political Philosophy of George Washington* (Baltimore: Johns Hopkins University Press, 2009); Glenn A. Phelps, *George Washington and American Constitutionalism* (Lawrence: University Press of Kansas, 1993); Robert F. Jones, *George Washington: Ordinary Man, Extraordinary Leader* (Bronx, NY: Fordham University Press, 2002); Edmund S. Morgan, *The Genius of George Washington* (Washington, DC: Society of the Cincinnati, 1980); Marcus W. Cunliffe, *George Washington: Man and Monument* (Boston: Little, Brown, 1958); and John F. Rhodehamel, ed., *George Washington: Writings* (New York: Library of America, 1997). For the Washington-Hamilton collaboration, see Richard B. Morris, "Washington and Hamilton: A Great Collaboration," *Proceedings of the American Philosophical Society* 102, no. 2 (April 30, 1958): 107–16. On John Marshall, see Charles F. Hobson, *The Great Chief Justice: John Marshall and the Rule of Law* (Lawrence: University Press of Kansas, 1996); R. Kent Newmyer, *The Supreme Court under Marshall and Taney*, 2nd ed. (Wheeling, IL: Harlan Davidson, 2006 [1968]); R. Kent Newmyer, *John Marshall and the Heroic Age of the Supreme Court* (Baton Rouge: Louisiana State University Press, 2001); Jean Edward Smith, *John Marshall: Definer of a Nation* (New York; Henry Holt, 1996); Charles F. Hobson, ed., *John Marshall: Writings* (New York: Library of America, 2010).

32. On other constitutional visions, see Ray Raphael, Alfred F. Young, and Gary B. Nash, eds., *Revolutionary Founders: Rebels, Radicals, and Reformers in the Making of the Nation* (New York: Alfred A. Knopf, 2011); Mark David Hall, *Roger Sherman and the Creation of the American Republic* (New York: Oxford University Press, 2013).

33. William E. Nelson, "Reason and Compromise in the Establishment of the Federal Constitution, 1787–1801," *William and Mary Quarterly*, 3rd ser., 44, no. 3 (July 1987): 458–84; Jack N. Rakove, "The Great Compromise: Ideas, Interests, and the Politics of Constitution Making," *William and Mary Quarterly*, 3rd ser., 44, no. 3 (July 1987): 424–57.

34. Since I wrote the first drafts of this preface, I have come across Rakove, *A Politician Thinking*. It is good to know that my thinking runs in parallel with that of one of the field's best scholars.

Chapter One

1. John Adams autobiography, part 1, "John Adams," through 1776, sheet 1 of 53, AFPEA/MHS.

2. Charles Francis Adams, *History of Braintree, Massachusetts (1639–1708) the North Precinct of Braintree (1708–1792) and the Town of Quincy (1732–1889)* (Cambridge, MA: Printed at the Riverside Press, 1891).

3. "Tablet for Henry Adams' Grave," *The Magazine of History, with Notes and Queries* 7, no. 5 (May 1908): 294–97 (quotation at 295).

4. Alfred F. Young, *The Shoemaker and the Tea Party: Memory and the American Revolution* (Boston: Beacon Press, 1999), 19, 29.

5. John Adams autobiography, part 1, "John Adams," through 1776, sheet 2 of 53, AFPEA/MHS.

6. Quoted in Gilbert Chinard, *Honest John Adams* (Boston: Little, Brown, 1935), 8.

7. John E. Ferling, *John Adams: A Life* (Knoxville: University of Tennessee Press, 1992; pbk. repr., New York: Henry Holt, 1993), 10.

8. Ferling, 9.

9. John Adams autobiography, part 1, "John Adams," through 1776, sheet 2 of 53, AFPEA/MHS.

10. John Adams autobiography, part 1, "John Adams," through 1776, sheet 2 of 53, AFPEA/MHS.

11. Chinard, *Honest John Adams*, 9.

12. John Adams autobiography, part 1, "John Adams," through 1776, sheet 2 of 53, AFPEA/MHS. All quotations in this paragraph and the next come from this source.

13. John Adams autobiography, part 1, "John Adams," through 1776, sheet 2 of 53, AFPEA/MHS. For the other version, Chinard, *Honest John Adams*, 11.

14. John Adams autobiography, part 1, "John Adams," through 1776, sheet 2 of 53, AFPEA/MHS.

15. John Adams autobiography, part 1, "John Adams," through 1776, sheet 2 of 53, AFPEA/MHS.

16. Robert C. Baron and Conrad Edick Wright, eds., *The Libraries, Leadership, and Legacy of John Adams and Thomas Jefferson* (Golden, CO: Fulcrum Publishing and Massachusetts Historical Society, 2010), esp. Beth Prindle,

"Thoughts, Care, and Money: John Adams Assembles His Library," 3–19, 260–61; and Zoltan Haraszti, *John Adams and the Prophets of Progress* (Cambridge, MA: Harvard University Press, 1952), 14–25. Adams's copy of Cicero's *Orationes* is available online at http://www.archive.org/stream/mtulliiciceronis00cice#page/n3/mode/2up.

17. I am grateful to James M. Farrell of the University of New Hampshire for sharing with me his superb studies of Cicero's importance to John Adams: James M. Farrell, "John Adams's *Autobiography*: The Ciceronian Paradigm and the Quest for Fame," *New England Quarterly* 62 (1989): 505–28; Farrell, "'Syren Tully' and the Young John Adams," *Classical Journal* 87 (1992): 373–90; Farrell, "Letters and Political Judgment: John Adams and Cicero's Style," *Studies in Eighteenth-Century Culture* 24 (1994): 137–53.

18. John Adams autobiography, part 1, "John Adams," through 1776, sheet 2 of 53, AFPEA/MHS.

19. Bainbridge Bunting, *Harvard: An Architectural History* (Cambridge, MA: Harvard University Press, 1998), esp. 318.

20. James Grant, *John Adams: Party of One* (New York: Farrar, Straus and Giroux, 2005), 24, citing Clifford K. Shipton, *Sibley's Harvard Graduates: Biographical Sketches of Those Who Attended Harvard College* (Boston: Massachusetts Historical Society, 1965), 13:512.

21. John Adams autobiography, part 1, "John Adams," through 1776, sheet 3 of 53, AFPEA/MHS; and see Chinard, *Honest John Adams*, 17–18.

22. I. Bernard Cohen, *Science and the Founding Fathers: Science in the Political Thought of Thomas Jefferson, Benjamin Franklin, John Adams, and James Madison*, rev. pbk. ed. (New York: W. W. Norton, 1997 [1995]), chap. 4.

23. Grant, *John Adams*, 22–25; Chinard, *Honest John Adams*, 12–17.

24. Alan Macfarlane, *The Family Life of Ralph Josselin: A Seventeenth-Century Clergyman: An Essay in Historical Anthropology* (Cambridge: Cambridge University Press, 19701), esp. 3–11.

25. Bernard Bailyn, "Notes and Documents: Butterfield's Adams: Notes for a Sketch," *William and Mary Quarterly*, 3rd ser., 19, no. 2 (April 1962): 238–56; Edmund S. Morgan, "Review Essay: John Adams and the Puritan Tradition," *New England Quarterly* 34, no. 4 (December 1961): 518–29; Dan Doll and Jessica Munns, eds., *Recording and Reordering: Essays on the Seventeenth-Century and Eighteenth-Century Diary and Journal* (Lewisburg, PA: Bucknell University Press, 2006).

Chapter Two

1. "From John Adams to Richard Cranch, 2 September 1755," FO/NA. See also "From John Adams to Nathan Webb, 1 September 1755," FO/NA.

2. "From John Adams to Nathan Webb, with Comments by the Writer Recorded in 1807," FO/NA. All quotations in this paragraph come from this letter.

3. Fred Anderson, *Crucible of War: The Seven Years' War and the Fate of Empire in British North America* (New York: Alfred A. Knopf, 2000).

4. In 1807, a kinsman of Nathan Webb returned this letter to Adams, who scribbled reflections on his friendship with Webb and on Webb's untimely death in 1760, which caused him great sorrow. He saw his letter as prophetic in its case for American claims to imperial status and its argument for the need to preserve the American Union.

5. Gordon S. Wood, *The Americanization of Benjamin Franklin* (New York: Penguin, 2004); and Carla J. Mulford, *Benjamin Franklin and the Ends of Empire* (New York: Oxford University Press, 2015). John A. Schutz and Douglass Adair, in *The Spur of Fame: Dialogues of John Adams and Benjamin Rush, 1805–1813* (San Marino, CA: Huntington Library Press, 1966), 81n13, point out that in 1755 Adams had been reading William Clarke's *Observations on the . . . Conduct of the French* (Boston, 1755), which included Franklin's essay "Observations Concerning the Increase of Mankind and the Peopling of Countries" (1751). "Observations Concerning the Increase of Mankind, 1751," FO/NA.

6. Entry for March 15, 1756, in John Adams diary 1, November 18, 1755–August 29, 1756, AFPEA/MHS.

7. Entry for February 16, 1756, in John Adams diary 1, November 18, 1755–August 29, 1756, AFPEA/MHS.

8. Entry for April 22, 1756, in John Adams diary 1, November 18, 1755–August 29, 1756, AFPEA/MHS.

9. John Adams autobiography, part 1, "John Adams," through 1776, sheet 4 of 53, AFPEA/MHS.

10. John Adams autobiography, part 1, "John Adams," through 1776, sheet 4 of 53, AFPEA/MHS.

11. On the quest for consensus, see Michael Zuckerman, *Peaceable Kingdoms: New England Towns in the Eighteenth Century* (New York: Alfred A. Knopf, 1972); on consensus and conflict in Massachusetts's evolving legal culture, see William E. Nelson, *Americanization of the Common Law: The*

Impact of Legal Change on Massachusetts Society, 1760–1830 (Cambridge, MA: Harvard University Press, 1975; repr. with new intro., Athens: University of Georgia Press, 1994).

12. On Adams's fascination with Cicero, see the sources cited in chapter 1, note 17. On his legal studies, see L. Kinvin Wroth and Hiller Zobel, eds., *The Legal Papers of John Adams*, 3 vols. (hereafter *LPJA*) (Cambridge, MA: Belknap Press of Harvard University Press, 1965). In *LPJA* 1:1–25, "Legal Study," two documents survive from Adams's early study of law, including fragments of his commonplace book. *LPJA* 1:26–86 appears to be Adams's collection of model pleadings and writs—in essence his private form book. Daniel R. Coquillette, ed., *Law in Colonial Massachusetts 1630–1800* (Boston: Colonial Society of Massachusetts, distributed by University of Virginia Press, 1984); and Nelson, *Americanization of the Common Law*.

13. Daniel R. Coquillette, "Justinian in Braintree: John Adams, Civilian Learning, and Legal Elitism, 1758–1775," in Coquillette, *Law in Colonial Massachusetts*, 359–418.

14. William E Nelson, "Court Records as Sources for Historical Writing," in Coquillette, *Law in Colonial Massachusetts*, 499–518 (esp. 502–16). See also Nelson, *Americanization of the Common Law*, 69–80. The leading treatment of colonial American legal history is William E. Nelson, *The Common Law in Colonial America*, 4 vols. (New York: Oxford University Press, 2008–18). See also the pathbreaking study by Richard B. Morris, *Studies in the History of American Laws with Special Reference to the Seventeenth and Eighteenth Centuries* (New York: Columbia University Press, 1930; 2nd ed., New York: Octagon Books, 1958).

15. Morris R. Cohen, "Legal Literature in Colonial Massachusetts," in Coquillette, *Law in Colonial Massachusetts*, 243–72; Sally Hadden, "Legal History Meets the History of the Book" (paper presented at 2015 annual meeting of the American Historical Association, New York, January 2, 2015). I thank Sally Hadden for permission to cite this unpublished paper.

16. These are diaries 3, 9, 10, and 14; http://www.masshist.org/digitaladams/archive/browse/diaries_by_number.php.

17. On Gridley, see *LPJA* 1:ci; John L. Sibley (continued by Clifford K. Shipton, Conrad Edick Wright, and Edward W. Hanson), *Sibley's Harvard Graduates: Biographical Sketches of Graduates of Harvard University . . .* , 16 vols. to date (Cambridge, MA: Charles William Sever, University Bookstore, 1873–; later Cambridge, MA: Harvard University Press), 7:518–30; Samuel Lorenzo Knapp, *Biographical Sketches of Eminent Lawyers, Statesmen, and Men of Letters*

(Boston: Published by Richardson and Lord; John H. A. Frost, Printer, 1821), 199–217. For a portrait identified as depicting Gridley, see Coquillette, *Law in Colonial Massachusetts*, 364. For sketches of Otis, Prat, and Thacher, see *LPJA* 1:cv (Otis), 1:cvi (Prat), and 1:cxi (Thacher). For Adams's mentor, Putnam, see *LPJA* 1:cvii. *LPJA* 1:xcv–cxiv provides a biographical register of the principal lawyers whom John Adams encountered in practice. Charles R. McKirdy, "Massachusetts Lawyers on the Eve of the American Revolution: The State of the Profession," in Coquillette, *Law in Colonial Massachusetts*, 313–58, esp. 348 (Otis) and 350 (Putnam); McKirdy, 339–58, Appendix IV, "Biographical Sketches of Lawyers Practicing in Massachusetts, 1775," including the two sketches already cited.

18. Entry for October 5, 1758, in John Adams diary 2, October 5, 1758–April 9, 1759, AFPEA/MHS.

19. Entries for October 25, 1758 (on meeting with Gridley) and for October 24–26 and November 6 (?), 1758, in John Adams diary 2, October 5, 1758–April 9, 1759, AFPEA/MHS. For the passage of his *Autobiography*, see John Adams autobiography, part 1, "John Adams," through 1776, sheets 6–7 of 53, AFPEA/MHS; Coquillette, "Justinian in Braintree," 362–63, 366; Adams's summary account of his education, stressing his legal education, in John Adams to Thomas Dawes, July 28, 1821, http://www.masshist.org/database/viewer.php?item_id=1514. In this letter, Adams sought to clarify an apparently common misunderstanding—that Gridley and not Putnam had been his mentor in his legal studies.

20. Entries for October 24–26, and November 6 (?), 1758, in John Adams diary 2, October 5, 1758–April 9, 1759, AFPEA/MHS.

21. Entries for October 13, 1758 and December 18 and 29, 1758, in John Adams diary 2, October 5, 1758–April 9, 1759, AFPEA/MHS.

22. Entry for December 18, 1758, in John Adams diary 2, October 5, 1758–April 9, 1759, AFPEA/MHS.

23. Entry for November 14, 1760, John Adams diary 4, October 1759–November 20, 1761, November 21, 1772, AFPEA/MHS.

24. On pettifoggers in the English legal profession, see C. W. Brooks, *Pettifoggers and Vipers of the Commonwealth: The Lower Branch of the Legal Profession in Early Modern England* (Cambridge: Cambridge University Press, 1986).

25. John Adams autobiography, part 1, "John Adams," through 1776, sheet 8 of 53, AFPEA/MHS.

26. Entry for August 1, 1761, John Adams diary 7, March 21–October 18, 1761, AFPEA/MHS. I am deeply grateful to William Chrystal for this reference. All quotations in the next paragraph are from this source.

27. *LPJA* 2:48–67 (case nos. 38–42).

28. Edward J. Dumbauld, *Thomas Jefferson and the Law* (Norman: University of Oklahoma Press, 1978); Frank J. Dewey, *Thomas Jefferson, Lawyer* (Charlottesville: University Press of Virginia, 1981).

29. Nelson, *The Common Law in Colonial America*; also Nelson, *Americanization of the Common Law.*

30. For the ancestor group including all nine "Humphrey Ploughjogger" letters, see https://founders.archives.gov/ancestor/ADMS-06-01-02-0045. On Adams's racist humor, see Arthur Scherr, *John Adams, Race, and Slavery: Ideas, Politics, and Diplomacy in an Age of Crisis* (Santa Barbara, CA: Praeger, 2018), 2–3.

31. Helen Saltzberg Saltman, "John Adams's Earliest Essays: The Humphrey Ploughjogger Letters," *William and Mary Quarterly*, 3rd ser., 37, no. 1 (January 1980): 125–35; Ryerson, *Republic*, 39–41, 43–44.

32. Carol Berkin, *Jonathan Sewall: Odyssey of an American Loyalist* (New York: Columbia University Press, 1974).

33. Entries for [October 27–30, 1758,] and January 1759, in John Adams diary 2, October 5, 1758–April 9, 1759, AFPEA/MHS.

34. John Ferling, *John Adams: A Life* (Knoxville: University of Tennessee Press, 1992), 26–27, and sources cited.

35. Edith Gelles, *Portia: The World of Abigail Adams* (Bloomington: Indiana University Press, 1992); Edith Gelles, *Abigail Adams: A Writing Life* (London: Routledge, 2002); Edith Gelles, *Abigail and John: Portrait of a Marriage* (New York: William Morrow, 2009); and Woody Holton, *Abigail Adams: A Life* (New York: Free Press, 2009).

36. Letter from John Adams to Abigail Smith, February 14, 1763,. *AFPEA* / MHS.

37. Gelles, *Abigail and John*, 16.

38. Letter from Abigail Smith to John Adams, April 8, 1764, AFPEA/MHS.

39. Letter from Abigail Smith to John Adams, April 16, 1764, AFPEA/MHS.

40. Letter from John Adams to Abigail Smith, May 7, 1764; letter from Abigail Smith to John Adams, May 9, 1764, AFPEA/MHS.

41. Gelles, *Abigail and John*, 18.

42. Letter from Abigail Smith to John Adams, October 4, 1764, AFPEA/MHS.

Chapter Three

1. Entry for January 1, 1766, John Adams diary 12, December 30, 1765–January 20, 1766, AFPEA/MHS.

2. "From John Adams to Thomas Jefferson, 24 August 1815," FO/NA [Early Access document].

3. Fred Anderson, *Crucible of War: The Seven Years' War and the Fate of Empire in British North America, 1754–1766* (New York: Alfred A. Knopf, 2000).

4. Fred Anderson, *A People's Army: Massachusetts Soldiers and Society in the Seven Years' War* (Chapel Hill: University of North Carolina Press for the Institute for Early American History and Culture, 1984).

5. Edmund S. Morgan, *The Meaning of Independence: John Adams, George Washington, and Thomas Jefferson* (1968; Charlottesville: University of Virginia Press, 2004).

6. "From John Adams to William Tudor, Sr., 29 March 1817," FO/NA [Early Access document]. Charles Francis Adams struck the italicized portion of the quotation from his published version of the letter.

7. M. H. Smith, *The Writs of Assistance Case* (Berkeley: University of California Press, 1978); L. Kinvin Wroth and Hiller B. Zobel, eds., *The Legal Papers of John Adams*, 3 vols. (hereafter *LPJA*) (Cambridge, MA: Belknap Press of Harvard University Press, 1965), 2:106–47: "Case No. 44: *Petition of Lechmere*"; James M. Farrell, "Writs of Assistance and Public Memory: John Adams and the Legacy of James Otis," *New England Quarterly* 89 (2006): 535–56; Farrell, "The Child Independence Is Born: James Otis and Writs of Assistance," in *Rhetoric, Independence and Nationhood*, ed. Stephen E. Lucas, vol. 2 of Martin J. Medhurst, ed., *A Rhetorical History of the United States: Significant Moments in American Public Discourse* (East Lansing: Michigan State University Press, forthcoming), available online at http://scholars.unh.edu/cgi/viewcontent.cgi?article=1004&context=comm_facpub.

8. "From John Adams to William Tudor, Sr., 29 March 1817," FO/NA [Early Access document].

9. "From John Adams to William Tudor, Sr., 29 March 1817," FO/NA [Early Access document].

10. Richard Archer, *As If an Enemy's Country: The British Occupation of Boston and the Origins of Revolution* (New York: Oxford University Press, 2010), 13–15.

11. Bernard Bailyn, *The Ordeal of Thomas Hutchinson* (Cambridge, MA: Belknap Press of Harvard University Press, 1974). For a legal-historical critique, see John Phillip Reid, "Book Review: The Ordeal by Law of Thomas Hutchinson," *New York University Law Review* 49 (October 1974): 593–613. For Bailyn's later reflections, see Bernard Bailyn, "Thomas Hutchinson in Context: The *Ordeal* Revisited," in Bailyn, *Sometimes an Art: Nine Essays on History* (New York: Alfred A. Knopf, 2015), 147–70 (notes at 284–85). On the Otises, see John J. Waters Jr., *The Otis Family in Provincial and Revolutionary Massachusetts* (Chapel Hill: University of North Carolina Press for Institute of Early American History and Culture, 1968).

12. "From John Adams to William Tudor, Sr., 29 March 1817," O/NA [Early Access document].

13. Akhil Reed Amar, *The Bill of Rights: Creation and Reconstruction* (New Haven, CT: Yale University Press, 1998), 66n*, accusing Adams of "historical revisionism." For the Virginia view, see Jon Kukla, *Patrick Henry: Champion of Liberty* (New York: Simon and Schuster, 2017), 39–46.

14. Rhys Isaac, "Religion and Authority: Problems of the Anglican Establishment in Virginia in the Era of the Great Awakening and the Parsons' Cause," *William and Mary Quarterly*, 3rd ser., 30, no. 1 (January 1973): 3–36; Arthur P. Scott, "The Constitutional Aspects of the 'Parson's Cause,'" *Political Science Quarterly* 31, no. 4 (December 1916): 558–77; Thad W. Tate, "The Coming of the Revolution in Virginia: Britain's Challenge to Virginia's Ruling Class, 1763–1776," *William and Mary Quarterly*, 3rd ser., 19, no. 3 (July 1962): 323–43.

15. Anderson, *Crucible of War*, 560–71; see also 572–616, 641–746.

16. Anderson, *A People's Army*.

17. Archer, *As If in an Enemy's Country*, 4.

18. Anderson, *Crucible of War*, 574–80.

19. Instructions dated May 24, 1764, in *Documents of the City of Boston, for the Year 1886, in Three Volumes: Volume II . . .* (Boston: Rockwell and Churchill, City Printers, 1887), *City Document No. 88: Boston Town Records*, 120–22 (quotation at 122).

20. Kevin Sharpe, *The Personal Rule of Charles I* (New Haven, CT: Yale University Press, 1996).

21. Steven Pincus, *1688: The First Modern Revolution* (New Haven, CT: Yale University Press, 2009).

22. Thomas Truxes, *Defying the Empire: Trading with the Enemy in Colonial New York* (New Haven, CT: Yale University Press, 2008).

23. Edward Porritt, assisted by Annie G. Porritt, *The Unreformed House of Commons: Parliamentary Representation before 1832*, 2 vols. (Cambridge: Cambridge University Press, 1903); John Cannon, *Parliamentary Reform, 1640–1832* (Cambridge: Cambridge University Press, 1973); and J. R. Pole, *Political Representation in England and the Origins of the American Republic* (London: Macmillan, 1966).

24. John Phillip Reid, *The Concept of Representation in the Age of the American Revolution* (Chicago: University of Chicago Press, 1989); Cannon, *Parliamentary Reform*; and Pole, *Political Representation*.

25. John Phillip Reid, *Constitutional History of the American Revolution*, 4 vols. (Madison: University of Wisconsin Press, 1986–1993; one-vol. abridged ed., 1995); Jack P. Greene, *The Constitutional Origins of the American Revolution* (Cambridge: Cambridge University Press, 2012).

26. Martin Loughrin, *The British Constitution: A Very Short Introduction* (Oxford: Oxford University Press, 2013).

27. John Phillip Reid, "Another Origin of Judicial Review: The Constitutional Crisis of 1776 and the Need for a Dernier Judge," *New York University Law Review* 64, no. 5 (November 1989): 963–89.

28. Archer, *As If an Enemy's Country*, 16.

29. Edmund S. Morgan and Helen M. Morgan, *The Stamp Act Crisis: Prologue to Revolution*, 3rd ed. (1955; Chapel Hill: University of North Carolina Press for the Institute of Early American History and Culture, 1991); Edmund S. Morgan, ed., *Prologue to Revolution: Sources and Documents on the Stamp Act Crisis, 1764–1766* (Chapel Hill: University of North Carolina Press for the Institute of Early American History and Culture, 1959); and Archer, *As If an Enemy's Country*, 20–22, 49–50.

30. John Adams autobiography, part 1, "John Adams," through 1776, sheet 10 of 53, AFPEA/MHS.

31. https://founders.archives.gov/ancestor/ADMS-06-01-02-0052. Ryerson, *Republic*, 47–49, 60–61; Howe, 40–43.

32. "III. Instructions as Printed in the *Massachusetts Gazette*, 10 October 1765," FO/NA. See Ryerson, *Republic*, 49–50.

33. Richard A. Samuelson, "The Constitutional Sanity of James Otis: Resistance Leader and Loyal Subject," *Review of Politics* 61, no. 3 (Summer 1999): 493–523; James R. Ferguson, "Reason in Madness: The Political Thought of James Otis," *William and Mary Quarterly*, 3rd ser., 36, no. 2 (April 1979): 194–214; Waters, *Otis Family*; and Ellen Elizabeth Brennan, "James Otis: Recreant and

Patriot," *New England Quarterly* 12, no. 4 (December 1939): 691–725. See also the studies by Farrell cited in note 7.

34. C. Bradley Thompson, *John Adams and the Spirit of Liberty* (Lawrence: University Press of Kansas, 1998), 24–87.

35. Benjamin C. Irvin, *Sam Adams: Son of Liberty, Father of Revolution* (New York: Oxford University Press, 2003); Pauline Maier, *The Old Revolutionaries: Political Lives in the Age of Samuel Adams* (New York: Alfred A. Knopf, 1980); John C. Miller, *Sam Adams: Pioneer in Propaganda* (Stanford, CA: Stanford University Press, 1960 [1936]). For context, see Pauline Maier, *From Resistance to Revolution: Colonial Radicals and the Development of American Opposition to Britain, 1765–1776* (New York: Alfred A. Knopf, 1972).

36. Archer, *As In an Enemy's Country*; Eric Hinderaker, *Boston's Massacre* (Cambridge, MA: Belknap Press of Harvard University Press, 2017).

37. Archer, *As If an Enemy's Country*, 179–81; Hinderaker, *Boston's Massacre*, 216, 234. On *Rex v. Richardson*, see *LPJA* 2:396–430.

38. Archer, *As If an Enemy's Country*, 182–206; Hinderaker, *Boston's Massacre*.

39. The engraving is in Archer, *As If an Enemy's Country*, 194, and in Hinderaker, *Boston's Massacre*, 228, 229, 232, 233.

40. John Adams autobiography, part 1, "John Adams," through 1776, sheet 12 of 53, AFPEA/MHS.

41. Entry for March 5, 1773, John Adams diary 19, December 16, 1772–December 18, 1773, AFPEA/MHS.

42. Archer, *As If an Enemy's Country*, 218; Hinderaker, *Boston's Massacre*, 189; and John Ferling, *John Adams: A Life* (Knoxville: University of Tennessee Press, 1992), 68. The surviving documents from the Boston Massacre Trials appear in *LPJA*, vol. 3. On Adams's fee, *Autobiography*, cited in note 41, but see also Hinderaker, *Boston's Massacre*, 189, suggesting that Adams's fee was higher than he remembered.

43. John Adams autobiography, part 1, "John Adams," through 1776, sheet 13 of 53, AFPEA/MHS.

44. John Adams, "Adams's Argument for the Defense [in *Rex v. Wemmes*]," *LPJA* 3:242–70 (quotations at 266 ["wretched conservators"], 246, 269, and 266 ["Molatto"]); Arthur Scherr, *John Adams, Race, and Slavery: Ideas, Politics, and Diplomacy in an Age of Crisis* (Santa Barbara, CA: Praeger, 2018), 4–5.

45. John Phillip Reid, "A Lawyer Acquitted: John Adams and the Boston Massacre Trials," *American Journal of Legal History* 18, no. 3 (July 1974): 189–207.

46. Reid, 207.

47. Adams, "Argument for the Defense," *LPJA* 3:269.

48. Archer, *As If an Enemy's Country*, 182–225; Hiller B. Zobel, *The Boston Massacre* (New York: W. W. Norton, 1970); contra Zobel, see Reid, "A Lawyer Acquitted."

49. John Phillip Reid, ed., *The Briefs of the American Revolution: Constitutional Arguments between Thomas Hutchinson, Governor of Massachusetts Bay, and James Bowdoin for the Council and John Adams for the House of Representatives* (New York: New York University Press, 1981), with excellent commentary. Ryerson, *Republic*, 104–14. For an account focusing on Hutchinson, see Bailyn, *Ordeal of Thomas Hutchinson*, 196–220 [esp. 207–11].

50. Richard D. Brown, *Knowledge Is Power: The Diffusion of Information in Early America, 1700–1865* (New York: Oxford University Press, 1989); Brown, *The Strength of a People: The Idea of an Informed Citizenry in America, 1650–1870* (Chapel Hill: University of North Carolina Press, 1996).

51. Maier, *From Resistance to Revolution*; Richard D. Brown, *Revolutionary Politics in Massachusetts: The Boston Committee of Correspondence and the Towns, 1772–1774* (Cambridge, MA: Harvard University Press, 1970).

52. Rogan Kersh, *Dreams of a More Perfect Union* (Ithaca, NY: Cornell University Press, 2001); Richard L. Merritt, *The Symbols of American Community, 1735 to 1755* (New Haven, CT: Yale University Press, 1968); Yehoshua Arieli, *Individualism and Nationalism in American Ideology* (Cambridge, MA: Harvard University Press, 1964); Henry Steele Commager, "The Origins and Nature of American Nationalism," in Henry Steele Commager, *Jefferson, Nationalism, and the Enlightenment* (New York: George Braziller, 1975), 187–96.

53. Ryerson, *Republic*, 101–4.

54. See Benjamin I. Carp, *Defiance of the Patriots: The Boston Tea Party and the Making of America* (New Haven, CT: Yale University Press, 2010); Alfred H. Young, *The Shoemaker and the Tea Party: Memory and the American Revolution* (Boston: Beacon Press, 1999); Joseph Crimmins, *Ten Tea Parties: Patriotic Protests That History Forgot* (Philadelphia: Quirk Books, 2012).

55. "Abigail Adams to Mercy Otis Warren, 5 December 1773," FO/NA.

56. Carp, *Defiance of the Patriots*; Young, *The Shoemaker and the Tea Party*. See also Benjamin Woods Larrabee, *The Boston Tea Party* (Boston: Northeastern University Press, 1979 (1964)).

57. Entry for December 17, 1773, John Adams diary 19, December 16, 1772–December 18, 1773, AFPEA/MHS.

58. Bailyn, *Ordeal of Thomas Hutchinson*, 221–374.

59. Carp, *Defiance of the Patriots*, 192–200.

60. Boston Port Act (Trade Act 1774), 14 Geo. III. c.19 (1774); Massachusetts Government Act, 14 Geo. III c.45 (1774); Administration of Justice Act 1774, 14 Geo III c.39 (1774); Quartering Act 1774, 14 Geo. III c.54; Quebec Act (Quebec Act 1774), 14 George III, c.83 (1774).

61. Willi Paul Adams, *The First American Constitutions: Republican Ideology and the Making of the State Constitutions in the Revolutionary Era*, expanded edition, trans. Rita Kimber and Robert Kimber (Lanham MD: Rowman and Littlefield, 2000 [1980]), 336–46.

62. Ferling, *John Adams*, 96–97.

63. Entry for June 20, 1774, John Adams diary 20, February 28–June 25, 1774, AFPEA/MHS.

Chapter Four

1. Harry M. Ward, *The United Colonies of New England, 1643–90* (New York: Vantage Press, 1961); Ward, *"Unite or Die": Intercolony Relations, 1690–1763* (Port Washington, NY: Associated Faculty Press, 1971); Edmund S. Morgan and Helen M. Morgan, *The Stamp Act Crisis*, 3rd ed. (Chapel Hill: University of North Carolina Press for the Institute of Early American History and Culture, 1991 [1955]).

2. Jack N. Rakove, *The Beginnings of National Politics: An Interpretive History of the Continental Congress* (New York: Alfred A. Knopf, 1979), 21–62; Edmund Cody Burnett, *The Continental Congress* (New York: ; W. W. Norton, 1964 [1941]), 33–59; Robert G. Parkinson, *The Common Cause: Creating Race and Nation in the American Revolution* (Chapel Hill: University of North Carolina Press for the Omohundro Institute of Early American History and Culture, 2018).

3. John Fea, *Was America Founded as a Christian Nation?*, rev. ed. (Westminster, MD: John Knox Press, 2016 [2011]), 122.

4. John Adams to Abigail Adams, September 8, 1774, AFPEA/MHS.

5. The ancestor group for the *Novanglus* essays is https://founders.archives.gov/ancestor/ADMS-06-02-02-0072. Two excellent discussions of the *Novanglus-Massachusettensis* essays are Joseph A. Dowling, "John Adams vs. Daniel Leonard: 'Novanglus' Opposes 'Massachusettensis,'" in *The Colonial Legacy*, vol. 2, *Some Eighteenth-Century Commentators*, ed. Lawrence H. Leder (New York: Harper and Row, 1971), 181–202; and Albert Furtwangler,

American Silhouettes: Rhetorical Identities of the Founders (New Haven, CT: Yale University Press, 1987), 35–63; Ryerson, *Republic,* chap. 5, for a contextualized discussion.

6. "V. To the Inhabitants of the Colony of Massachusetts-Bay, 20 February 1775," FO/NA.

7. Ray Raphael and Marie Raphael, *The Spirit of '74: How the American Revolution Began* (New York: New Press, 2015); Ray Raphael, *The First American Revolution: Before Lexington and Concord* (New York: New Press, 2002).

8. David Hackett Fischer, *Paul Revere's Ride* (New York: Oxford University Press, 1994); Robert A. Gross, *The Minutemen and Their World* (New York: Hill and Wang, 2001 [1976]).

9. Letter from Abigail Adams to John Adams, June 18–20, June 1775, AFPEA/ MHS; Christian Di Spigna, *Founding Martyr: The Life and Death of Dr. Joseph Warren, the American Revolution's Lost Hero* (New York: Crown, 2018).

10. Joseph J. Ellis, *His Excellency: George Washington* (New York: Alfred A. Knopf, 2004), 68–69, 289n49, on the conflict of authorities. Edward G. Lengel, *General George Washington: A Military Life* (New York: Random House, 2005), and Robert Middlekauff, *Washington's Revolution: The Making of America's First Leader* (New York: Alfred A. Knopf, 2015), focus on Washington's decision to accept the command without mentioning Adams's claimed efforts to secure the command for him. David McCullough, *John Adams* (New York: Simon and Schuster, 2001), 27–28, accepts Adams's view.

11. The text of the Olive Branch Petition, from the *Journals of Congress* edited by Worthington Chauncey Ford, appears online at http://avalon.law.yale.edu/ 18th_century/contcong_07-08-75.asp.

12. Henry St. John, Viscount Bolingbroke, *Bolingbroke: Political Writings,* ed. David Armitage (1738; Cambridge: Cambridge University Press, 1997), 217–94. On Adams's lifelong reading of Bolingbroke, see Zoltan Haraszti, *John Adams and the Prophets of Progress* (Cambridge, MA: Harvard University Press, 1952), 49–79..

13. Jane Calvert, *Quaker Constitutionalism and the Political Thought of John Dickinson* (Cambridge: Cambridge University Press, 2009), 233–34.

14. "From John Adams to James Warren, 24 July 1775," FO/NA.

15. For example, "From John Adams to Timothy Pickering, 6 August 1822," FO/NA [Early Access document].

16. John Adams autobiography, part 1, "John Adams," through 1776, sheet 21 of 53 [electronic edition], AFPEA/MHS.

17. Abigail Adams to John Adams, March 31, 1776, AFPEA/MHS.

18. John Adams to Abigail Adams, April 14, 1776, AFPEA/MHS.

19. John Adams to James Sullivan, May 26, 1776, AFPEA/MHS.

20. John Adams to Abigail Adams, April 15, 1776, AFPEA/MHS.

21. Abigail Adams to John Adams, May 9, 1776, AFPEA/MHS.

22. "III. Thoughts on Government, April 1776," FO/NA; Ryerson, *Republic*, chap. 6, for a contextualized discussion; Howe, 80ff.

23. "III. Thoughts on Government, April 1776," FO/NA.

24. "III. Thoughts on Government, April 1776," FO/NA.

25. John Adams to Abigail Adams, March 19, 1776, AFPEA/MHS.

26. "[In Congress, Spring 1776, and Thomas Paine]," FO/NA. For a discussion taking Paine's part, see Jett B. Conner, *John Adams vs. Thomas Paine: Rival Plans for the Early Republic* (Yardley, PA: Westholme Publishing, 2018). Eric Foner, *Tom Paine and Revolutionary America* (New York: Oxford University Press, 1976; exp. edition, 2001), esp. 120–23, offers a nuanced and thoughtful approach.

27. On American exceptionalism, see Godfrey Hodgson, *The Myth of American Exceptionalism* (New Haven, CT: Yale University Press, 2009) (skeptical assessment); Seymour Martin Lipset, *American Exceptionalism: A Double-Edged Sword* (New York: W. W. Norton, 1996) (more favorable view).

28. "V. Preamble to Resolution on Independent Governments, 15 May 1776," FO/NA; Ryerson, *Republic*, 184, 187.

29. John Adams autobiography, part 1, "John Adams," through 1776, sheet 35 of 53, AFPEA/MHS.

30. "From John Adams to James Lloyd, 29 March 1815," FO/NA [Early Access document].

31. Pauline Maier, *American Scripture: Making the Declaration of Independence* (New York: Alfred A. Knopf, 1997; pbk, with corrections, Vintage Books, 1998), esp. chaps. 1 and 2.

32. "From John Adams to Henry Knox, 2 June 1776," FO/NA.

33. John Adams autobiography, part 1, "John Adams," through 1776, sheet 24 of 53, AFPEA/MHS. On their friendship, see Lester J. Cappon, ed., *The Adams Jefferson Letters: The Complete Correspondence between Thomas Jefferson and John*

and Abigail Adams, 2 vols. (Chapel Hill: University of North Carolina Press for Institute for Early American History and Culture, 1959); Merrill D. Peterson, *Adams and Jefferson: A Revolutionary Dialogue* (Athens: University of Georgia Press, 1976); and Gordon S. Wood, *Friends Divided: John Adams and Thomas Jefferson* (New York: Penguin, 2017).

34. "From John Adams to Timothy Pickering, 6 August 1822," FO/NA [Early Access document].

35. John Adams autobiography, part 1, "John Adams," through 1776, sheet 24 of 53, AFPEA/MHS.

36. Daniel Webster, "Eulogy Pronounced at Boston, Massachusetts, August 2, 1826 . . . ," in *A Selection of Eulogies Pronounced in the Several States, in Honor of Those Illustrious Patriots and Statesmen, John Adams and Thomas Jefferson* (Hartford, CT: D. F. Robinson and Co., 1826), 212, quoted in Wood, *Friends Divided*, 106.

37. Maier, *American Scripture*, 97–153.

38. John Adams to Abigail Adams, July 3, 1776, "Had a Declaration . . . ," AFPEA/MHS.

39. "III. Plan of Treaties as Adopted (with Instructions), 17 September 1776," FO/NA. Two excellent commentaries are Gregg L. Lint, "John Adams and the 'Bolder Plan,' " in *John Adams and the Founding of the Republic*, ed. Richard Alan Ryerson (Boston: Massachusetts Historical Society/Northeastern University Press, 2001), 105–14; Lint, "John Adams on the Drafting of the Treaty Plan of 1776," *Diplomatic History* 2, no. 3 (July 1978): 313–20. On Adams's four-part plan analyzed in the text,, see the excellent discussion by Daniel J. Hulsebosch, "The Revolutionary Portfolio: Constitution-Making and the Wider World in the American Revolution," *Suffolk University Law Review* 47 (2014): 759–822, esp. 770–800. I thank Dan Hulsebosch for sharing a copy of this article with me.

40. John Adams to Abigail Adams, August 14, 1776, AFPEA/MHS.

41. John Adams autobiography, part 1, "John Adams," through 1776, sheets 43–44 of 53, AFPEA/MHS.

42. John Adams to Abigail Adams, April 26, 1777, AFPEA/MHS.

43. Abigail Adams to John Adams, April 1777, AFPEA/MHS.

44. "John Adams to Thomas Boylston Adams, 6 May 1777," FO/NA.

45. Abigail Adams to John Adams, July 2, 1777, AFPEA/MHS.

46. Abigail Adams to John Adams, July 9, 1777, AFPEA/MHS.

47. John Adams to Abigail Adams, July 10, 1777, AFPEA/MHS.

48. Abigail Adams to John Adams, July 16 1777, AFPEA/MHS.

49. John Adams to Abigail Adams, July 28, 1777, AFPEA/MHS.

50. John Adams to Abigail Adams, July 26, 1777, AFPEA/MHS.

51. Edith Gelles, *Abigail and John: Portrait of a Marriage* (New York: William Morrow, 2009).

52. See, e.g., "[Memorandum of Measures to Be Pursued in Congress, February? 1776]," FO/NA; John Adams, "Notes on Relations with France," March–April 1776, FO/NA.

Chapter Five

1. H. James Henderson, "Congressional Factionalism and the Attempt to Recall Benjamin Franklin," *William and Mary Quarterly*, 3rd ser., 27, no. 2 (April 1970): 246–67; Henderson, *Party Politics in the Continental Congress* (New York: McGraw-Hill, 1974).

2. John E. Ferling, "John Adams, Diplomat," *William and Mary Quarterly*, 3rd ser., 51, no. 2 (April 1994): 227–52. Ferling wrote in skeptical response to James H. Hutson's combative monograph, *John Adams and the Diplomacy of the American Revolution* (Lexington: University Press of Kentucky, 1980). See generally Richard B. Morris, *The Peacemakers: The Great Powers and American Independence* (New York: Harper and Row, 1965). The most recent study of the Deane affair is Joel Richard Paul, *Unlikely Allies: How a Merchant, a Playwright, and a Spy Saved the American Revolution* (New York: Riverhead Books/Penguin Group, 2009); Julian P. Boyd, "Silas Deane: Death by a Kindly Teacher of Treason?," *William and Mary Quarterly*, 3rd Ser., 16 (1959), 165–87, 319–42, 515–50; William Stinchcombe: "Notes and Documents: A Note in Silas Deane's Death," *William and Mary Quarterly*, 3rd ser., 32 (1975): 619–24.

3. Ferling, "John Adams, Diplomat," 250.

4. Gerald Stourzh, *Benjamin Franklin and American Foreign Policy*, rev. ed. (Chicago: University of Chicago Press, 1969 [1954]). On Franklin as a colonial agent, see Michael G. Kammen, *A Rope of Sand: Colonial Agents, British Politics, and the American Revolution* (Ithaca, NY: Cornell University Press, 1968); on Franklin as a scientist, see I. Bernard Cohen, *Benjamin Franklin's Science* (Cambridge, MA: Harvard University Press, 1991 [1990]).

5. Jack N. Rakove, *The Beginnings of National Politics: An Interpretive History of the Continental Congress* (New York: Alfred A. Knopf, 1979); Rogan Kersh, *Dimensions of a More Perfect Union* (Ithaca, NY: Cornell University Press, 2001).

6. Morris, *Peacemakers*; Bradford Perkins, *The Cambridge History of American Foreign Relations*, vol. 1, *The Creation of a Republican Empire, 1765–1865* (Cambridge: Cambridge University Press, 1993), 17–53; William Earl Weeks, *The New Cambridge History of American Foreign Relations*, vol. 1, *Dimensions of the Early American Empire, 1754–1865* (Cambridge: Cambridge University Press, 2013), 1–33; Felix Gilbert, *To the Farewell Address: Ideas of Early American Foreign Policy* (Princeton, NJ: Princeton University Press, 1961), ; Paul E. Varg, *Foreign Policies of the Founding Fathers* (East Lansing: Michigan State University Press, 1963).

7. Letter from Abigail Adams to John Adams, June 30, 1778, draft, AFPEA/MHS.

8. Letter from John Adams to Abigail Adams, February 13, 1778, AFPEA/MHS.

9. John Adams diary 47, February 13, 1778–April 26, 1779, AFPEA/MHS.

10. "[April 21. Tuesday. 1778.]," FO/NA.

11. Letter from Abigail Adams to John Adams, June 18. 1778, AFPEA/MHS.

12. John Adams autobiography, part 2, "Travels, and Negotiations," 1777–1778, sheet 9 of 37, AFPEA/MHS.

13. Robert Middlekauff, *Benjamin Franklin and His Enemies* (Berkeley: University of California Press, 1996), 173–201, 204–6.

14. "From John Adams to James Warren, 4 August 1778," FO/NA; Ferling, "John Adams, Diplomat," 228–29.

15. John Adams autobiography, part 2, "Travels, and Negotiations," 1777–78, sheet 13 of 37, AFPEA/MHS.

16. "From John Adams to Elbridge Gerry, 5 December 1778," FO/NA; Abigail Adams to John Adams, May 18, 1778, AFPEA/MHS.

17. Ferling, "John Adams, Diplomat," 234–35.

18. John Adams diary 47, February 13, 1778–April 26, 1779 [entry for February 11, 1779], AFPEA/MHS.

19. Middlekauff, *Benjamin Franklin and His Enemies*, 193.

20. John Adams to Abigail Adams, December 3, 1778, AFPEA/MHS; Ferling, "John Adams, Diplomat," 235.

21. John Adams to Abigail Adams, February 28, 1779, AFPEA/MHS.

22. John Adams to Abigail Adams, February 20, 1779, AFPEA/MHS.

23. Abigail Adams to John Adams, February 13, 1779, AFPEA/MHS.

24. Richard B. Bernstein, "The Massachusetts Constitution of 1780," in *Roots of the Republic: American Founding Documents Interpreted*, ed. Stephen L. Schechter, Richard B. Bernstein, and Donald S. Lutz (Madison, WI: Madison House, 1990), 188–94 (the constitution follows on pages 195–226); Ryerson, *Republic*, 212–27.

25. Richard B. Bernstein, "John Adams's *Thoughts on Government* (1776)," in Schechter, Bernstein, and Lutz, *Roots of the* Republic, 118–37, and sources cited.

26. Robert J. Taylor, ed., *Massachusetts, Colony to Commonwealth: Documents on the Foundation of the Constitution 1775–1780* (Chapel Hill: University of North Carolina Press for the Institute of Early American History and Culture, 1960), 45.

27. Oscar Handlin and Mary Handlin, *The Popular Sources of Political Authority: Documents on the Massachusetts Constitution of 1780* (Cambridge, MA: Belknap Press of Harvard University Press, 1966), 190.

28. The November 1 *Report of a Constitution* appears in "The Report of a Constitution or Form of Government for the Commonwealth of Massachusetts, 28–31 October 1779," FO/NA. The finished version appears in Schechter, Bernstein, and Lutz, *Roots of the Republic*, 195–226, derived from its appearance in *The Journal of the Convention, for Framing a Constitution of Government for the State of Massachusetts-Bay . . .* (Boston: Dutton and Wentworth, Printer to the State, 1832), 222–49.

29. Quoted in Schechter, Bernstein, and Lutz, *Roots of the Republic*, 202.

30. Robert C. Palmer, "Liberties as Constitutional Provisions, 1776–1791," in *Liberty and Community: Constitution and Rights in the Early American Republic*, ed. William E. Nelson and Robert C. Palmer (New York: Oceana, 1988), 55–148.

31. Quoted in Schechter, Bernstein, and Lutz, *Roots of the Republic*, 221.

32. Wood *JA 1775–1783*, 764 note.

33. Samuel Eliot Morison, "The Struggle over the Adoption of the Massachusetts Constitution of 1780," *Proceedings of the Massachusetts Historical Society* 50 (1916–17): 353–411.

34. Letter from Abigail Adams to John Adams, January 18, 1780, letterbook copy, AFPEA/MHS.

35. "From John Adams to Samuel Adams, 23 February 1780," FO/NA.

36. "From John Adams to Samuel Adams, 15 June 1782," FO/NA.

37. Ronald M. Peters, *The Massachusetts Constitution of 1780: A Social Compact* (Amherst: University of Massachusetts Press, 1980), 14; "Symposium—The

Massachusetts Constitution of 1780," *Suffolk University Law Review* 14, no. 4 (Summer 1980): 841–1010, esp. John Phillip Reid, "In the Taught Tradition: The Meaning of Law in Massachusetts-Bay Two Hundred Years Ago," 931–74.

38. Charles Warren, *Congress, the Constitution, and the Supreme Court*, rev. ed. (Boston: Little, Brown, 1935 [1925]), 30–34); Willi Paul Adams, *The First American Constitutions: Republican Ideology and the Making of the State Constitutions in the Revolutionary Era*, expanded edition, trans. Rita Kimber and Robert Kimber (Lanham, MD: Rowman and Littlefield, 2001 [1980]), 3; George Dargo, *Law in the New Republic: Private Law and Public Estate* (New York: Alfred A. Knopf, 1983), 13.

39. "To John Adams from Henry Laurens, 4 October 1779," FO/NA.

40. "From John Adams to Henry Laurens, 25 October 1779," FO/NA.

41. Edith B. Gelles, *Abigail and John: Portrait of a Marriage* (New York: William Morrow, 2009), 124.

42. Abigail Adams to John Adams, November 14, 1779, AFPEA/MHS.

43. Adams appended copies of these letters to his diary entry. "[February 4–March 21, 1780]," FO/NA.

44. Ferling, "John Adams, Diplomat," 241–44, and sources cited; Morris, *Peacemakers*, 199.

45. Ferling, "John Adams, Diplomat," 244–45, and sources cited.

46. "From Benjamin Franklin to Samuel Huntington, 9 August 1780," FO/NA.

47. Ferling, "John Adams, Diplomat," 245.

48. Wood *JA 1775–1783*, 768–69 note. For the list of links to relevant pages on FO for the *Adams Papers* edition of the *Memorial*, see https://founders.archives.gov/ancestor/ADMS-06-09-02-0115.

49. Wood *JA 1775–1783*, 769–70 note. John Adams, *Letters from a Distinguished American: Twelve Essays by John Adams on American Foreign Policy*, ed. James H. Huston (Washington, DC: Library of Congress, 1978); Hutson's introduction discusses the questionable Jennings. For the list of links to relevant pages on FO for the *Adams Papers* edition of the *Letters*, see https://www.founders.archives.gov/ancestor/ADMS-06-09-02-0312.

50. For the list of links to relevant pages on FO for the *Adams Papers* edition of the "Replies to Hendrik Calkoen," see https://founders.archives.gov/ancestor/ADMS-06-10-02-0117.

51. "John Quincy Adams to Abigail Adams, 26 December 1778," FO/NA.

52. See the references scattered throughout their correspondence, and through the pages of Gelles, *Abigail and John*; Edith B. Gelles, *Abigail Adams: A Writing Life* (New York: Routledge, 2002), and Gelles, *Portia: The World of Abigail Adams* (Bloomington: Indiana University Press, 1991). See also Woody Holton, *Abigail Adams: A Life* (New York: Free Press, 2009).

53. Gelles, *Abigail and John*, 114–15.

54. On Amsterdam, see Russell Shorto, *Amsterdam: A History of the World's Most Liberal City* (New York: Doubleday, 2017); on the Netherlands, see Simon Schama, *Patriots and Liberators: Revolution in the Netherlands 1780–1813*, 2nd ed. (London: Pimlico, 1992 [1977]).

55. John Adams to Abigail Adams, July 11, 1781, AFPEA/MHS.

56. Abigail Adams to John Adams, August 1, 1781, AFPEA/MHS; Ferling, "John Adams, Diplomat," 245–46, and sources cited at 246–47nn63–69.

57. Morris, *Peacemakers*, 211–17.

58. J. W. Schulte Nordholt, *The Dutch Republic and American Independence* (Chapel Hill: University of North Carolina Press, 1982); Nordholt, *Till I Knew John Adams: A Sketch of John Adams' Diplomacy in the Netherlands, 1781–1782, & of His house in Quincy, Massachusetts* (The Hague: Joint Esso Companies in the Netherlands, 1981); Nordholt, "The Recognition of the United States by the Dutch Republic," *Proceedings of the Massachusetts Historical Society* 94 (January 1982): 37–48.

59. James Grant, *John Adams: Party of One* (New York: Farrar, Straus and Giroux, 2005), 268–76, gives an excellent analysis of the negotiations and the results.

60. Middlekauff, *Benjamin Franklin and His Enemies*, 197; Herbert E. Klingelhofer, "Notes and Documents: Matthew Ridley's Diary during the Peace Negotiations of 1782," *William and Mary Quarterly*, 3rd ser., 20, no. 1 (January 1963): 95–133 (esp. 123).

61. Walter Stahr, *John Jay: Founding Father* (New York: Hambledon and London, 2005); Elizabeth Nuxoll, Mary E. Y. Gallagher, and Jenn Steenshorne, eds., *John Jay: Selected Papers*, 5 vols. of 8 projected (Charlottesville: University of Virginia Press, 2010–). This new edition draws on the edition by Richard B, Morris, *John Jay: Unpublished Papers* (New York: Harper and Row, 1980–84); those volumes (succeeded by vols. 1–3 of the Nuxoll edition) covered the period 1745–84.

62. Morris, *Peacemakers*, 288–310.

63. See the analysis in Morris, 382–84.

64. Morris, *Peacemakers*, 408–10, 435–37; Ronald Hoffman and Peter J. Albert, eds., *Peace and the Peacemakers of 1783* (Charlottesville: University Press of Virginia, 1985). For the treaty's text, see "Preliminary Peace Treaty between the United States and Great Britain, 30 November 1782," FO/NA; Morris, *Peacemakers*, 461–65; Wood *JA 1775–1783*, 691–96.

65. Morris, *Peacemakers*, 435–36.

66. Ferling, "John Adams, Diplomat," 245–46, and sources cited.

67. "From Benjamin Franklin to Robert R. Livingston, 22[–26] July 1783," FO/NA.

Chapter Six

1. "From John Adams to Robert R. Livingston, 4 December 1782," FO/NA.

2. Abigail Adams to John Adams, December 15, 1783, AFPEA/MHS.

3. "From John Adams to the President of Congress, 13 November 1783," FO/NA.

4. "Instructions to the American Peace Commissioners, 29 October 1783," FO/NA. The supplementary instructions are "Instructions to the American Commissioners, May–June 1784," FO/NA.

5. Cappon, 1:12–238.

6. Abigail Adams to John Adams, February 11, 1784, AFPEA/MHS.

7. "Abigail Adams to Elizabeth Smith Shaw, 11 July 1784," FO/NA.

8. Abigail Adams to John Adams, July 23, 1784, AFPEA/MHS.

9. John Adams to Abigail Adams, July 26, 1784, AFPEA/MHS.

10. Edith B. Gelles, *Abigail and John: Portrait of a Marriage* (New York: William Morrow, 2009), 150–56.

11. "John Adams' Commission as Minister to Great Britain, 24 February 1785," FO/NA. For John Jay's cover letter, see "John Jay to John Adams, 15 March 1785," FO/NA.

12. Andrew Oliver, *Portraits of John and Abigail Adams* (Cambridge, MA: Belknap Press of Harvard University Press, 1967), 23–38.

13. "From John Adams to John Jay, 2 June 1785," FO/NA.

14. "From John Adams to John Jay, 2 June 1785," FO/NA.

15. "John Adams' Instructions as Minister to Great Britain, 7 March 1785," FO/NA.

16. Henry Steele Commager, *Empire of Reason: How Europe Imagined and America Realized the Enlightenment* (Garden City, NY: Anchor Books/Doubleday, 1977), 236–40 (on the meaning of the term "philosophe"), and 241–45 (on the contrast between the European and American Enlightenments).

17. Bernard Peach with Jon Erik Larson, eds., *Richard Price and the Ethical Foundations of the American Revolution* (Durham, NC: Duke University Press, 1979). The pamphlet appears at 177–214; Turgot's letter appears at 215–24.

18. "From John Adams to Richard Price, 8 April 1785," FO/NA.

19. Zoldan Haraszti, *John Adams and the Prophets of Progress* (Cambridge, MA: Harvard University Press, 1952), 149.

20. David Szatmary, *Shays' Rebellion: The Making of an Agrarian Insurrection* (Amherst: University of Massachusetts Press, 1980); Robert A. Gross, ed., *In Debt to Shays: The Bicentennial of an Agrarian Rebellion* (Charlottesville: University Press of Virginia for the Colonial Society of Massachusetts, 1993).

21. "From Thomas Jefferson to Abigail Adams, 22 February 1787," FO/NA.

22. John Adams, *A Defence of the Constitutions of Government*, 3 vols. (London, 1787–88). The work is reprinted in *WJA*, vols. 4–6. Charles Francis Adams edited and revised that version without indicating his revisions. I have used the third edition, published in 1797: *A Defence of the Constitutions of Government of the United States of America, against the Attack of M. Turgot in His Letter to Dr. Price Dated the Twenty-Second Day of March, 1778*, 3rd ed. in 3 vols. (Philadelphia: Printed by Budd and Bartram for William Cobbett, 1797). (The 1797 third edition exists in two modern reprint editions—Aalen, Germany: Scientia Verlag, 1979, and Union, NJ: Lawbook Exchange, 2001.) The third edition of 1797 is closest to Adams's intentions. On the composition of the *Defence*, see Haraszti, *John Adams and the Prophets of Progress*, 139–64. Luke Mayville, *John Adams and the Fear of American Oligarchy* (Princeton, NJ: Princeton University Press, 2016), makes the *Defence* the focus of his illuminating, invaluable study of Adams's political thought. Ryerson, *Republic*, focuses on the *Defence* at 280–309. The analysis here is deeply indebted to Mayville and Ryerson, and to Howe, chaps. 5 and 6.

23. Adams, *Defence*, 3rd ed. 1797, 3: 503

24. For an analysis of the rhetorical design of the *Defence*, see John E. Paynter, "The Rhetorical Design of John Adams's Defence of the Constitutions of... America," *Review of Politics* 16, no. 3 (Summer 1996): 531–60.

25. Stephen G. Kurtz, "The Political Science of John Adams: A Guide to His Statecraft," *William and Mary* Quarterly, 3rd ser., 25, no. 4 (October 1968): 605–13. Every student of Adams and the political thought and arguments of his time should study Kurtz's fine article with care.

26. Adams, *Defence*, 3rd ed. (1797), 3:503.

27. Thomas Jefferson, *Notes on the State of Virginia* (1787). There are two scholarly editions—one edited by William Peden (Chapel Hill: University of North Carolina Press for the Institute of Early American History and Culture, 1955; Norton pbk. repr.), and one edited by Frank Shuffelton (New York: Penguin, 1998). See also David Tucker, *Enlightened Republicanism: A Study of Jefferson's Notes on the State of Virginia* (Lanham, MD: Lexington Books, 2008).

28. John Adams to Thomas Jefferson, May 22, 1785, FO/NA.

29. Mayville, *John Adams and the Fear of American Oligarchy*, is excellent on this point.

30. "From James Madison to Thomas Jefferson, 6 June 1787," FO/NA.

31. "Notes on Ancient and Modern Confederacies, [April–June?] 1786," FO/NA.

32. Max Farrand, *The Records of the Federal Convention of 1787*, 4 vols. (New Haven, CT: Yale University Press, 1911, 1937, 1966, 1987), 1:134–36 (Madison's notes for June 6, 1787, specifically his speech on factionalism).

33. Jack N. Rakove, *A Politician Thinking: The Creative Mind of James Madison* (Norman: University of Oklahoma Press, 2017), presents an excellent discussion of what it means to view Madison as a thinking politician.

34. Rakove, *A Politician Thinking*,; Trevor Colbourn, ed., *Fame and the Founding Fathers: Essays of Douglass Adair* (New York: W. W. Norton for the Institute of Early American History and Culture, 1974; repr. ed., Indianapolis: Liberty Fund, 1998); Lance Banning, *The Sacred Fire of Liberty: James Madison and the Founding of the Federal Republic* (Ithaca, NY: Cornell University Press, 1995); Drew R. McCoy, *The Last of the Fathers: James Madison and the Republican Legacy* (Cambridge: Cambridge University Press, 1989).

35. Richard B. Bernstein with Kym S. Rice, *Are We to Be a Nation? The Making of the Constitution* (Cambridge, MA: Harvard University Press, 1987), esp. chap. 6; Richard B. Morris, *The Forging of the Union, 1781–1789*

(New York: Harper and Row, 1987); Richard R. Beeman, *Plain, Honest Men: The Making of the American Constitution* (New York: Random House, 2009); Clinton L. Rossiter III, *1787: The Grand Convention* (New York: Macmillan, 1966); Carol Berkin, *A Brilliant Solution: Inventing the American Constitution* (New York: Harcourt, 2002).

36. [James Madison], *The Federalist No. 10, The Federalist*, ed. Jacob E. Cooke (Middletown, CT: Wesleyan University Press, 1961), 56–65 (quotation at 59)

37. Larry D. Kramer, "Madison's Audience," *Harvard Law Review* 112, no. 3 (January 1999): 611–79.

38. McCoy, *The Last of the Fathers*, is particularly good on Madison's thinking on this point.

39. This point is the focus of Gordon S. Wood's discussion of Adams's relevance and irrelevance. See Gordon S. Wood, *The Creation of the American Republic, 1776–1787* (Chapel Hill: University of North Carolina Press for the Institute of Early American History and Culture, 1969; with new preface, 1998), 567–92 (chap. 14: "The Relevance and Irrelevance of John Adams"). See the epilogue.

40. Adams, *Defence*, 3rd ed. 1797, 3:505–6, with the Constitution reprinted as an appendix at 507–28. On the creation of the Senate by the Federal Convention, see R. B. Bernstein, "Parliamentary Principles, American Realities: The Continental and Confederation Congresses, 1774–1789," in *Inventing Congress: Origins and Establishment of the First Federal Congress*, ed. Kenneth R. Bowling and Donald R. Kennon (Athens: Published for the United States Capitol Historical Society by Ohio University Press, 1999), 76–105.

41. "From John Adams to John Jay, 24 January 1787," FO/NA [Early Access document]; "From John Adams to John Jay, 25 January 1787," FO/NA [Early Access document].

42. "To John Adams from John Jay, 31 July 1787," FO/NA [Early Access document].

43. "To John Adams from John Jay, 16 October 1787," FO/NA [Early Access document].

44. "From John Adams to John Jay, 21 February 1788," FO/NA [Early Access document].

45. "To Thomas Jefferson from John Adams, 10 November 1787," FO/NA.

46. "From Thomas Jefferson to John Adams, 13 November 1787," FO/NA.

47. "To Thomas Jefferson from John Adams, 6 December 1787," FO/NA.

48. I base the statement in the text on a search of the online version of the *Documentary History of the Ratification of the Constitution and the Bill of Rights, 1787–1791*, https://uwdc.library.wisc.edu/collections/history/constitution/.

49. "From John Adams to George Clinton, 26 March 1788," FO/NA [Early Access document].

50. [John Stevens], *Observations on government: including some animadversions on Mr. Adams's Defence of the constitutions of government of the United States of America: and on Mr. De Lolme's Constitution of England. By a farmer, of New-Jersey* (New York: Printed by W. Ross, in Broad-Street, [1787]); R. R. Palmer, *The Age of the Democratic Revolution: A Political History of Europe and America, 1760–1800* (Princeton, NJ: Princeton University Press, 159, 1964; one-volume ed., 2014), 210–11.

Chapter Seven

1. Douglass Adair, *Fame and the Founding Fathers: Essays of Douglass Adair*, ed. Trevor Colbourn (New York: W. W. Norton for the Institute of Early American History and Culture, 1974; repr., Indianapolis: Liberty Fund, 1998), chap. 1.

2. James Grant, *John Adams: Party of One* (New York: Farrar, Straus and Giroux, 2005), 343–44.

3. Diana Jacobs, *Dear Abigail: The Intimate Lives and Revolutionary Ideas of Abigail Adams and Her Two Remarkable Sisters* (New York: Ballantine Books/Random House, 2014), 280.

4. Jacobs, 280–82; Woody Holton, *Abigail Adams: A Life* (New York: Free Press, 2009), 256–58.

5. Holton, *Abigail Adams*; see also Woody Holton, "Abigail Adams, Bond Speculator," *William and Mary Quarterly*, 3rd ser., 64, no. 4 (October 2007): 821–38; Woody Holton, "The Battle against Patriarchy That Abigail Adams Won," in *Revolutionary Founders: Rebels, Radicals, and Reformers in the Making of the Nation*, ed. Alfred F. Young, Gary B. Nash, and Ray Raphael (New York: Alfred A. Knopf, 2011), 273–87 (notes at 419–20).

6. Grant, *John Adams*, 344–45.

7. Peter Shaw, *The Character of John Adams* (Chapel Hill: University of North Carolina Press for the Institute of Early American History and Culture, 1975), 225 (on Adams's election to the Confederation Congress in 1788); "To James Madison from Tench Coxe, 27 January 1789," FO/NA. See Edmund Cody

Burnett, *The Continental Congress* (New York: W. W. Norton, 1964 [1941]), 725 (on Adams as prospect for president of the Confederation Congress in 1789).

8. Joseph J. Ellis, *His Excellency: George Washington* (New York: Alfred A. Knopf, 2004), 182–84.

9. Steven R. Boyd, *The Politics of Opposition: Antifederalists and the Acceptance of the Constitution* (Millwood, NY: KTO Press, 1979).

10. John P. Kaminski, *George Clinton: Yeoman Politician of the New Republic* (Lanham, MD: Rowman and Littlefield, 1989), 166–77.

11. The smoking gun is "From Alexander Hamilton to James Wilson, [25 January 1789]," FO/NA.

12. Grant, *John Adams*, 346–47, offers an interpretation from Adams's perspective. For a pro-Hamilton version, stressing Hamilton's desire to protect Washington and referring to the process of depleting Adams's electoral-vote total without mentioning Adams, see Forrest McDonald, *Alexander Hamilton: A Biography* (New York: W. W. Norton, 1979), 124 and sources cited in 391n12.

13. John Ferling, *John Adams: A Life* (Knoxville: University of Tennessee Press, 1992), 299, 491–92nn7–8.

14. Linda Grant De Pauw, Charlene Bangs Bickford, and LaVonne Marlene Siegel, eds., *The Documentary History of the First Federal Congress*, vol. 1, *Senate Legislative Journal* (Baltimore, MD: Johns Hopkins University Press, 1972), 9 (entries for April 6, 1789).

15. Linda Dudik Guerrero, *John Adams' Vice Presidency: The Neglected Man in the Forgotten Office* (New York: Arno Press, 1972). See also Jack D. Warren Jr., "In the Shadow of Washington: John Adams as Vice President," in *John Adams and the Founding of the Republic*, ed. Richard Alan Ryerson (Boston: Massachusetts Historical Society, 2001), 117–41; Harry C. Thompson, "The Second Place in Rome: John Adams as Vice President," *Presidential Studies Quarterly* 10, no. 2 (Spring 1980): 171–78.

16. "The Vice-President's Speech: Extract from the Journal of the Senate of the United States, Tuesday, 21 April, 1789," in *WJA* 8:485–87 (quotation at 487).

17. "From George Washington to Henry Knox, 1 April 1789," FO/NA.

18. R. B. Bernstein, "Parliamentary Principles, American Realities: The Continental and Confederation Congresses, 1774–1789," in *Inventing*

Congress: Origins and Establishment of the First Federal Congress, ed. Kenneth R. Bowling and Donald R. Kennon (Athens: Published for the United States Capitol Historical Society by Ohio University Press, 1999), 76–105.

19. Charlene Bangs Bickford and Kenneth R. Bowling, *Birth of the Nation: The First Federal Congress, 1879–1791* (New York: Published for the New York State Commission on the Bicentennial of the United States Constitution and United States Capitol Historical Society by the First Federal Congress Project and the Second Circuit Committee on the Bicentennial of the United States Constitution, 1989), 23–24.

20. "From John Adams to Thomas Jefferson, 6 December 1787," FO/NA [Early Access document].

21. For the members of the First Federal Congress, see Carol Berkin, *The Bill of Rights: James Madison and the Politics of the Parchment Barrier* (New York: Simon and Schuster, 2015), Appendix: "Biographies."

22. Quoted by William Maclay in diary entry for April 25, 1789, in *The Diary of William Maclay and Other Notes on Senate Debates, March 4, 1789—March 3, 1791,* ed. Kenneth R. Bowling and Helen E. Veit, vol. 9 of Linda Grant DePauw, Charlene Bangs Bickford, Kenneth R. Bowling, and Helen E. Veit, eds., *The Documentary History of the First Federal Congress . . . ,* 20 vols. to date (Baltimore: Johns Hopkins University Press, 1972–), 9:5–6 (quotation at 6).

23. Quoted by William Maclay in diary entry for April 25, 1789 (quotation at 6).

24. Quoted by William Maclay in diary entry for April 25, 1789. For a distilled life of Maclay, see Maclay, *Diary,* 431–41; Joanne B. Freeman, *Affairs of Honor: National Politics in the New Republic* (New Haven, CT: Yale University Press, 2001), 11–61.

25. Kathleen Bartoloni-Tuazon, *For Fear of an Elective King: George Washington and the Presidential Titles Controversy of 1789* (Ithaca, NY: Cornell University Press, 2014).

26. Maclay, *Diary,* 4–5 (entry for April 24, 1789); 16–19 (entry for May 1, 1789); 26–29 (entry for May 8, 1789); 29–32 (entry for May 9, 1789). See also Freeman, *Affairs of Honor,* 40–42.

27. Bickford and Bowling, *Birth of the Nation,* 17–18; Daniel N. Hoffman, *Governmental Secrecy and the Founding Fathers: A Study in Constitutional Controls* (Westport, CT: Greenwood Press, 1981), 47–55 (House), 55–69 (Senate).

28. Maclay, *Diary,* 33–34 (entry for May 11, 1789 [quotation at 33]).

29. Maclay, 35–40 (entry for May 14, 1789 [esp. 37]).

30. Ferling, *John Adams*, 310–11.

31. Warren, "In the Shadow of Washington," esp. 127–28. For the encounter between Washington and the Senate, see Maclay, *Diary*, 128–31 (entry for August 22, 1789).

32. Freeman, *Affairs of Honor*, 48, 304n77, quoting and citing John Adams to John Trumbull, April 25 and April 2, 1790.

33. See Ellis, *His Excellency*, 190–91.

34. "To George Washington from James McHenry, 28 June 1789," FO/NA.

35. See the editorial headnote, "William Jackson to Clement Biddle, 2 May 1790," FO/NA.

36. "From George Washington to David Stuart, 15 June 1790," FO/NA.

37. Guerrero, *John Adams' Vice Presidency*, 128 (reporting thirty-one tie-breaking votes); US Congress, Senate, *The Senate 1789–1989*, by Robert C. Byrd, S. Doc. No. 100-20, 100th Cong., 1st Sess., vol. 4, *Historical Statistics, 1789–1992*, 1993, at 640 (reporting 29). See also Mark O. Hatfield, with the Senate Historical Office, *Vice Presidents of the United States, 1789–1993* (Washington, DC: US Government Printing Office, 1997), 3–13, esp. 12n1. For the figure of fifteen tie-breaking votes during the First Congress alone, see Warren, "In the Shadow of Washington," 132.

38. John Adams to Abigail Adams, December 19, 1793, AFPEA/MHS.

39. On the relationship between the *Defence* and the *Discourses on Davila*, see John E. Paynter, "The Rhetorical Design of John Adams's 'Defence of the Constitutions of . . . America,'" *Review of Politics* 58, no. 3 (Summer 1996): 531–60.

40. In *John Adams and the Fear of American Oligarchy* (Princeton, NJ, Princeton University Press, 2016), Luke Mayville presents a brilliant analysis of Adams's thinking on aristocracy and oligarchy, concentrating on his *Defence of the Constitutions of Government*—including insightful reflections on *Discourses on Davila* (see, e.g., 100ff.). Richard Alan Ryerson's analysis parallels Mayville's and mine. Ryerson, *Republic*, 324–36. See also Arthur O. Lovejoy, *Reflections on Human Nature* (Baltimore: Johns Hopkins Press, 1961), 197–207.

41. Henrico Caterino Davila, *The Historie of the Civil Warres of France . . .* (London: Printed by R. Raworth, and are to be sold by W. Lee, D. Pakeman, and G. Bedell [II: Printed by Ruth Raworth, and are to be sold by Thomas Heath], 1647–48).

42. Mack F. Holt, *The French Wars of Religion, 1562–1629* (Cambridge: Cambridge University Press, 1995); J. H. M. Salmon, *The French Religious Wars in English Political Thought* (Oxford: Clarendon Press of Oxford University Press, 1959).

43. Zoltan Haraszti, *John Adams and the Prophets of Progress* (Cambridge, MA: Harvard University Press, 1952), 168–71; Adam Smith, *The Theory of Moral Sentiments*, ed. Ryan Patrick Hanley, intro. by Amyarta Sen (London: Penguin, 2009); Adam Smith, *The Theory of Moral Sentiments*, ed. D. D. Raphael and Adam Macfie (Oxford: Oxford University Press, 1976; repr. pbk. ed., Indianapolis: Liberty Fund, 1984).

44. Marginal note in Adams's copy of the *Discourses*, quoted in Haraszti, *John Adams and the Prophets of Progress*, 179.

45. Albert Iacuzzi, *John Adams, Scholar* (New York: S. F. Vanni, 1952), 266–67, and see 135–57; Haraszti, *John Adams and the Prophets of Progress*, 165–79; Zoltan Haraszti, "The 32nd Discourse on Davila," *William and Mary Quarterly*, 3rd ser., 11, no. 1 (January 1954): 89–92. The fragment appeared in the Federalist *Gazette of the United States* on April 27, 1791.

46. Ryerson, *Republic*, 336, reaches the same conclusion.

47. R. B. Bernstein, *The Founding Fathers Reconsidered* (New York: Oxford University Press, 2009), 32–38 and notes at 196–98.

48. Michael S. Foley, *Law, Men and Machines: Modern American Constitutionalism and the Appeal of Newtonian Mechanics* (London: Routledge, 1990).

49. Bernstein, *The Founding Fathers Reconsidered*, 120–21.

50. R. B. Bernstein, *Thomas Jefferson* (New York: Oxford University Press, 2003), 79–80.

51. Alexis de Tocqueville, *Democracy in America*, ed. J. P. Mayer, trans. George Lawrence (New York: Harper and Row, 1966), 12.

52. Lynton K. Caldwell, *The Administration Theories of Hamilton and Jefferson*, 2nd ed. (New York: Holmes and Meier, 1988 [1944]); Bernstein, *Thomas Jefferson*, 88–91.

53. "To John Adams from Thomas Jefferson, 17 July 1791," FO/NA. See also Bernstein, *Thomas Jefferson*, 92.

54. "X. John Adams to Thomas Jefferson, 29 July 1791," FO/NA.

55. Lynn Hudson Parsons, *John Quincy Adams* (Madison, WI: Madison House, 1999), 41–48.

56. Haraszti, *John Adams and the Prophets of Progress*; H. J. Jackson, "John Adams's Marginalia, Then and Now," in *The Libraries, Leadership, and Legacy of John Adams and Thomas Jefferson*, ed. Robert C. Baron and Conrad Edick Wright (Golden, CO: Fulcrum Books and Massachusetts Historical Society, 2010), 59–79 and notes at 264.

57. John Adams to Benjamin Rush, June 9, 1789, in *Old Family Letters: Copied from the Originals for Alexander Biddle, Series A* (Philadelphia: Press of J. B. Lippincott Company, 1892), 36–38 (quotation at 38). Compare "X. John Adams to Thomas Jefferson, 29 July 1791," FO/NA.

58. Kenneth R. Bowling, *The Creation of Washington, D.C.: The Idea and Location of the American Capital* (Fairfax, VA: George Mason University Press, 1991).

59. John H. Powell, *Bring Out Your Dead: The Great Plague of Yellow Fever in Philadelphia in 1793*, new ed. (Philadelphia: University of Pennsylvania Press, 1993 (1949)).

60. John Adams to Abigail Adams, April 1, 1796, AFPEA/MHS.

61. Warren, "In the Shadow of Washington," 133–34. Warren relies on Shaw, *Character of John Adams*, 240–46, but Ferling has an opposite reading of this period of Adams's life. Ferling, *John Adams*, 299, 318–19.

62. John Adams to Abigail Adams, March 12, 1794, AFPEA/MHS.

63. John Adams to Abigail Adams, January 5, 1796, AFPEA/MHS.

64. George Washington, "Farewell Address, 19 September 1796," FO/NA.

65. Joanne B. Freeman, "The Presidential Election of 1796," in *John Adams and the Founding of the Republic*, ed. Richard Alan Ryerson (Boston: Massachusetts Historical Society, 2001), 142–67 (esp. 144–49 on choosing candidates); Jeffrey A. Pasley, *The First Contested Presidential Election: 1796 and the Founding of American Democracy* (Lawrence: University Press of Kansas, 2013), esp. 182–223 on choosing candidates.

66. Samuel Flagg Bemis, *Pinckney's Treaty: America's Advantage from European Distress*, revised ed. (New Haven, CT: Yale University Press, 1960 [1925]).

67. "The Vice-President's Speech: Extract from the Journal of the Senate of the United States, Wednesday, 15 February, 1797," in *WJA* 8:525–27 (quotation at 527).

68. Garry Wills, *Nixon Agonistes: The Crisis of the Self-Made Man* (Boston: Houghton Mifflin, 1970), 115–16 (on the vice presidency's victims).

69. Bernstein, *Thomas Jefferson*, 117–18.

Chapter Eight

1. John Adams, Inaugural Address, March 4, 1797, in *A Compilation of the Messages and Papers of the Presidents, 1789–1897*, 10 vols., ed. James D. Richardson (Washington, DC: Government Printing Office, 1896), 1:228–32 (quotation at 231).

2. John Adams to Abigail Adams, March 5, 1797, AFPEA/MHS.

3. On Washington as president, see Ralph Ketcham, *Presidents above Party: The First American Presidency, 1789–1829* (Chapel Hill: University of North Carolina Press for the Institute of Early American History and Culture, 1984), 89–93; Ray Raphael, *Mr. President: How and Why the Founders Created a Chief Executive* (New York: Alfred A. Knopf, 2012), 156–98; and Barry Schwartz, *George Washington: The Making of an American Symbol* (New York: Free Press/ Macmillan, 1987), 41–89. On the creation of the presidency, see Ketcham, *Presidents above Party*, , and Raphael, *Mr. President*. On FDR's influence on his successors, see William E. Leuchtenburg, *In the Shadow of FDR: From Harry Truman to Barack Obama*, 4th ed. (Ithaca, NY: Cornell University Press, 2009 [1983]).

4. Schwartz, *George Washington*; and Garry Wills, *Cincinnatus: George Washington and the Enlightenment* (New York: Doubleday, 1984); Edmund S. Morgan, *The Genius of George Washington (Third George Rogers Clark Lecture)* (Washington, DC: Society of the Cincinnati, 1980); Charles S. Sydnor, *Gentlemen Revolutionaries: Political Practices in George Washington's Virginia* (Chapel Hill: University of North Carolina Press for the Institute of Early American History and Culture, 1952); Ketcham, *Presidents above Party*, 89–93; and John E. Ferling, *The Ascent of George Washington: The Political Genius of an American Icon* (New York: Bloomsbury Press, 2009). Glenn A. Phelps, *George Washington and American Constitutionalism* (Lawrence: University Press of Kansas, 1993), is indispensable.

5. Quoted in Joanne B. Freeman, *Affairs of Honor: National Politics in the New Republic* (New Haven, CT: Yale University Press, 2001), 105. From James McHenry to Oliver Wolcott, November 9, 1800, in *Memoirs of the Administrations of Washington and John Adams, Edited from the Papers of Oliver Wolcott*, 2 vols., ed. George Gibbs (New York: Printed for the Subscribers, 1840), 2:445.

6. Ketcham, *Presidents above Party*, 93–99, on Adams.

7. Bruce Miroff, "John Adams and the Presidency," in *Inventing the American Presidency*, ed. Thomas Cronin (Lawrence: University Press of Kansas, 1989), 304–25.

8. John Adams to Benjamin Rush, April 22, 1812, in *The Spur of Fame: Dialogues of John Adams and Benjamin Rush, 1805–1813*, ed. John G. Schutz and Douglass Adair (San Marino, CA: Huntington Library, 1966), 212–15 (quotation at 214).

9. On Pickering, see Gerald Clarfield, *Timothy Pickering and American Diplomacy, 1795–1800* (Columbia: University of Missouri Press, 1969); Clarfield, *Timothy Pickering and the Republic* (Pittsburgh: University of Pittsburgh Press, 1980). On McHenry, see Karen E. Robbins, *James McHenry: Forgotten Federalist* (Athens: University of Georgia Press, 2013). There is no modern life of Wolcott or of Lee.

10. Charles O. Jones, *The U.S. Presidency: A Very Short Introduction*, 2nd ed. (New York: Oxford University Press, 2016 [2007]), 80–84; Kathryn Dunn Tenpas, "President Obama's Second Term: Staffing Challenges and Opportunities," *Brookings Issues in Governance Studies*, no. 57 (February 2013), http://www.brookings.edu/~/media/research/files/papers/2013/02/obama%20second%20term%20staffing%20tenpas/obama%20second%20term%20staffing%20tenpas.pdf.

11. Robert L. Scheina, "Benjamin Stoddert, Politics, and the Navy," *American Neptune* 36, no. 1 (January 1976): 54–69; Robert F. Jones, "The Naval Thought and Policy of Benjamin Stoddert, First Secretary of the Navy," *American Neptune* 24, no. 1 (January 1964): 61–69; John J. Carigg, "Benjamin Stoddert," in *American Secretaries of the Navy*, ed. Paolo E. Coletta (Annapolis, MD: Naval Institute Press, 1980), 58–75. See also sources cited in note 21 of this chapter.

12. Jean S. Holder, "The Sources of Presidential Power: John Adams and the Challenge to Executive Primacy," *Political Science Quarterly* 101, no. 4 (1986): 601–16 (quotation at 603).

13. Richard Hofstadter, *The Idea of a Party System: The Rise of Legitimate Opposition in the United States, 1780–1840* (Berkeley: University of California Press, 1969), ; Daniel Sisson, *The American Revolution of 1800* (New York: Alfred A. Knopf, 1974); and Freeman, *Affairs of Honor*, 261, 284–87.

14. Marie-Jeanne Rossignol, *The Nationalist Ferment: The Origins of U.S. Foreign Policy, 1792–1812*, trans. Lillian A. Parrott (Columbus: Ohio State University Press, 2004). On France, see William Doyle, *The Oxford History of the French Revolution*, 3rd ed. (New York: Oxford University Press, 2018).

15. Ralph Adams Brown, *The Presidency of John Adams* (Lawrence: University Press of Kansas, 1971), 153–55.

16. Daniel H. Unser, "'A Savage Feast They Made of It': John Adams and the Paradoxical Origins of Federal Indian Policy," *Journal of the Early Republic* 33, no. 4 (Winter 2013): 607–41, esp. 614, 622–33; Rossignol, *The Nationalist Ferment*, 92–115.

17. John Adams, "Special Message to Congress, May 16, 1797," in Richardson, *Messages and Papers of the Presidents*, 1:233–39 (quotation at 235).

18. William Stinchcombe, *The XYZ Affair* (New York: Praeger, 1980).

19. Gordon S. Wood, *Empire for Liberty: A History of the Early American Republic, 1789–1815* (New York: Oxford University Press, 2009), 241–43; Rossignol, *The Nationalist Ferment*, 60–62.

20. Alexander de Conde, *The Quasi-War: The Undeclared Naval War with France* (New York: Charles Scribner's Sons, 1958); Rossignol, *The Nationalist Ferment*, 99–101.

21. Frederick C. Leiner, *Millions for Defense: The Subscription Warships of 1798* (Annapolis, MD: Naval Institute Press, 2000); Ian W. Toll, *Six Frigates: The Epic History of the Founding of the U.S. Navy* (New York: W. W. Norton, 2006), esp. pt. 1.

22. Michael Durey, *Transatlantic Radicals and the Early American Republic* (Lawrence: University Press of Kansas, 1997); Durey, *With the Hammer of Truth: James Thomson Callendar and America's Early National Heroes* (Charlottesville: University Press of Virginia, 1990).

23. Joanne B. Freeman, "Explaining the Unexplainable: The Cultural Origins of the Sedition Act," in *The Democratic Experiment: New Directions in American Political History*, ed. Meg Jacobs, William J. Novak, and Julian E. Zelizer (Princeton, NJ: Princeton University Press, 2003), 20–49.

24. 1798 Naturalization Act (An act supplementary to and to amend the act, entitled "An act to establish an uniform rule of naturalization, and to repeal the act heretofore passed on that subject"), Sess. II, Chap. 54; 1 Stat. 566, 5th Congress, June 17, 1798; 1798 Alien Enemies Act (An act respecting alien enemies), Sess. II, Chap. 66; 1 Stat. 570, 5th Congress, July 6, 1798; 1798 Alien Friends Act (An act concerning aliens), Sess. II, Chap. 58; 1 Stat. 577, 5th Congress, June 25, 1798; and 1798 Sedition Act (An act in addition to the Act, entitled "An Act for the punishment of certain crimes against the United States"), Sess. II., Chap. 74, 5th Congress, July 14, 1798.

25. I am indebted to Kelly Garner, a graduate of New York Law School, and Joel Collins Sati, a graduate of CCNY (now at Yale Law School), for excellent research papers illuminating these statutes. For a list of contemplated uses of the Alien Acts, see Wendell Bird, *Criminal Dissent: Prosecutions Under the Alien*

and Sedition Acts of 1798 (Cambridge, MA: Harvard University Press, 2020), appendix, table A.4, pp. 386–87, also discussion at 321–57.

26. Phillip I. Blumberg, *Repressive Jurisprudence in the Early American Republic: The First Amendment and the Legacy of English Law* (Cambridge: Cambridge University Press, 2010), 82–90, and sources cited. But see Wendell Bird, *Press and Speech under Assault: The Early Supreme Court Justices, the Sedition Act of 1798, and the Campaign against Dissent* (New York: Oxford University Press, 2016); Bird, "New Light on the Sedition Act of 1798: The Missing Half of the Prosecutions," *Law and History Review* 34 (August 2016): 541–614; Bird, *Criminal Dissent: Prosecutions under the Alien and Sedition Acts of 1798* (Cambridge, MA: Harvard University Press, 2020; and Freeman, "Explaining the Unexplainable,".

27. Blumberg, *Repressive Jurisprudence*, 92–99.

28. Cappon, 1:265–82 (seven letters, May 20 to October 25, 1804, between Abigail Adams and Thomas Jefferson, with Abigail beginning and ending the exchange); Woody Holton, *Abigail Adams* (New York: Free Press, 2009), 241–43. On the Terror in American thought, see Rachel Hope Cleeves, *The Reign of Terror in America: Visions of Violence from Anti-Jacobinism to Antislavery* (Cambridge: Cambridge University Press, 2009).

29. Blumberg, *Repressive Jurisprudence*, 99–147; James Morton Smith, *Freedom's Fetters: The Alien and Sedition Acts and Civil Liberties*, rev. ed. (Ithaca, NY: Cornell University Press, 1963 [1955]); and Durey, *With the Hammer of Truth*. See also the sources cited in note 79 of this chapter.

30. Blumberg, *Repressive Jurisprudence*, 90–92 (criticism of Adams); David McCullough, *John Adams* (New York: Simon and Schuster, 2001), 506–7 (unconvincing defense of Adams). For overviews of Adams and the press, see Walt Brown, *John Adams and the American Press: Politics and Journalism at the Birth of the Republic* (Jefferson, NC: McFarland, 1995), ; and Richard D. Brown, "The Disenchantment of a Radical Whig: John Adams Reckons with Free Speech," in *John Adams and the Founding of the Republic*, ed. Richard Alan Ryerson (Boston: Northeastern University of Press for MHS, 2001), 171–85.

31. Brown, *John Adams and the American Press*; Freeman, *Affairs of Honor*, 105–58; Jeffrey L. Pasley, *The Tyranny of Printers: Newspaper Politics in the Early American Republic* (Charlottesville: University of Virginia Press, 2001); and Brown, "The Disenchantment of a Radical Whig."

32. Leonard W. Levy, *Emergence of a Free Press* (New York: Oxford University Press, 1985), chaps. 9–10. On the difference between law on the books and

law as applied, see Levy, *Emergence of a Free Press*; Jeffery A. Smith, *Printers and Press Freedom: The Ideology of Early American Journalism* (New York: Oxford University Press, 1988); and Smith, *Franklin and Bache: Enlightening the Early Republic* (New York: Oxford University Press, 1990). Compare also the monographs by Blumberg and by Bird, cited in note 26 of this chapter.

33. "From Thomas Jefferson to John Taylor, 4 June 1798," FO/NA.

34. Ethelbert Dudley Warfield, *The Kentucky Resolutions of 1798: A Historical Study* (New York: G. P. Putnam's Sons, 1887); Andrew C. Lenner, *The Federal Principle in American Politics, 1790–1833* (Lanham, MD: Rowman and Littlefield/Madison House, 2001), esp. chap. 2.

35. *The Virginia report of 1799–1800, touching the alien and sedition laws; together with the Virginia resolutions of December 21, 1798, including the debate and proceedings thereon in the House of Delegates of Virginia and other documents illustrative of the report and resolutions* (New York: Da Capo Press, 1970; repr. of 1850 ed.); *The address of the minority in the Virginia legislature to the people of that state: containing a vindication of the constitutionality of the Alien and Sedition laws* ([Richmond, VA?]: [Printed by Augustine Davis?], [1799?]).

36. Morris D. Forkosch, "Freedom of the Press: Croswell's Case," *Fordham Law Review* 33 (1989): 415.

37. Uriah Forrest to John Adams, April 28, 1799, in *WJA* 8:637–38, quoted in Brown, *Presidency of John Adams*, 135.

38. In 1797, the Adamses left Philadelphia on July 19, returning on November 10. In 1798, they left Philadelphia on July 25, with Adams returning alone about November 20, leaving Abigail in Quincy. In 1799, Adams left Philadelphia on March 11, returning on October 10. In 1800, Adams left Washington before June 30 to return to Quincy; he arrived back in Washington on November 1, the first president to serve in the nation's permanent national capital. Brown, *Presidency of John Adams*, 134–37; White, *The Federalists*, 42n23.

39. George Boudreau, *Independence: A Guide to Historic Philadelphia* (Yardley, PA: Westholme, 2012), 307–14.

40. "From John Adams to Uriah Forrest, 13 May 1799," FO/NA [Early Access document].

41. Manning J. Dauer, *The Adams Federalists*, 2nd ed. (Baltimore: Johns Hopkins Press, 1968 [1953]).

42. On Vans Murray, see Peter P. Hill, *William Vans Murray: Federalist Diplomat* (Syracuse, NY: Syracuse University Press, 1961). In 1787, Vans Murray dedicated a pamphlet to Adams: [William Vans Murray], *Political Sketches,*

Inscribed to His Excellency John Adams . . . , by a Citizen of the United States (London: Printed for C. Dilly, 1787). The letters from Vans Murray appear in the appendix to volume 8 of *WJA*.

43. Robin Blackburn, "Haiti, Slavery, and the Age of the Democratic Revolution," *William and Mary Quarterly*, 3rd ser., 63, no. 4 (October 2006): 643–74; Donald R. Hickey, "America's Response to the Slave Revolt in Haiti, 1791–1806," *Journal of the Early Republic* 2, no. 4 (Winter 1982): 361–79; David Brion Davis, *The Problem of Slavery in the Age of Emancipation* (New York: Alfred A. Knopf, 2014), 45–82; Don E. Fehrenbacher (completed and edited by Ward A. McAfee), *The Slaveholding Republic: An Account of the United States Government's Relations to Slavery* (New York: Oxford University Press, 2001), 111–18; and Rossignol, *Nationalist Ferment*, 119–40. Laurent DuBois, *Avengers of the New World: The Story of the Haitian Revolution* (Cambridge, MA: Harvard University Press, 2004); DuBois, *A Colony of Citizens: Revolution and Slave Emancipation in the French Caribbean, 1787–1804* (Chapel Hill: University of North Carolina Press for the Omohundro Institute for Early American History and Culture, 2004); DuBois, *Haiti: The Aftershocks of History* (New York: Henry Holt, 2012); Arthur Scherr, *John Adams, Race, and Slavery: Ideas, Politics, and Diplomacy in an Age of Crisis* (Santa Barbara, CA: Praeger, 2018), 43–136, 172–74 (notes at 201–33, 244). Nancy Isenberg and Andrew Burstein, *The Problem of Democracy: The Presidents Adams Confront the Cult of Personality* (New York: Viking, 2019), 416–17, offers a more muted assessment of Adams's views.

44. James Grant, *John Adams: Party of One* (New York: Farrar, Straus and Giroux, 2005), 422; Edith B. Gelles, *Abigail and John: Portrait of a Marriage* (New York: William Morrow, 2009), 260–62.

45. For a pro-Hamilton account, see Forrest McDonald, *Alexander Hamilton: A Biography* (New York: W. W. Norton, 1979), 347–48, and sources at 445nn37–39. For a pro-Adams version, see Grant, *John Adams*, 421–23.

46. James Hart, *The American Presidency in Action, 1789: A Study in Constitutional History* (New York: Macmillan, 1948), 178–84; Leonard D. White, *The Federalists: A Study in Administrative History, 1789–1801* (New York: Macmillan, 1948), 19–25; and Gerhard Casper, *Separating Power: Essays on the Founding Period* (Cambridge, MA: Harvard University Press, 1997), 33–44.

47. John E. Ferling, *John Adams: A Life* (Knoxville: University of Tennessee Press, 1992), 393–94, and sources cited.

48. R. Kent Newmyer, *John Marshall and the Heroic Age of the Supreme Court* (Baton Rouge: Louisiana State University Press, 2001); and Jean Edward Smith, *John Marshall: Definer of a Nation* (New York: Henry Holt, 1997).

49. Paul Douglas Newman, *Fries' Rebellion: The Enduring Struggle for the American Revolution* (Philadelphia: University of Pennsylvania Press, 2004).

50. Freeman, *Affairs of Honor*, 199–261; see also Joanne B. Freeman, "The Election of 1800: A Study in the Logic of Political Change," *Yale Law Journal*: 108, no. 8 (June 1999): 1959–94. See also Susan Dunn, *Jefferson's Second Revolution: The Election Crisis of 1800 and the Triumph of Republicanism* (Boston: Houghton Mifflin, 2004); John Ferling, *Adams vs. Jefferson: The Tumultuous Election of 1800* (New York: Oxford University Press, 2004); Edward J. Larson, *A Magnificent Catastrophe: The Tumultuous Election of 1800, America's First Presidential Campaign* (New York: Free Press, 2007); James Horn, Jan Ellen Lewis, and Peter S. Onuf, eds., *The Revolution of 1800: Democracy, Race, and the New Republic* (Charlottesville: University of Virginia Press, 2002); Peter S. Onuf, *Jefferson's Empire: The Language of American Nationhood* (Charlottesville: University Press of Virginia, 2000), 80–108; Bernard A. Weisberger, *America Afire: Jefferson, Adams, and the Revolutionary Election of 1800* (New York: William Morrow, 2000); James Roger Sharp, *The Deadlocked Election of 1800: Jefferson, Burr, and the Union in the Balance* (Lawrence: University Press of Kansas, 2010). This literature focuses on the contest between Jefferson and Burr, omitting Adams once the electoral ballots were cast and counted. See also R. B. Bernstein, *Thomas Jefferson* (New York: Oxford University Press, 2003), 128–34; Raphael, *Mr. President*, 199–229.

51. "Letter from Alexander Hamilton, Concerning the Public Conduct and Character of John Adams, Esq. President of the United States, [October 24, 1800]," FO/NA. It is also available in Joanne B. Freeman, ed., *Alexander Hamilton: Writings* (New York: Library of America, 2001), 934–71. On this pamphlet, and on its continuing effects on Adams, see Freeman, *Affairs of Honor*, 105–9, 148–58; Raphael, *Mr. President*, 221–23.

52. Freeman, *Affairs of Honor*, 199–261; Joanne B. Freeman, "The Presidential Election of 1796," in Ryerson, *John Adams and the Founding of the Republic*, 142–70.

53. Brown, *Presidency of John Adams*, 193.

54. George William Van Cleve, *A Slaveholders' Union: Slavery, Politics, and the Constitution in the Early American Republic* (Chicago: University of Chicago Press, 2010), 139–41.

55. Gelles, *Abigail and John*, 261–62.

56. Ferling, *John Adams*, 405–6.

57. Freeman, *Affairs of* Honor, 241–53; Bernstein, *Thomas Jefferson*, 128–34.

58. "From John Adams to William Tudor, Sr., 13 December 1800," FO/NA [Early Access document].

59. McDonald, *Alexander Hamilton*, 352–53.

60. "Thomas Jefferson to Benjamin Rush, 16 January 1811," FO/NA.

61. Wythe Holt, "'To Establish Justice': Politics, the Judiciary Act of 1789, and the Invention of the Federal Courts," *Duke Law Journal* 1989, no. 6 (1989): 1421–531; Holt, "'Federal Courts Have Enemies in All Who Fear Their Influence on State Objects': The Failure to Abolish Supreme Court Circuit-Riding in the Judiciary Acts of 1792 and 1793," *Buffalo Law Review* 36, no. 2 (1987): 301–40; Holt, "'Federal Courts as the Asylum to Federal Interests': Randolph's Report, the Benson Amendment, and the 'Original Understanding' of the Federal Judiciary," *Buffalo Law Review* 36, no. 2 (1987): 341–72. See also Wilfred J. Ritz, *Rewriting the History of the Judiciary Act of 1789: Exposing Myths, Challenging Premises, and Using New Evidence*, ed. Wythe Holt and L. H. LaRue (Norman: University of Oklahoma Press, 1990).

62. Mary Sarah Bilder, Maeva Marcus, and R. Kent Newmyer, eds., *Blackstone in America: Selected Essays of Kathryn Preyer* (Cambridge: Cambridge University Press, 2009), 7–91.

63. Ritz, Holt, and LaRue, *Rewriting the History of the Judiciary Act of 1789*, 27–52. See also Maeva Marcus, ed., *Origins of the Federal Judiciary: Essays on the Judiciary Act of 1789* (New York: Oxford University Press, 1992). On the changes to federal question jurisdiction and the amount in controversy limitation, see William E. Nelson, *Marbury v. Madison: The Origins and Legacy of Judicial Review*, 2nd rev. ed. (Lawrence: University Press of Kansas, 2018 [2000]), 92–93.

64. Joshua Glick, "On the Road: The Supreme Court and the History of Circuit Riding," *Cardozo Law Review* 24 (2003): 1735; and articles by Holt cited in note 61; Marcus, *Origins of the Federal Judiciary*, .

65. Kathryn Turner, "Federalist Policy and the Judiciary Act of 1801," *William and Mary Quarterly*, 3rd ser., 22 (January 1965): 3–32, reprinted in *Blackstone in America*, 10–38.

66. Kathryn Turner, "The Midnight Judges," *University of Pennsylvania Law Review* 109, no. 4 (February 1961): 494–523, reprinted in *Blackstone in America*, 59–91.

67. Kathryn Turner, "The Appointment of Chief Justice Marshall," *William and Mary Quarterly*, 3rd ser., 17, no. 2 (April 1960): 143–63, reprinted in *Blackstone in America*, 39–58 (from perspective of the judiciary); and R. B. Bernstein, "President John Adams and Four Chief Justices: An Essay for James F. Simon," *New York Law School Law Review* 57, no. 3 (2012/13), 441–63 (from perspective of Adams).

68. John Adams to John Jay, December 19, 1800, in *The Documentary History of the Supreme Court of the United States*, 8 vols., ed. Maeva Marcus (New York: Columbia University Press, 1985–2007), 1:145–46 (hereafter *DHSC*).

69. John Jay to John Adams, January 2, 1801, in Marcus, *DHSC*, 1:146–47.

70. Quoted in Marcus, *DHSC* 1:928; see also 1:152–55.

71. I am indebted to Kevin Arlyck for this view of the Court's role in national security issues in the early republic, the subject of a dissertation at New York University that I hope will soon take book form.

72. Brown, *Presidency of John Adams*, 206–8.

73. "From John Adams to Thomas Jefferson, 20 February 1801," FO/NA [Early Access document].

74. "From John Adams to Thomas Jefferson, 24 March 1801," FO/NA [Early Access document], answering "To John Adams from Thomas Jefferson, 8 March 1801," FO/NA [Early Access document].

75. Letter from John Adams to Abigail Adams, November 2, 1800, AFPEA/ MHS.

76. "From Thomas Jefferson to Elbridge Gerry, 13 May 1797," FO/NA.

77. "From John Adams to John Marshall, 17 August 1825," FO/NA [Early Access document].

78. On Marshall, see R. Kent Newmyer, *The Supreme Court under Marshall and Taney*, 2nd ed. (Wheeling, IL: Harlan Davidson, 2006 [1968]); R. Kent Newmyer, *John Marshall and the Heroic Age of the Supreme Court* (Baton Rouge: Louisiana State University Press, 2001); Charles F. Hobson, *The Great Chief Justice: John Marshall and the Rule of Law* (Lawrence: University Press of Kansas, 1996); and Jean Edward Smith, *John Marshall: Definer of a Nation* (New York: Henry Holt, 1996).

79. Leonard W. Levy, *Legacy of Suppression: Freedom of Speech and Press in Early American History* (Cambridge, MA: Belknap Press of Harvard University Press, 1960); Levy, *Jefferson and Civil Liberties: The Darker Side*,

repr. with new intro. (Chicago: Ivan R. Dee, 1989 [1963]); Levy, *Emergence of a Free Press*. See also James Morton Smith, *Freedom's Fetters: The Alien and Sedition Acts and American Civil Liberties*, rev. ed. (Ithaca, NY: Cornell University Press, 1963 [1955]); Smith, *Printers and Press Freedom*; Smith, *Franklin and Bache*; and Jeffery A. Smith, *War and Press Freedom: The Problems of Prerogative Power* (New York: Oxford University Press, 1999); Durey, *Transatlantic Radicals*; Durey, *With the Hammer of Truth*; Aleine Austin, *Matthew Lyon: "New Man" of the American Revolution, 1749–1822* (University Park: Penn State University Press, 1981); Geoffrey Stone, *Perilous Times: Free Speech in Wartime from the Sedition Act of 1798 to the War on Terror* (New York: W. W. Norton, 2004); John C. Miller, *Crisis in Freedom: The Alien and Sedition Acts* (Boston: Atlantic/Little, Brown, 1955); Irving N. Brant, *The Bill of Rights: Its Origin and Meaning* (Indianapolis: Bobbs-Merrill, 1965); Juhani Rudanko, *The Forging of Freedom of Speech: Essays on Argumentation in Congressional Debates on the Bill of Rights and the Sedition Act* (Lanham, MD: University Press of America, 2003); Brown, *John Adams and the American Press*; Pasley, *Tyranny of Printers*; and Blumberg, *Repressive Jurisprudence*. See also the works by Wendell Bird cited in note 26.

Chapter Nine

1. For Adams's letters to Jefferson written between 1819 and 1823 dated from "Montezillo Alias the little Hill," see Cappon, 2:547–86 (quotation at 2:547, from John Adams to Thomas Jefferson, November 23, 1819).

2. R. B. Bernstein, "Review of *The Papers of Thomas Jefferson: Retirement Series, Volume I: 4 March—15 November 1801* (J. Jefferson Looney, ed.)," *Journal of the Early Republic* 26, no. 4 (Winter 2006): 682–98.

3. Barry Schwartz, *George Washington: The Making of an American Hero* (New York: Free Press/Macmillan, 1987), esp. 91–103.

4. John Adams to Benjamin Rush, June 12, 1812, in *The Spur of Fame: Dialogues of John Adams and Benjamin Rush, 1805–1813*, ed. John A. Schutz and Douglass Adair (San Marino, CA: Huntington Library Press, 1966; repr., Indianapolis: Liberty Fund, 2001), 224–26 (esp. 226 numbered paragraph 5). I have used the original 1966 edition; the Liberty Fund reprint differs in pagination. Schutz and Adair presented a carefully edited, excerpted version of the correspondence as it was published in 1892: *Old Family Letters: Copied from the Originals for Alexander Biddle, Series A* (Philadelphia: Press of J. B. Lippincott Company, 1892). I cite mostly to *Spur of Fame* but occasionally to *Old Family Letters*.

5. John E. Ferling, *John Adams: A Life* (Knoxville: University of Tennessee Press, 1992), 418; see also James Grant, *John Adams: Party of One* (New York: Farrar, Straus and Giroux, 2005), 432.

6. Grant, *John Adams*, 432, 495n8. On John Quincy Adams's efforts on his parents' behalf, see Fred Kaplan, *John Quincy Adams: American Visionary* (New York: Harper, 2014), 195–96; S. R. Coppe, *Bird, Savage, and Bird* (London: Corp. of London, 1981).

7. Joanne B. Freeman, *Affairs of Honor: National Politics in the New Republic* (New Haven, CT: Yale University Press, 2001), 274–88; Douglass Adair, *Fame and the Founding Fathers: Essays of Douglass Adair*, ed. Trevor Colbourn (New York: W. W. Norton for the Institute of Early American History and Culture, 1974; repr., Indianapolis: Liberty Fund, 1998), 3–36.

8. Ryerson, *Republic*, 355–58.

9. *Spur of Fame*. On Rush, see Stephen Fried, *Rush: Revolution, Madness, and Benjamin Rush: The Doctor Who Became a Founding Father* (New York: Crown, 2018); David Freeman Hawke, *Benjamin Rush: Revolutionary Gadfly* (Indianapolis: Bobbs-Merrill, 1971); Donald J. D'Elia, *Benjamin Rush: Philosopher of the American Revolution*, Transactions of the American Philosophical Society, n.s., vol. 64, part 5 (Philadelphia: American Philosophical Society, 1974).

10. John Adams to Benjamin Rush, March 26, 1806, in *Spur of Fame*, 51–52 (quotation at 52).

11. John Adams to Benjamin Rush, November 11, 1807, in *Spur of Fame*, 97–99 (esp. 98). Recent studies of Washington have shown that Adams's barb, though amusing, was deeply unfair. Kevin Hayes, *George Washington: A Life in Books* (New York: Oxford University Press, 2017); Adrienne M. Harrison, *A Powerful Mind: The Self-Education of George Washington* (Lincoln: Potomac Books/University of Nebraska Press, 2015).

12. John Adams to Benjamin Rush, December 25, 1811, in *Spur of Fame*, 200–202 (esp. 201–2).

13. John Adams to Benjamin Rush, July 23, 1806, in *Spur of Fame*, 59–61 (esp. 59); John Adams to Benjamin Rush, November 11, 1807, in *Old Family Letters*, 167–73 (esp. 170).

14. "From John Adams to Joseph Ward, 8 January 1810," FO/NA [Early Access document]; Annette Gordon-Reed, *Thomas Jefferson and Sally Hemings: An American Controversy* (Charlottesville: University Press of Virginia, 1997; with new introduction, 1999); and Jan Ellen Lewis and Peter

S. Onuf, eds., *Sally Hemings and Thomas Jefferson: History, Memory, and Civic Culture* (Charlottesville: University Press of Virginia, 1999). On Callendar, see Michael Durey, *"With the Hammer of Truth": James Thomas Callendar and America's Early National Heroes* (Charlottesville: University Press of Virginia, 1990).

15. Worthington Chauncey Ford, ed., *Statesman and Friend: Correspondence of John Adams with Benjamin Waterhouse, 1784–1822* (Boston: Little, Brown, 1927). On Waterhouse, see Stefan C. Schatzki, "Benjamin Waterhouse," *American Journal of Roentgenology*, no. 187 (August 2006): 585, www.ajronline. org/doi/full/10.2214/AJR.05.2125.

16. John Adams to Benjamin Waterhouse, February 13, 1805, and February 19, 1805, in Ford, *Statesman and Friend*, 11–12, 13–16.

17. John Adams to Benjamin Waterhouse, July 5, 1811, in Ford, *Statesman and Friend*, 55–58 (quotation at 56–57).

18. John Adams to Benjamin Waterhouse, August 7, 1805, in Ford, *Statesman and Friend*, 22–31 (quotation at 31).

19. Harry F. Jackson, *Scholar in the Wilderness: Francis Adrian Van der Kemp* (Syracuse, NY: Syracuse University Press, 1963); see also Helen Lincklain Fairchild, *Francis Adrian Van der Kemp, 1752–1829: An Autobiography Together with Extracts from His Correspondence* (New York: G. P. Putnam's Sons, 1903).

20. Mercy Otis Warren, *History of the Rise, Progress, and Termination of the American Revolution, Interspersed with Biographical, Political, and Moral Observations* (orig. ed. in 3 vols, Boston: printed by Manning and Loring, for E. Larkin; edited and annotated by Lester H. Cohen, 2 vols., Indianapolis: Liberty Fund, 1998 [1805]).

21. "From Thomas Jefferson to Mercy Otis Warren, 8 February 1805," FO/ NA.

22. Warren, *Rise, Progress, and Termination* (1805 ed.), 3:392–93.

23. This correspondence was published in Charles Francis Adams, ed., "Correspondence between John Adams and Mercy Warren," *Collections of the Massachusetts Historical Society*, 5th ser., 4:321–511 (1870). I used the 1972 reprint edition in the series *American Women: Images and Realities: Correspondence between John Adams and Mercy Warren, Including an Appendix of Specimen Pages from the "History"* (New York: Arno Press, 1972). The pagination for the correspondence is identical to that of the original 1870 edition. The pagination of the selected pages from Warren's *History* is from the 1805 edition.

24. John Adams to Mercy Otis Warren, July 20, 1807, in *Correspondence between John Adams and Mercy Otis Warren*, 332–54 (quotation at 336).

25. Mercy Warren to John Adams, August 27, 1807, in *Correspondence between John Adams and Mercy Warren* 479–91 (quotation at 490–91).

26. An appendix to *Correspondence between John Adams and Mercy Warren*, at 493–511, presents letters between Abigail Adams and Mercy Otis Warren preceding the conflict, letters between Elbridge Gerry and Mrs. Warren addressing the conflict and Gerry's advice to Mrs. Warren as to her proper course of conduct (*"silence"*), and an abortive attempt in 1814 by John Adams, rebuffed by Mrs. Warren, to restore good relations.

27. The best and most thoughtful discussion is Freeman, *Affairs of Honor*, chap. 3. See also Ryerson, *Republic*, 359ff.

28. The correspondence is collected in *Correspondence between the Hon. John Adams, Late President of the United States, and the Late William Cunningham, Esq. Begun in 1803, and Ending in 1812* (Boston: Published by E. M. Cunningham, Son of the Late Wm. Cunningham, Esq., and Tree and Greene, Printers, 1823). Charles Francis Adams omitted these letters from his edition of his grandfather's *Works* (1850–56). Freeman, *Affairs of Honor*, 130–41, 148–57, gives an excellent analysis; see also Cappon, 2:600n77. Further discussion of the aftermath appears in chapter 10.

29. Lyman Butterfield, "The Dream of Benjamin Rush: The Reconciliation of John Adams and Thomas Jefferson," *Yale Review* 40 (1951): 297–319.

30. Abigail Adams to Thomas Jefferson, May 20, 1804, in Cappon, 1:268–69 (quotation at 269).

31. Thomas Jefferson to Abigail Adams, June 23, 1804, in Cappon, 1:269–71.

32. Abigail Adams to Thomas Jefferson, July 1, 1804, in Cappon, 1:271–74.

33. Abigail Adams to Thomas Jefferson, October 25, 1804, in Cappon, 1:280–82 (quotation at 282). The entire correspondence is at 1:268–82; see also the editor's commentary at 1:265–68.

34. Abigail Adams to Thomas Jefferson, July 1, 1804, in Cappon, 1:271–74 (quotation at 274).

35. John Adams, note dated November 19, 1804, in Cappon, 1:282.

36. "Thomas Jefferson to Benjamin Rush, 16 January 1811," FO/NA.

37. John Adams to Benjamin Rush, December 25, 1811, in *Spur of Fame*, 200–202 (quotation at 202).

38. Cappon, 2:286–87. John Quincy Adams, *Lectures on Rhetoric and Oratory, Delivered to the Classes of Senior and Junior Sophisters in Harvard University*, 2 vols. (Boston: Hilliard and Metcalf, 1810).

Chapter Ten

1. Henry David Thoreau, *Walden, or, Life in the Woods*, ed. Jeffrey S. Cramer (New Haven, CT: Yale University Press, 2006 [1854]), 2.

2. For now, the definitive edition is Cappon. *The Papers of Thomas Jefferson, The Papers of Thomas Jefferson: Retirement Series*, and *The Papers of John Adams* will publish letters that Cappon apparently did not find. An excellent interim means of checking these editions is http://www.founders.archives.gov. Gordon S. Wood, *Friends Divided: John Adams and Thomas Jefferson* (New York: Penguin, 2017); Merrill D. Peterson, *Adams and Jefferson: A Revolutionary Dialogue* (Athens: University of Georgia Press, 1976). For an excellent brief discussion, see Joanne B, Freeman, "Jefferson and Adams: Friendship and the Power of the Letter," in *The Cambridge Companion to Thomas Jefferson*, ed. Frank Shuffelton (Cambridge: Cambridge University Press, 2009), 168–78.

3. "Thomas Jefferson to John Adams, 21 January 1812," FO/NA.

4. "Thomas Jefferson to John Adams, 23 January 1812," FO/NA.

5. "From John Adams to Thomas Jefferson, 15 July 1813," FO/NA [Early Access document]. On Rush, see Stephen Fried, *Rush: Revolution, Madness, and the Visionary Doctor Who Became a Founding Father* (New York: Crown, 2018).

6. "Thomas Jefferson to John Adams, 27 May 1813," FO/NA.

7. "Thomas Jefferson to John Adams, 29 May 1813," FO/NA.

8. "Thomas Jefferson to John Adams, 5 July 1814," FO/NA.

9. "From John Adams to Thomas Jefferson, 16 July 1814," FO/NA [Early Access document].

10. "From John Adams to Thomas Jefferson, 13 July 1813," FO/NA [Early Access document].

11. "From John Adams to Thomas Jefferson, 19 April 1817," FO/NA [Early Access document].

12. "Thomas Jefferson to John Adams, 11 January 1817," FO/NA.

13. "To John Adams from Thomas Jefferson, 14 October 1816," FO/NA [Early Access document].

14. "John Adams to Thomas Jefferson, 9 July 1813," FO/NA.

15. "John Adams to Thomas Jefferson, 15 September 1813," FO/NA.

16. "John Adams to Thomas Jefferson, 2 March 1816," FO/NA.

17. "From John Adams to Thomas Jefferson, 30 July 1815," FO/NA [Early Access document].

18. "From John Adams to Thomas Jefferson, 24 August 1815," FO/NA [Early Access document].

19. "From John Adams to Thomas Jefferson, 16 July 1814," FO/NA [Early Access document].

20. "From John Adams to William Tudor, Sr., 9 February 1819," FO/NA [Early Access document].

21. "John Adams to Thomas Jefferson, [ca. 14] August 1813, with Postscript, 16 August 1813," FO/NA.

22. "From Abigail Smith Adams to Thomas Jefferson, 20 September 1813," FO/NA [Early Access document].

23. "Thomas Jefferson to John Adams, 12 October 1813," FO/NA.

24. "From John Adams to Thomas Jefferson, 20 October 1818," FO/NA [Early Access document].

25. "To John Adams from Thomas Jefferson, 13 November 1818," FO/NA [Early Access document].

26. "From John Adams to Thomas Jefferson, 8 December 1818," FO/NA [Early Access document].

27. David L. Holmes, *The Faiths of the Founding Fathers* (New York, Oxford University Press, 2006), 73–78; Amy Kittelstrom, *The Religion of Democracy: Seven Liberals and the American Moral Tradition* (New York: Penguin, 2016 [2015]), 17–55 (notes 365–71); and esp. Sara Georgini, *Household Gods: The Religious Lives of the Adams Family* (New York: Oxford University Press, 2019), 7–40 (notes 210–23).

28. *Journal of debates and proceedings in the Convention of delegates, chosen to revise the constitution of Massachusetts, begun and holden at Boston, November 15, 1820, and continued by adjournment to January 9, 1821. Reported for the Boston daily advertiser* (Boston: Published at the office of the Daily Advertiser, 1821) (hereafter cited as *Journal 1821* with page numbers).

29. *Journal 1821*, 11–12.

30. *Journal 1821*, 9–10.

31. *Journal 1821*, 209, and see also 193.

32. "To Thomas Jefferson from John Adams, 3 February 1821," FO/NA [Early Access document].

33. "To Thomas Jefferson from John Adams, 3 February 1821," FO/NA [Early Access document].

34. See chapter 9.

35. "From John Adams to Richard Rush, 20 November 1813," FO/NA [Early Access document].

36. Arthur Scherr, *John Adams, Slavery, and Race: Ideas, Politics, and Diplomacy in an Age of Crisis* (Santa Barbara, CA: Praeger, 2018); John R. Howe Jr., "John Adams's Views of Slavery," *Journal of Negro History* 49, no. 3 (1964): 201–6; Charles R. Lawrence III, "The Id, the Ego, and Equal Protection: Reckoning with Unconscious Racism," *Stanford Law Review* 39, no. 2 (January 1987): 317–88; Charles R. Lawrence III, "Unconscious Racism Revisited: Reflections on the Impact and Origins of 'The Id, the Ego, and Equal Protection,'" *Connecticut Law Review* 40, no. 4 (July 2008): 931–77. I am indebted to my students at CCNY, particularly Joel Sati, Tiffany Scruggs, and those taking our course on African American Political Thought and my course on Early American Political Development, for discussions of this topic. I am also indebted to Annette Gordon-Reed and to my former teacher Charles R. Lawrence III.

37. *Correspondence between the Hon. John Adams, Late President of the United States, and the Late Hon. Wm. Cunningham, Esq., Beginning in 1803, and Continuing until 1823* (Boston: Published by E. M. Cunningham, son of the late Wm. Cunningham/Tree and Greene, Printers, 1823).

38. "To John Adams from Thomas Jefferson, 12 October 1823," FO/NA [Early Access document].

39. "From John Adams to Thomas Jefferson, 10 November 1823," FO/NA [Early Access document]. Both the previous quotation and this quotation come from this letter.

40. "To John Adams from Thomas Jefferson, 15 February 1825," FO/NA [Early Access document].

41. "From John Adams to John Quincy Adams, 18 February 1825," FO/NA [Early Access document].

42. "From John Adams to Thomas Jefferson, 1 December 1825," FO/NA [Early Access document].

43. "From John Adams to John Whitney, 7 June 1826," FO/NA [Early Access document]; "From John Adams to Roger Chew Weightman, 22 June 1826,"

FO/NA [Early Access document]; "From Thomas Jefferson to Roger Chew Weightman, 24 June 1826," FO/NA [Early Access document].

44. Andrew Burstein, *America's Jubilee* (New York: Alfred A. Knopf, 2001), chap. 11.

45. For a contemporary newspaper's coverage of the funeral and other ceremonies marking the passing of John Adams in 1826, see Wood *JA 1784–1826*, 873–78.

46. On the concept of law-mindedness, see R. B. Bernstein, "Legal History's Pathfinder: The Quest of John Phillip Reid," in *Law as Culture and Culture as Law: Essays in Honor of John Phillip Reid*, ed. Hendrik Hartog, William E. Nelson, and Barbara Wilcie Kern (Madison, WI: Madison House, 2000), 10–37.

Epilogue

1. John Adams to Benjamin Rush, March 23, 1809, in *Old Family Letters: Copied from the Originals for Alexander Biddle, Series A* (Philadelphia: Press of J. B. Lippincott, 1892), 224–28 (quotation at 226).

2. "John Adams to Thomas Jefferson, 1 May 1812," FO/NA.

3. For a list of monuments to John Adams, see https://en.wikipedia.org/wiki/List_of_memorials_to_John_Adams.

4. See Nancy Isenberg and Andrew Burstein, "The Adamses on Screen," in *A Companion to John Adams and John Quincy Adams*, ed. David Waldstreicher (Malden, MA: Wiley-Blackwell, 2013), 487–509.

5. See R. B. Bernstein, "John Adams: The Life and the Biographers," in Waldstreicher, *A Companion to John Adams and John Quincy Adams*, 5–35 (esp. 24–34); Nancy Isenberg and Andrew Burstein, "The Adamses on Screen," in Waldstreicher, *A Companion to John Adams and John Quincy Adams*, 487–509.

6. For an example following September 11, 2001, see Jeffrey L. Pasley, "Publick Occurrences: Federalist Chic," *Common-Place* 2, no. 2 (January 2002): http://www.common-place.org/publick/200202.shtml (accessed February 16, 2008). For the leading critique that appeared before September 11, 2001, see Sean Wilentz, "Review: America Made Easy: John Adams Is Not the Hero We Need and David McCullough Is Not the Historian We Need," *New Republic*, July 2, 2001, 40ff. A book-length example is Richard Rosenfeld, *American Aurora: The Suppressed History of Our Nation's Beginnings*

and the Heroic Newspaper That Tried to Report It (New York: St. Martin's Press, 1996). See the review by Joanne B. Freeman for H-LAW: Joanne B. Freeman. "Recapturing the Sense of Crisis": Review of Rosenfeld, Richard N., *American Aurora: A Democratic-Republican Returns. The Suppressed History of Our Nation's Beginnings and the Heroic Newspaper That Tried to Report It*, H-Law, H-Net Reviews, August 1998, http://www.h-net.org/reviews/showrev. php?id=2252.

7. "Rebecca West once said that to understand is not to forgive. It is only to understand. It is not an end but a beginning. Knowledge is power." Victoria Glendinning quoting Rebecca West, quoted in R. B. Bernstein, *Thomas Jefferson* (New York: Oxford University Press, 2003), xviii.

8. On this concept, see R. B. Bernstein, *The Founding Fathers Reconsidered* (New York: Oxford University Press, 2009), esp. 3–11.

9. On this concept, see Henry Steele Commager, *The Search for a Usable Past: And Other Essays in Historiography* (New York: Alfred A. Knopf, 1966).

10. See Parker's wonderful essay on John Adams in Theodore Parker, *Historic Americans* (Boston: American Universalist Association, 1908 [1870]), 97–157 (quotation at 142).

11. The most splenetic example of this view is Rosenfeld, *American Aurora*.

12. Even now, nearly a century after its appearance, the best study of the subject of monarchism in this period remains Louise B. Dunbar, *A Study of "Monarchical" Tendencies in the United States from 1776 to 1801*, in *University of Illinois Studies in the Social Sciences* 10, no. 1 (March 1922), reprinted with new preface (New York: Johnson Reprint Corporation, 1970), esp. 129–34 (on John Adams). Eric Nelson, *The Royalist Revolution: Monarchy and the American Founding* (Cambridge, MA: Harvard University Press, 2014), came to hand too late for use in this book but should be viewed with skepticism. On aristocracy, see William Doyle, *Aristocracy and Its Enemies in the Age of Revolution* (Oxford: Oxford University Press, 2009); Doyle, *Aristocracy: A Very Short Introduction* (Oxford: Oxford University Press, 2011); and Jonathan Powys, *Aristocracy* (Oxford: Basil Blackwell, 1984). See also the discussion in R. R. Palmer, *The Age of the Democratic Revolution: A Political History of Europe and America, 1760–1800*, one vol. ed. (Princeton, NJ: Princeton University Press, 2014 [1959, 1964]), 22–63.

13. Arthur Scherr, *John Adams, Slavery, and Race: Ideas, Politics, and Diplomacy in an Age of Crisis* (Santa Barbara, CA: Praeger, 2018), bashes Adams but takes even more pleasure in bashing modern scholars whom the author regards as

unduly kind to Adams on this subject. On the doughfaces, I am grateful to Professor Joanne B. Freeman for many discussions of the subject.

14. Joanne Pope Melish, *Disowning Slavery: Gradual Emancipation and "Race" in New England, 1780–1860* (Ithaca, NY: Cornell University Press, 1998); Jared Ross Hardesty, *Unfreedom: Slavery and Dependence in Eighteenth-Century Boston* (New York: New York University Press, 2017). One possibility is the influence of the Broadway musical (later a film) *1776*, which portrays John Adams as a near abolitionist. Sherman Edwards and Peter Stone, *1776* (New York: Viking, 1970).

15. See Robert N. Wiebe, *The Search for Order, 1877–1920* (New York: Hill and Wang, 1967); Richard White, *The Republic for Which It Stands: The United States during Reconstruction and the Gilded Age, 1865–1896* (New York: Oxford University Press, 2017).

16. On this aspect of Jefferson's thought, see Hannah Spahn, *Thomas Jefferson, Time and History* (Charlottesville: University of Virginia Press, 2012). On Adams's immersion in history and on his inability or disinclination to consider evolution of political and constitutional ideas over time, see John R. Howe Jr., *The Changing Political Thought of John Adams* (Princeton, NJ: Princeton University Press, 1966), esp. 209–10; and H. Trevor Colbourn, *The Lamp of Experience: Whig History and the Intellectual Origins of the American Revolution*, rept. ed. (Indianapolis: Liberty Fund, 1998 [1965]), 100–28

17. Arnold Rampersad, in interview, quoted in Gail Porter Mandell, *Life into Art: Conversations with Seven Contemporary Biographers* (Fayetteville: University of Arkansas Press, 1991), 45. See also Arnold Rampersad, *The Art and Imagination of W. E. B. Du Bois* (Cambridge, MA: Harvard University Press, 1976).

18. Lester J. Cappon, "American Historical Editors before Jared Sparks: 'they will plant a forest . . . ,'" *William and Mary Quarterly*, 3rd ser., 30, no. 3 (July 1973): 375–400. On Charles Francis Adams as historical editor, see Haraszti, *John Adams and the Prophets of Progress*, 9, 10, 12, 13, 46–47.

19. Haraszti, *John Adams and the Prophets of Progress*, 13.

20. See Correa M. Walsh, *The Political Science of John Adams: A Study in the Theory of Mixed Government and Bicameralism* (New York: G. P. Putnam's Sons, 1915).

21. See, for example, Russell Kirk, *The Conservative Mind: From Burke to Eliot*, 3rd ed. (Chicago: Regnery, 2001 [1953]), 71–74. See also Clinton Rossiter, *Conservatism in America: The Thankless Persuasion*, 2nd rev. ed.

(New York: Alfred A. Knopf, 1962 [1955]). For a scholarly treatment that occasionally parallels conservative arguments, see Haraszti, *John Adams and the Prophets of Progress.* John E. Ferling, *John Adams: A Life* (Knoxville: University Press of Tennessee, 1992), 3, identifies Page Smith as an Adams biographer responding to Cold War concerns.

22. Crane Brinton, *The Anatomy of Revolution,* revised and expanded edition (New York: Vintage Books, 1965, [1938]); Hannah Arendt, *On Revolution* (New York: Penguin, 2006 [1963]). Arendt devotes extensive, favorable attention to Adams, as part of her general preference for the gradualist, incremental nature of the American Revolution.

23. Zoltan Haraszti, *John Adams and the Prophets of Progress* (Cambridge, MA: Harvard University Press, 1952). For a fascinating essay that digs further into Adams's marginalia, see H. J. Jackson, "John Adams's Marginalia, Then and Now," in *The Libraries, Leadership, and Legacy of John Adams and Thomas Jefferson,* ed. Robert C. Baron and Conrad Edick Wright (Golden, CO: Fulcrum Publishing and Massachusetts Historical Society, 2010), 59–79, with notes at 264.

24. On the "documentary-editing revolution," see William W. Freehling, *The Reintegration of American History: Slavery and the Civil War* (New York: Oxford University Press, 1994), chap. 1. This chapter originally appeared as William W. Freehling, "The Editorial Revolution, Virginia, and the Coming of the Civil War: A Review Essay," *Civil War History* 16, no. 1 (March 1970): 64–72. On the influence of the 1954 Internal Revenue Code, I am indebted to Professor Daniel J. Hulsebosch of New York University School of Law for pointing out this possible causal factor.

25. US Cong., House Committee on Resources, Subcommittee on National Parks, Recreation, and Public Lands, Legislative Hearing, H.R. 271, H.R. 980, and H.R. 1668, 107th Cong., 1st Sess. (Washington, DC: Government Printing Office, 2001), 41–43 (testimony of David McCullough, June 12, 2001); H.R. 1668, 107th Cong., 1st Sess., "To authorize the Adams Memorial Foundation to establish a commemorative work on Federal land in the District of Columbia and its environs to honor former President John Adams and his legacy," introduced on May 1, 2001, adopted in House June 25, 2001, adopted in Senate October 17, 2001, signed into law November 5, 2001, as Public Law 107-62. See also Senate Report 107-77, 107th Cong., 1st Sess., October 1, 2001. Trevor Parry-Giles, "Fame, Celebrity, and the Legacy of John Adams," *Western Journal of Communication* 72, no. 1 (January–March 2008): 83–101.

26. William Dawson Johnston, *History of the Library of Congress*, vol. 1, *1800–1864* (Washington, DC: Government Printing Office, 1904), 275–87.

27. John Y. Cole, "On These Walls: Inscriptions and Quotations in the Buildings of the Library of Congress," http://www.loc.gov/loc/walls/ (accessed February 16, 2008). This is the online version of John Y. Cole, *On These Walls: Inscriptions and Quotations in the Buildings of the Library of Congress* (Washington, DC: Printed for the Library of Congress by the US Government Printing Office, 1995; repr., New York: SCALO, 2008). Senate Report 107-77 wrongly claims that the building in question is named for John Quincy Adams. Statement of John G. Parsons, Associate Regional Director for Lands, Resources, and Planning, National Capital Region, National Park Service, Department of the Interior, in Senate Report 107-77, 4–5 (esp. 5).

FURTHER READING

To understand the Adamses, begin with their writings. The Note on Sources lists the best online and print editions. The Adamses were extraordinary writers, especially in their letters; reading their own words is still the best way to get to know them.

The best modern biographies are John E. Ferling, *John Adams: A Life* (Knoxville: University Press of Tennessee, 1993), and James Grant, *John Adams: Party of One* (New York: Farrar, Straus & Giroux, 2005). The best older biography is Gilbert Chinard, *Honest John Adams* (Boston: Little, Brown, 1935). Peter Shaw, *The Character of John Adams* (Chapel Hill: University of North Carolina Press for the Institute of Early American History and Culture, 1975), is an insightful character study. Page Smith, *John Adams* (Garden City, NY: Doubleday, 1962), is badly organized and poorly documented; the book lacks a table of contents and a reliable index. The highly uncritical David McCullough, *John Adams* (New York: Simon & Schuster, 2001), elevates John Adams's character over his mind. Joseph J. Ellis, *Passionate Sage: The Character and Legacy of John Adams* (New York: W. W. Norton, 1993), is a well-written examination of Adams's later years.

The best studies of Abigail Adams are Woody Holton, *Abigail Adams: A Life* (New York: Free Press, 2009); Edith B. Gelles, *Portia: The World of Abigail Adams* (Bloomington: Indiana University Press, 1991); and Edith B. Gelles, *Abigail Adams: A Writing Life* (New York: Routledge, 2002; originally *First Thoughts: Life and Letters of Abigail Adams* [New York: Twayne, 1998]). Edith B. Gelles, *Abigail and John: Portrait of a Marriage* (New York: William Morrow, 2009), is the best study of its subject. Diane Jacobs, *Dear Abigail: The Intimate Lives and Revolutionary Ideas of Abigail Adams and Her Two Remarkable Sisters* (New York: Ballantine Books, 2014), views Abigail within the context of her relationships with her sisters and her other relatives.

Three fine essay collections are David Waldstreicher, ed., *A Companion to John Adams and John Quincy Adams* (Malden, MA: Wiley-Blackwell, 2013); Richard Alan Ryerson, ed., *John Adams and the Founding of the Republic* (Boston: Massachusetts Historical Society/Northeastern University Press, 2001); and Conrad Edick Wright and Robert X. Baron, eds., *The Libraries, Leadership, and Legacy of John Adams and Thomas Jefferson* (Golden, CO: Fulcrum Publishing; Boston: Massachusetts Historical Society, 2010).

For political history, see James H. Hutson, *John Adams and the Diplomacy of the American Revolution* (Lexington: University Press of Kentucky, 1980); Leonard D. White, *The Federalists: A Study in Administrative History* (New York: Macmillan, 1948); Linda Dudik Guerrero, *John Adams' Vice Presidency: The Neglected Man in the Forgotten Office* (New York: Arno Press, 1982); Manning J. Dauer, *The Adams Federalists* (Baltimore: Johns Hopkins Press, 1968 [1953]); Stephen G. Kurtz, *The Presidency of John Adams: The Collapse of Federalism, 1795–1800* (Philadelphia: University of Pennsylvania Press, 1957); Ralph Adams Brown, *The Presidency of John Adams* (Lawrence: University Press of Kansas, 1975); Walt Brown, *John Adams and the American Press: Politics and Journalism at the Birth of the Republic* (Jefferson, NC: McFarland, 1995); Jeffrey A. Pasley, *The First Presidential Contest: 1796 and the Founding of American Democracy* (Lawrence: University Press of Kansas, 2013); Merrill D. Peterson, *Adams and Jefferson: A Revolutionary Dialogue* (Athens: University Press of Georgia, 1976); John P. Kaminski and Jonathan M. Reid, eds., *Adams and Jefferson: Contrasting Anxieties and Aspirations from the Founding* (Madison, WI: Published for the Center for the Study of the American Constitution by Parallel Press, 2013); and Gordon S. Wood, *Friends Divided: John Adams and Thomas Jefferson* (New York: Penguin, 2017).

For John Adams's intellectual life, a focus of this biography, see Luke Mayville, *John Adams and the Fear of American Oligarchy* (Princeton, NJ: Princeton University Press, 2016), and Richard Alan Ryerson, *John Adams's Republic: The One, the Few, and the Many* (Baltimore: Johns Hopkins University Press, 2016). Also see C. Bradley Thompson, *John Adams and the Spirit of Liberty* (Lawrence: University Press of Kansas, 1998); John R. Howe Jr., *The Changing Political Thought of John Adams* (Princeton, NJ: Princeton University Press, 1965); Edward Handler, *America and Europe in the Thought of John Adams* (Cambridge, MA: Harvard University Press, 1964); Zoltan Haraszti, *John Adams and the Prophets of Progress* (Cambridge, MA: Harvard University Press, 1952); and Alfred Iacuzzi, *John Adams, Scholar* (New York: S. F. Vanni, 1952).

Three new studies deserve mention. Sara Georgini, *Household Gods: The Religious Lives of the Adams Family* (New York: Oxford University Press, 2019), is a beautifully crafted, formidably researched, and enlightening study of the evolving relationship of the Adamses with religion, by a senior editor of the *Adams Papers* project. Arthur Scherr, *John Adams, Race, and Slavery: Ideas, Politics, and Diplomacy in an Age of Crisis* (Santa Barbara, CA: Praeger, 2018), is intemperate in denouncing John Adams's views of slavery and race, but Scherr has done a valuable job in presenting the evidence, with which all scholars should deal. Both books show the immense value of close, serious research in the papers left by John Adams and his family. Nancy Isenberg and Andrew Burstein, *The Problem of Democracy: The Presidents Adams Confront the Cult of Personality* (New York: Viking, 2019), appeared just as this book was being readied for publication.

Consult this book's endnotes for specialized monographs of value.

ACKNOWLEDGMENTS

I am thankful to those who have helped me along the way. I absolve them from any mistakes and errors of judgment remaining in these pages.

This book began more than forty-five years ago, thanks to a movie and a mentor. In 1971, I saw the film *1776* (based on the Broadway musical by Sherman Edwards and Peter Stone); I was captivated by William Daniels's portrayal of John Adams and the late, great Virginia Vestoff's portrayal of Abigail Adams. I decided that I had to know more about John and Abigail. When I was a student at Amherst and a research assistant to my first mentor, Henry Steele Commager (1902–98), he paused in the midst of working on page proofs and said, "Someday, young Bernstein, you must write a book on John Adams." Decades later, here it is. I'm sorry it took so long, but books wait until you're ready to write them.

My family, those who have passed on and those who are still here, have stood by me with this book as with all my earlier books. I also acknowledge my mentors and role models—Henry Steele Commager, Richard B. Morris (1904–89), Arthur R. Miller (once at the Harvard Law School, now at NYU Law School), John Phillip Reid, and William E. Nelson.

Nancy E. Toff, my peerless editor at Oxford University Press, continues to muster patience, faith, encouragement, and goading in dealing with me regarding this book; there are more to come. Many thanks also to her colleagues at Oxford: Julia Turner, who oversaw the book's production; James Peralis, designer of the magnificent dust jacket; Susan Ecklund, whose copyediting is the best I have ever received in over thirty years of authorship; and Brent Matheny.

I remain indebted to the New York University Legal History Colloquium, a group founded by Bill Nelson in 1981 and presided over by him ever since. Professor John Phillip Reid inspired in his own unique way (including his insistence that I consult the unpublished monograph by Franklin Pierce claiming that he was a better and more successful one-term president than John Adams). This book has made appearances before the colloquium in evolving forms, and the colloquialists' comments and advice have kept it moving forward.

Professor Joanne B. Freeman of Yale University and I have been talking and writing about the "founding guys" for longer than either of us will admit; she has taught me far more about history and the founding guys than I can recount. Joanne's mentor, Peter S. Onuf, now the Thomas Jefferson Foundation Professor of History Emeritus at the University of Virginia, continues to be "mentor from heaven" (Joanne's phrase) to us all. Professor Charles L. Zelden of Nova Southeastern University, my scholarly brother, continues to have more faith in me and in my work than I do. His sage counsel and his collegial friendship are indispensable to me (especially as he was writing his superb life of Thurgood Marshall as I was working on John Adams, giving us many chances to discuss men of law.) That is true, as well, of other faithful friends, including Professor Felice Batlan of Chicago-Kent Law School; Professor Annette Gordon-Reed of the Harvard Law School; the late Dr. Gaspare J. Saladino of the *Documentary History of the Ratification of the Constitution and the Bill of Rights* and his colleagues John P. Kaminski, Richard Leffler, and Charles Schoenleber; the redoubtable team guiding the *Documentary History of the First Federal Congress*, Charlene Bangs Bickford, Kenneth Russell Bowling, Helen E. Veit, and Charles DiGiacomantonio; Dr. Maeva Marcus of the Institute for Constitutional History at the New-York Historical Society and George Washington University; Professor Marian Ahumada of the Universidad Autónoma de Madrid (Spain); Professor Carla J. Mulford of Pennsylvania State University; the late George Athan Billias, professor of history emeritus at Clark University and his wife, Margaret; Julie Silverbrook of ConSource; Carol Berkin, newly retired from Baruch College, CUNY; and many others in the community of historians and other scholars who make study of the founding guys so rewarding.

I record here my abiding gratitude to three fine scholars who shared their work with me at critical times for this book; James M. Farrell's superb articles on Cicero and Adams were of inestimable importance to me in illuminating Adams's mind, and Luke Mayville and Richard Alan Ryerson, who shared pre-publication versions of their grand books.

I have given talks and lectures on the subject of this book at, among other places, Turin, Italy, under the auspices of George Washington's Mount Vernon; Amsterdam, the Netherlands, under the auspices of the John Adams Institute; Vienna, Austria, and Prague, the Czech Republic, under the auspices of the International Association for Law and Mental Health; the Fifth Annual Leon

Levy Biography Conference, Graduate Center, CUNY, New York, New York; Blinn College in Brenham, Texas; Cabrini College, Radnor, Pennsylvania; Nova Southeastern University, Ft. Lauderdale, Florida; the University of Richmond, Richmond, Virginia; and Oklahoma City University School of Law, Oklahoma City, Oklahoma. I am profoundly grateful to all those who organized those events and trusted me to come through. That includes the spirited audiences (including those, such as Peter S. Onuf and Woody Holton, who forced me to think things through on my feet, to my abiding benefit).

My friends, the "usual suspects" in my life, have never stinted in insight, encouragement, and patience: Phillip A. Haultcoeur; Maralyn Lowenheim; Hedy A. Lowenheim; Maureen K. Phillips and Joseph Newpol; Maureen's children, Kathleen Spencer and Nathan Spencer, and their families; the documentarians extraordinaire Ron Blumer and Muffie Meyer, and their daughter, Emma; April Holder and Michelle Waites; Kevin Griffin and Elissa Wynn; Edward D. Young III, his wife, Gina Tillman-Young, and their children, Christa, Adam, Noah (and his wife, Allison, and their children, Selah and Daniel), Luke, Mary Maya, Peter, and Moses; Molly Myers and Hasan Rizvi and their sons, Zane and Jehan; and internet friends Karen Spisak, Natalie D. Brown, Patrick Feigenbaum, Marion Pavan, Robert K. Folkner, Philip Whitford, Cynthia E. Nowak, and Kevin J. Hutchison.

Clark's Restaurant in Brooklyn Heights was a nursery for this book and a refuge for its author. To the Sgantzos family and those who work for them, my deepest thanks. So also to Xiu Bin Weng and Ming Hui Lin, who oversee the famed Amsterdam Sushi with grace and artistry.

In 2011, I became an adjunct professor at the City College of New York's Colin Powell School for Civic and Global Leadership; in 2016, I became a full-time lecturer in law and politics there. I am profoundly grateful to my colleagues in the political science department, Daniel DiSalvo, Bruce Cronin, John Krinsky, Carlo Invernizzi Accetti, Karen Struening, Rajan Menon, Nicholas Rush Smith, Jean Krasno, Mira Morgenstern, and Diana Greenwald—and to Jacqueline Williams Mose, who kept us all in line and who has been succeeded by the able and kind Jenifer Roman. I am grateful also to Vincent Boudreau, whom I now salute as president of CCNY and former dean of the Powell School. I also give a special shout-out to my CCNY rabbi, Harold Forsythe. I have worked closely with the Skadden, Arps Honors Program in Legal Studies and those who make it work: Andrew Rich, Jen Light, Nildania Perez, and Matt Longo. I am also deeply indebted to my students here at CCNY, past and present. To list them all would take another book, so I limit myself to Anna Sacerdote, Tiffany Scruggs, Joel Sati, Johnnie L. Fielder, Fatjon

Kaja, Cem Uyar, Sobiha Ahmed, Kathlen Dos Santos, Rokia Diabi, Rachel Lomax, Fatimah Barrie, Tyler Walls, Sultan Mirzhalilov, Emily Graham, Sagar Sharma, Natasha Levy, Brian Valladares, Aisha Meah, Maftuna Zaidova, Grace Isabel Rosado, Zachary Pious, Herut Tekilu, Angela Porwick, Celine Agard, and so many others. Special thanks to the Richard B. Morris Fellows who worked with ConSource on our online database of colonial charters and state constitutions: Kathlen Dos Santos, Sobiha Ahmed, Brian Ruiz, Anna Sacerdote, and Sindi Cela. You know that you are at a world-class college when your students teach you as much as you try to teach them.

For more than twenty-five years, I have been a member of the adjunct faculty of New York Law School, moving from assistant adjunct professor to distinguished adjunct professor. My two rabbis on the faculty there have been Bill LaPiana and Ed Purcell.

Writing an acknowledgments section is often a pleasure, but just as often it is a melancholy business, in that you realize who is no longer in your life, for whatever reason. One person who is gone is my mother, Marilyn Bernstein (1927–2015), who always inspired me and taught me how to teach and who succeeded my father, the late Fred Bernstein (1922–2001), as my demon proofreader and editor. A second is the late Marilee B. Huntoon (1956–2011), my dearest friend and the best and wisest person I've ever known, to whom I dedicate this book. I also miss my uncle Seymour F. Bernstein (1929–2018) and my aunt Shirley Bernstein (1938–2018), who always gave me love, moral support, encouragement, and the warmth of family. I miss Boo Freeman (2001–14), the world's best bird. Last but by no means least, is Danielle J. Lewis, who, while we were together, helped me to understand what John and Abigail had and what they saw in each other, intellectually and emotionally.

INDEX

*For the benefit of digital users, indexed terms that span two pages (e.g., 52–53)
may, on occasion, appear on only one of those pages.*

Abbreviations:
AA = Abigail Adams
AH = Alexander Hamilton
GW = George Washington
JA = John Adams
JM = James Madison
JQA = John Quincy Adams
TJ = Thomas Jefferson